1964

For the Rushbrooke family

1964

THE YEAR THE
SWINGING
SIXTIES
BEGAN

CHRISTOPHER SANDFORD

The
History
Press

First published 2024

The History Press
97 St George's Place, Cheltenham,
Gloucestershire, GL50 3QB
www.thehistorypress.co.uk

British Library Cataloguing in Publication Data.
A catalogue record for this book is available from the British Library.

ISBN 978 1 80399 123 8

Typesetting and origination by The History Press
Printed and bound in Great Britain by TJ Books Limited, Padstow, Cornwall.

Trees for LYfe

ALSO BY CHRISTOPHER SANDFORD

HISTORY

Houdini and Conan Doyle
The Final Over
Harold and Jack
The Man Who Would be Sherlock
Union Jack
The Zeebrugge Raid
The Final Innings
The Man Who Conned the World
Midnight in Tehran

MUSIC BIOGRAPHIES

Mick Jagger
Eric Clapton
Kurt Cobain
David Bowie
Sting
Bruce Springsteen
Keith Richards
Paul McCartney
The Rolling Stones

FILM BIOGRAPHIES

Steve McQueen
Roman Polanski

SPORT

The Cornhill Centenary Test
Godfrey Evans
Tom Graveney
Imran Khan
John Murray
Laker and Lock

FICTION

Feasting with Panthers
Arcadian
We Don't Do Dogs

PLAYS

Comrades

'We believe we are able to change the things around us. We forget the solution that generally comes to pass: we do not succeed in changing things according to our desire, but gradually our desire changes. The situation that we hoped to change because it was intolerable becomes unimportant. We have not managed to surmount the obstacle, but life has taken us round it, led us past it, and then if we turn round to gaze at the remote past, we can barely catch sight of it, so imperceptible has it become.'

Marcel Proust, *The Sweet Cheat Gone*

'Anything worth doing is worth overdoing.'

Mick Jagger

CONTENTS

ACKNOWLEDGEMENTS

This is yet another lockdown book, at least in part, though I hope the reader won't notice any conspicuous falling off from the modest standards of the ones written before the sanitary dictatorship clamped down for all time here in the American west, where I mostly live. For structural reasons I've divided the story into four main chapters that broadly follow the annual seasons, though with no superhuman effort to keep the compartments watertight; Vietnam might surface in February as well as in November, for instance; the joyous derangement of the Beatles and others cut right across the calendar; and the most brutal crime rarely seems to take a holiday. More importantly, it goes without saying that neither our current political rulers, nor any of the names listed below, can be blamed for the shortcomings of the text. They're mine alone.

For archive material, input or advice I should thank, professionally: AbeBooks; the Acton Institute; *America*; Mark Beynon; the British Library; the British Newspaper Library; Companies House; the *Cricketer International*; Emerald Downs; the FBI, Freedom of Information Division; the General Register Office; Tony Gill; Hansard; *Hedgehog Review*; The History Press; Barbara Levy; the Library of Congress; Christine McMorris; the Mitchell Library, Glasgow; Mitre House Hotel; Modern Age; The National Archives; Peter Noone; *The Oldie*; Bill Payne; *Plough*; Tim Reidy; Renton Public Library; Seattle Central College; *The Seattle Times*; *The Spectator*; Surrey History Centre; Sussex CCC; Derek Turner; Vital Records; and Simon Wright.

And personally: Rev. Maynard Atik; the late Sam Banner; Pete Barnes; the late David Blake; Rob Boddie; the Brazen Head; Robert and Hilary Bruce; Don Carson; Monty Dennison; the Dowdall family; Barbara and the late John Dungee; Mike and Roger Fisher; Steve Fossen; Malcolm Galfe; Simon George; James Graham; Steve and Jo Hackett; Duncan Hamilton; the late John Hastings; Alastair Hignell; Charles Hillman; Alex Holmes; Jo Jacobius; Julian James; Robin B. James; Tommy James; Jo Johnson; the late Wilko Johnson; Lincoln Kamell; Terry Lambert; Belinda Lawson; the Lorimer family; Robert Dean Lurie; Les McBride; Linda McBride; the Macris; Lee Mattson; Jim Meyersahm; Jerry Miller; the Morgans; Harry Mount; the Murray family; Greg Nowak; Phillip Oppenheim; Valya Page; Robin and Lucinda Parish; Owen Paterson; Roman Polanski; the Prins family; Matt Purple; Bill Reader; the late Ailsa Rushbrooke; Debbie Saks; the late Sefton Sandford; Peter Scaramanga; Fred and Cindy Smith; the Smith family; Sparks; Jack Surendranath; Nick Tudball; Derek Turner; the late Diana Villar; Lisbeth Vogl; Phil Walker; *Wisden Cricket Monthly*; Rogena and the late Alan White; Debbie Wild; the Willis Fleming family; and the Zombies.

My deepest thanks, as always, to Karen and Nicholas Sandford.

C.S.
2024

LIST OF ILLUSTRATIONS

See pages 143–158 for illustrations.

1.   The Beatles land in New York in February 1964 for the 'Big Bang' moment of pop music. The cap just visible behind Paul McCartney's head belongs to the record producer Phil Spector. It was a symbolic position for Spector, whose own career would also be obscured by those of the new arrivals. (Library of Congress)

2.   Ronan O'Rahilly, the young Irish nightclub owner who launched Radio Caroline.

3.   The police intervene in one of the clashes between rival gangs of Mods and Rockers that enlivened Margate and other English seaside towns in the chilly spring of 1964. (Trinity Mirror/Mirrorpix/Alamy Stock Photo)

4.   The early Rolling Stones; you would have got long odds in 1964 that they would still be in business sixty years later. (Archive PL/Alamy Stock Photo)

5.   Princess Margaret gets around.

6.   Alec Douglas-Home, Britain's accidental prime minister for a year, who against the odds nearly won a general election. (Wikimedia Commons/Allan Warren)

7.   George Brown visits President Kennedy in the White House, at least proving they once met. (Robert Knudsen/White House Photographs/John F. Kennedy Presidential Library and Museum, Boston)

8.   Bruce Reynolds (right) and other future Great Train Robbers celebrate a successful job with their wives. (Wikimedia Commons/Karen Hogan)

9.   Peter Sellers and Britt Ekland. He had a series of heart attacks, she was fired from a film and between them they lost their dog during the excitement of their whirlwind romance. (Allstar Picture Library Ltd/Alamy Stock Photo)

10.   Elizabeth Taylor and Richard Burton: Hollywood royalty, if in his case at consort level.

11.   Stanley Kubrick, who apart from being a revolutionary film-maker remains one of the few people ever to emigrate from Beverly Hills to suburban Watford.

12.   Cassius Clay, at age 22, defied pre-fight predictions to become world heavyweight boxing champion in February 1964. Two days later, Clay let it be known that he would answer only to the name Muhammad Ali. (Library of Congress)

13.   Terence Conran in his element. (Independent/Alamy Stock Photo)

14.   Mary Quant.

15.   Britain's briefly famous vocal trio The Paper Dolls, seen wearing Quant's most celebrated design. The miniskirt offered women a chance to feel bold and enfranchised, and provided a tantalising hint of underwear for men.

16.   England's enterprising cricket captain Ted Dexter (right) strides to the wicket with his Sussex County teammate Jim Parks. (PA Images/Alamy Stock Photo)

17. The swashbuckling Dexter figure of the jet-propelled racing world Donald Campbell, who broke both land- and water-speed records in 1964. (GP Library Limited/Alamy Stock Photo)

18. Ken Russell, who directed his first feature film, a soggy seaside comedy called *French Dressing*, in 1964. He's seen here on the set of another film with Michael Caine.

19. Peter Cook, who developed his monotonal alter ego E.L. Wisty in 1964. Rebuffed in his ambition to become a judge after his lack of Latin had caused him to fail 'the rigorous judging exams', Wisty opted for a career as a coal miner instead.

20. The American comic Lenny Bruce, later said to have died of 'an overdose of police'. (Archive PL/Alamy Stock Photo)

21. Simultaneously terrifying and absurd, Nikita Khrushchev began his term as Soviet leader in 1953 expounding his vision of a new communist world order, and ended it eleven years later obsessing about the construction of Moscow lavatory seats. (Library of Congress)

22. Perhaps Khrushchev's most enduring legacy was the so-called Anti-Fascist Protection Device, or Berlin Wall, as others came to know it. (Library of Congress)

23. Winston Churchill, who bowed out of the House of Commons in July 1964 at the age of 89, seen here with the American financier Bernard Baruch. (Library of Congress)

24. Robert Boothby, a fitfully brilliant Tory MP who combined formidable oratorical skills with the morals of an alley cat. (Wikimedia Commons/Allan Warren)

25. Sean Connery during the filming of *Goldfinger*. (ETH-Bibliothek Zürich, Bildarchiv/Fotograf: Comet Photo AG (Zürich)/Com_C13-035-006/CC BY-SA 4.0)

26. Roman Polanski with his young actress wife Sharon Tate, who later became a victim of the psychotic Manson cult.

27.   Clint Eastwood in *A Fistful of Dollars*, the first in his celebrated spaghetti-western trilogy.

28.   The eye-catching 'monokini', worn here by the model Peggy Moffitt, which attracted widespread public interest but never quite found a mass market in the British climate. (© William Claxton, via WENN Rights Ltd/Alamy Stock Photo)

29.   Tyneside schoolchildren waiting excitedly for Harold Wilson on the election campaign trail. Wilson's Pied Piper effect on the young was unprecedented in British politics, although America had seen it all before with John F. Kennedy. (Tyne & Wear Archives & Museums)

30.   The pipe-smoking Wilson (he preferred a cigar in private) who duly took Labour back into power in 1964 after thirteen years of opposition, seen with President Lyndon Johnson. Johnson won the US election that year in a landslide, even if it all went wrong for him from there.

31.   Sam Cooke, the wildly popular American singer whose December 1964 death was ruled justifiable homicide, despite evidence to the contrary.

32.   Stanley Matthews, whose thirty-three-year-long football career ended only after he was knighted at the age of 49 on New Year's Day 1965.

INTRODUCTION

ALL OUR YESTERDAYS

I spent most of 1964 as a 7-year-old schoolchild in an unprepossessing ghetto of south London, amid bricks and soot and cratered streets, where milk bottles, which sometimes spontaneously exploded in the cold, were delivered each morning by a man in an apron riding a horse-drawn cart. My mother went to the shops almost every day, not because we were gluttons but because our fridge was roughly the size of a small suitcase and we lacked a freezer. Our local grocery store, which went by the perhaps leading name of Mr Crooke's, was staffed by two or three middle-aged men also in aprons, had sawdust on the floor and closed early each Thursday. For Sunday lunch we generally treated ourselves to a joint of Mr Crooke's sweaty pink beef accompanied by a salad soaked in a brown oil that doubled as earwax remover. Our house was a poorly ventilated semi with postage-stamp-sized rooms patched together by crumbling plaster walls, although we aspired to that era's defining domestic status symbol of full indoor plumbing. 'Bloody lucky, too,' my father, then a landbound navy officer, remarked. The hint of amused irony behind the genuine conviction that we could have been much worse off was unmistakable.

Each weekday morning my father caught a commuter train for its last couple of stops into Waterloo, an experience he rarely spoke of fondly, and then walked over the bridge to his desk job in the Stalinist-looking bulk of the Ministry of Defence. A long-running power dispute involving the Amalgamated Engineering Union and their demand for a maximum forty-hour week periodically plunged all the houses in our street into total darkness, and when this happened we sat around in unheated rooms, the TV set – which, reversing the formula of the fridge, was the size of a coffin – shut off, reading flimsily printed newspapers by candlelight. My school classroom, about a mile away, included a pot-bellied stove and a row of wooden desks with a communal inkwell, into which we dipped our blue Osmiroid nibs. There was a framed official portrait of a youthful-looking Queen on the wall. The water emerged from the school's bathroom taps, to a cacophony of clanking pipes, with the consistency of sticky red hair oil and at only one temperature: glacial. You had to break the ice some winter afternoons when taking a knee-bath after playing compulsory football or rugby. There may have been no village in the Carpathians quite as primitive as our part of London in the immediate run-up to the Swinging Sixties.

Even so, there was evidence that certain individuals might soon come to inject a splash of colour into the sepia tones that seemed to wash over the British landscape like a Victorian group photograph. By the spring of 1964 you could almost see their hopeful little heads poking out of the soil. There were the Beatles, to give just the most obvious example. The four impish Scousers had closed out the old year with a thirty-seven-date tour of Britain's art deco fleapits from Carlisle to Portsmouth. At each stop a ruffle-shirted compère would bound on stage and demand, 'Do you want to see John?' (Roars). 'Paul?' (Roars). 'George?' (Roars). 'Ringo?' (Mayhem). A frantic pop party then ensued, with stretcher cases and arrests. As the curtain fell each night there was generally a full-scale riot in progress, suddenly ended, as if by a thrown switch, by everyone freezing in place for the national anthem. Early in the new year, the band went off to play in Paris and Paul McCartney had them send up a grand piano to his hotel room, the better to work on some of the songs that became *A Hard Day's Night*. That the quartet were each reportedly making £100 a week (£1,500 today) didn't slow them down: just the reverse. Later that winter McCartney turned up for a brainstorming session at John Lennon's suburban home, as it happened not too far from ours, with the words, 'Let's write ourselves a swimming pool.' Meanwhile, George Harrison was worried about keeping up payments on his new car, and Ringo just wanted to make enough to open his own hair salon. All four Beatles thought the band was a gas, but that it would be forgotten again in a year or two.

Harold Macmillan had resigned as Britain's prime minister in October 1963, ostensibly on health grounds but really a victim of that year's Profumo scandal, with its cast of characters including the eponymous Secretary of State for War, a society osteopath and sexual procurer named Stephen Ward, the assistant Soviet naval attaché, a pair of exotic, spliff-smoking West Indians, and two equally free-spirited young women of, as the parlance of the day had it, doubtful reputation. The press wasn't slow to build the affair into a cause célèbre that linked not only senior members of the Macmillan Cabinet but Britain's ruling elite as a whole to an underworld of prostitutes, pimps, spies, topless go-go dancers and unusual household practices. 'The whole United Kingdom government has become a sort of brothel,' *The Times* was left to sigh. I remember my father reading his evening paper around this time, grunting when he came to a certain passage, and remarking in a hushed tone to my mother that the news was all about 's-e-x' those days. At that my mother had glanced hastily in my direction and put a finger to her lips. I respected the effort, but as it happened I'd recently learned the word for myself. I discovered it at school, where another boy had gravely informed me that 'all the grown-ups – including the people in the Cabinet' were at it like rabbits, a statement he illustrated by producing a pack of playing cards adorned by photographs of well-upholstered young women. The concept was reinforced via my passing acquaintance with a neighbour by the name of Lulu, whom I sometimes saw waiting for a bus at the end of our street wearing a dress of singularly sparing cut.

For a while in the summer of 1963, the Macmillan government tottered, seemingly fatally wounded. Although it survived, it lost its former aura of respectability. Deference was never quite the same again. Macmillan's successor in office was the 60-year-old 14th Earl of Home (or plain Sir Alec Douglas-Home, as he became), a man whose misfortune it was in the television age to resemble a prematurely hatched bird and whose Adam's apple danced rapidly up and down his narrow neck. His selection was not noticeably a step in the direction of modernising Britain. It was thought the wily, 47-year-old Labour leader Harold Wilson, ostentatiously puffing his pipe in public while enjoying a good cigar in private, understood the medium rather better. TV was 'open to abuse by any charlatan capable of manipulating it properly, and so it proved in 1964,' Wilson's future opponent Edward Heath noted.

Both major political parties continued to struggle with the fallout of the tragicomic Suez affair of November 1956, when the British forces were comprehensively reverse-ferreted from their attempt to seize control of the canal zone amidst a disastrous run on sterling and the unexpected opposition of the Americans, and had since committed to phasing out their bases, harbours and other imperial-era establishments throughout the Middle East. Both also grappled with their stance on what was then called the European Common Market, the French having just vetoed Britain's latest application to join the club. To a certain generation of Britons, it must seem as if their whole lives have been spent in the shadow of a stale and still not wholly resolved debate about their nation's proper place on the Continent. As a whole, Macmillan's premiership from 1957–63 falls broadly into a first half, where he appeared to be in charge of events, and a second half, which was increasingly devoted to dealing with domestic and foreign disasters. Coming to power at a time when respect for one's 'betters' still predominated in all walks of life, and leaving it amidst a satirical firestorm that lampooned the PM as a broken-down figure presiding over an inept and sexually incontinent regime, Macmillan's seven-year tenure was the trigger point for Britain's 1960s modernisation crisis.

Aside from the accelerating plague of rock and roll, British parents were confronted by certain other unmistakable signs that the rallying legacy represented by the Dunkirk Spirit and the illusion of continuing post-war unity was starting to crack. Films as diverse as *Dr Strangelove*, *Girl With Green Eyes*, *The Chalk Garden*, *King & Country*, *Of Human Bondage*, *The Pumpkin Eater* and *Zulu* all appeared on British screens in 1964, each offering at least a hint of social commentary or satire about class distinctions. Joe Orton's first play *Entertaining Mr Sloane* was an immediate *succès de scandale* when performed at London's Arts Theatre that May. The opening act, in which a dowdy, middle-aged woman picks up a young, good-looking psychopath and informs him how positively she would react to any romantic overtures he might care to make to her gave notice that this was something other than traditional, all-round family entertainment. *Top of the Pops*, *Match of the Day* and *Crossroads* all made their debut on British television that year. The Rolling Stones released their first album in April, another key moment in blasting the parochial shackles off British pop music, perhaps even more so than the Beatles. Around the Stones in 1964 there was always the sound of fans braying and squealing, MCs sternly calling for order and police chiefs rumbling 'Disgraceful!' The headlines followed suit: 'Thugs', 'Cavemen', 'Apes' was the consensus, another sign that Britain as a whole might be a rather more divided place than the self-sufficient island nation of, say, 1954.

The national press for 2 January 1964, the day marking the beginning of the end of the extended festive season, showed some of the country's new spirit of egalitarianism alongside an icy touch of old-school class sensitivity. The *Daily Herald* led with the perennial 'Drive Drink Off The Road!' as its takeaway message, along with a variety of other such slogans that seemed to have been lifted direct from a local police authority press release. Over at the *Mirror*, 'The Spirit of 1964' was the splash, which the paper illustrated by a picture of a donkey-jacketed man sitting atop a high-rise beam on a building site in central Manchester with a 'glass of bubbly', thus literally straddling the two worlds. Elsewhere, we learn that Prince Charles and Princess Anne had enjoyed a 'fab twist session'. The royals, aged 15 and 13 respectively, had gone to a 'beat dance at the mansion home of Major and Mrs. John Bagge at Stradsett Hall, near Sandringham', with more than 100 other youths; the prince wore a 'casual sweater and tapered trousers', while his sister sported a 'light-coloured dress' of daring cut, a mere 'two or three inches below the knee'. The *Daily Express* carried the grim news that carpet prices were set to increase by a rather precise 7.5 per cent during the year, while there were more traffic-related concerns at the *Telegraph*, with the prospect of the 'compulsory destruction of hundreds of homes and the displacement of their unfortunate inhabitants to make way for new speedways to accommodate an eternal procession of gargantuan lorries and cars travelling at over 50 miles an hour'.

There was more elsewhere in the tabloids about the world of floor coverings, with the repeated invitation to buy one of Ulster-based Cyril Lord's 'fabulous, quality products' at direct-from-the-factory prices, with a free bottle of Swift Rug Shampoo thrown in. Meanwhile, Pontins was offering DIY holidays in one of its luxury chalets, each with 'lounge, bedroom, fully fitted kitchen, bathroom and even a TV!' at such exclusive resorts as Skegness or Rockey Sands in Dorset, starting at just £3 per person per week. For the more adventurous, there were the charms of fourteen days on the Bulgarian Riviera priced from 32½ guineas, exclusive of flights. If you wanted, you could buy a state-of-the art Imperial washing machine – still a novelty in many

British households, partly because the electricity grid in much of the country could only support a limited number of appliances in each home – for just £85 (£1,275 today), or 12s 11d a week on the three-year instalment plan. Or you could treat yourself to a pair of extravagantly heeled 'Cuban Bootle Boots' for 79s 11d (around £60 today); a 'stylish elastic corselet' to 'banish that spare tyre look' for 59s; or some modish Directoire Knickers, 'warm and comfortable where it counts for the chilly days ahead' at five bob each. There was a good deal more in the press promoting the virtues of cars, cameras, cold remedies, cod-liver oil, denture repairs, trusses and medical aids in general. National expenditure on retail advertising rose from £102 million in 1952 to £1.8 billion in 1964.

To judge from the press, Britain's employment landscape then hung in a sort of extended Georgian limbo. The 'Wanted' columns still had rows of openings for household servants, private chauffeurs ('only well-spoken men need apply') and 'boys' or 'girls' for unspecified immediate menial labour. Recruitment to the Prison Service was apparently a par-ticular issue, because many of the papers carried invitations to apply for a position as a guard or other officer, at rates starting at £12 10s a week for men and £9 10s for women, which compared to the average white-collar wage of the day of £15 and £11 10s respectively.

Scanning the real-estate columns, you could find a 'magnificent 4-bedroom villa' for sale in Sutton Coldfield, near Birmingham, for £5,150 o.n.o., or one of the same size in Banstead, Surrey, for £7,800. A new Morris Oxford car without extras would set you back around £750, although you could drive off in a Reliant three-wheeler, unheated, for just £480. Many of the displays for goods and services retained their essential 1950s air of apology for the tastelessness of having to promote their wares in the first place, with taglines such as 'If we have a rival in our field, we should be glad to hear of it,' or 'Any Interested Parties are invited to correspond, or call by appointment at our Premises.' There was a splash of the exotic to some of the adver-tisements for credit cards, flared trousers, Cuban boots and foreign holidays, but what strikes one most about the lives of most ordinary Britons is that they seemed to have changed so little, not so much, from the protracted aftermath of the Second World War, an era char-acterised by icy nights in gaslit rooms, a diet of whale fat and Spam, and all the other comically vile ingredients of a serious sacrifice none of those who endured it ever forgot.

Of course it's almost always a mistake to try and assemble random historical facts into a neatly unified pattern that few people would have recognised at the time. Whether in their claim that Britain over-night became a socialist mecca with the advent of the welfare state in 1945, or that the country abruptly succumbed to a priapic frenzy characterised by the sight of bare-thighed young women swaggering around Carnaby Street in their Mary Quant miniskirts to a backdrop of herbally-tinged joss sticks and the wafted strains of the Grateful Dead in the so-called Summer of Love twenty-two years later – with a sort of communal nervous breakdown triggered by the Suez Crisis at the midpoint between the two poles – social historians are always keen to identify what seem to them to be the transformative shifts in our national life. Such judgements are generally only feasible with the aid of hindsight. Few of those confronted by the individual pieces of the jigsaw can picture the completed puzzle.

In that spirit, perhaps the best way to briefly refresh our memories of 1964 is not to display a list of dates of domestic or international events, but to follow a modestly well-off young couple living in Dartford, or Luton, or Pontefract, or Dundee – it hardly matters which – through the routine of an ordinary day in January 1964. To do so may be nostalgic, but it isn't necessarily to mourn the lost Eden of a communitarian past.

From the appearance of the man of the house as he comes to the breakfast table on this winter morning, you would hardly know you weren't in the 1950s; the movement of male fashion since the war is glacial. His young wife, as life partners were then called, might con-ceivably have made a gesture toward the coming sartorial whirligig of the Sixties with some gaudily coloured knee socks or stockings, or a pair of platform heels, but wasn't yet likely to have abandoned herself to what Mary Quant evocatively described as her ideal of a modern woman dressed in 'a bouillabaisse of clothes and accessories [that] were much more for life, much more for real people, much more for being young and alive in'.

Breakfast over, the male half of the sketch might get in his car – the Morris, perhaps, or an equally sensible Vauxhall Victor or Ford Consul – or entrust himself to the only mixed charms of British Railways, as the system was then called, which was in the process of axing a third of its passenger services as well as 4,200 of its 7,000 stations. At that time, rail fares were still calculated not as a result of the party

INTRODUCTION **21**

in charge having ingested some mind-altering drug, but by the simple expedient of using a flat rate for the distance travelled, which in 1964 was threepence per mile second class, and 4s 2d per mile first class, meaning a single journey between Guildford and Waterloo would have cost you about eighty-four pence, or seven shillings, roughly £5.25 in today's money.

London itself, if that's where our man ended up, was an inexhaustible space, a labyrinth of narrow, serpentine streets and then home to about 8 million people, which represented a slow but steady downward population trend that continued until the early 1980s. The Underground system at that time favoured an unpainted aluminium carriage as its rolling stock, and as a rule would have been about half as congested as it is today. In 1964 the total distance travelled by all passengers on the Tube stood at around 3.1 billion miles, compared with nearly 7 billion miles just before the onset of the Covid pandemic in 2020. The ambient smell on the train itself would have been one of stale or active tobacco smoke, among other, less immediately identifiable aromas: although there were many honourable exceptions, the average British adult in 1964 (though far less likely to be obese than his modern counterpart) tended not to overdo it in terms of personal hygiene, with 31 per cent of those discreetly surveyed by the Metropolitan Water Board revealing that they preferred to bathe only on a Sunday.

The frivolous side of the Sixties – fashion, pop culture, sex – was unlikely to have asserted itself in our protagonist's place of work, which, again with significant exceptions, was apt to be a sober-minded retreat that was predominantly white and male, with women largely confined to their traditional roles as objects for decorative and secretarial purposes. The general rule was that the bosses expected absolute female subservience, total discretion, and the demurely efficient supervision of the office kitchen.

In the course of his day on the front lines, our man might have the opportunity to discuss prevailing business conditions. It seems things are generally looking up: the *Financial Times* 30-share index, the precursor to today's FTSE, continued to show modest gains, and the pound was then worth roughly three times more than the dollar on the foreign exchange. The Bank of England report for the twelve months ending 29 February 1964 began on a sanguine note:

The year under review was one of rapid development in the domestic economy, and of expanding markets abroad for British goods. The challenge is to ensure that demand does not expand faster than output can satisfy, and that costs and prices not rise unduly ... At the very end of the period, on 27 February 1964, Bank rate was raised to 5 per cent.

It seemed everybody was talking about the bright prospects for overseas trade and the exciting new opportunities for the ordinary British consumer to avail themselves of luxury goods such as deep freezes, televisions and fitted carpets. There were too many strikes, it was true, and the long-running industrial action by Britain's 128,000 electrical power workers would periodically seem to recede only to flare up again, like a repeatedly treated but never fully cured virus. The labouring classes as a whole were considered capital, as opposed to 'human resources', although homelessness, that unfortunate waste product of an economic system increasingly designed to exploit workers for the benefit of *Eyes Wide Shut* partying overlords, didn't seem to be much of an issue.

As it turned out, the Bank of England's rosy forecast for the year ahead proved something of a misjudgement. What the Bank tactfully referred to as a 'period of rapid development' in 1964 seems in retrospect to have been one of reckless boom, with Britain's current account sliding ever further into the red. When the new Labour chancellor Jim Callaghan took office in October, he imagined that the nation's balance of payments might be as much as £500m in arrears. Waiting for him on his desk was an elegant folder prepared by his new permanent secretary, Sir William Armstrong, containing a two-page summary of the true state of affairs. It opened with the time-honoured salutation: 'We greet the esteemed Chancellor', but rapidly went downhill from there. The actual deficit in Britain's trade figures was just over £805m. According to Callaghan, as he sat contemplating the full horror of the document in front of him, his predecessor in office, Reginald Maudling, walked past on his way out, carrying a pile of suits over his arm, and paused to stick his head in the door of his old study. "'Good luck, old cock,' Maudling said cheerfully. "Sorry to leave it in such a mess." Then he smiled, stuck his trilby on his head and sauntered off.'

Our leading man would have known little or none of this as he stepped outside for lunch, where he might have encountered a few self-consciously 'with it' displays of primary-coloured shirts, ruffled and splayed open at the chest as if for imminent heart surgery, or some tentative signs of the new vogue for geometric-shaped skirts made of tinsel-like PVC, a material that fitted 'into current fashion like an astronaut into his capsule,' *Queen* magazine informed its readers. Of course, most people, of all ages and at every walk of life, oblivious to the great anthropomorphic trends they were later said to embody, simply dressed in their old utilitarian way. In most small towns and villages in the Britain of 1964 you still saw children with hair cut close to the scalp to avoid lice and nits, with teeth uneven, broken or missing, wrapped in sack-like garments that looked like the family dog had just vomited on them, and as often as not reared in neighbourhoods cross-hatched by rows of Victorian terraced slums with a back door that opened directly onto an outhouse, and largely distinguished by their stagnant canals, endless one-way systems and mortuaries, with an air of fatigue and chronic naffness ('Fresh AND Frozen', 'REAL Imitation Antiques!') that revealed a nation poised between its baroque past and modern tat so richly characteristic of Britain's provincial outposts. As the actor Michael Caine noted to a friend after a working trip to the industrial northeast, 'The press is always going on about this Cockney-git image I've got and so on, but now I've been to Newcastle I realise I'm middle class.'

Our protagonist's midday meal, if taken at one of the new Chinese or Indian restaurants springing up around the UK, or perhaps aspiring to the full, three-course Berni Inn Family Platter, might have cost eleven or twelve shillings, with an accompanying pint of tepid lager at 2s 3d, respectively some £9 and £1.75 today. If he smoked, as over 70 per cent of British men and 40 percent of women then did, a packet of twenty Rothmans would have knocked him back around five shillings (£3.75), roughly the same as a gallon of high-octane petrol to speed him on his drive home. No one really spoke about the toxic, ashes-to-ashes risks we associate with cigarettes today, although in December 1963 one local authority in the south-west of England daringly prepared a cautionary leaflet for distribution in schools. The following is a representative extract of the language used:

Always puffin' a fag – squares, Never snuffin' the habit – squares, Drop it, doll, be smart, be sharp! Cool cats wise, And cats remain, Non-smokers, doll, in this campaign.

Not for the last time, an official government initiative may conceivably have produced the opposite result to the one intended.

Back home, meanwhile – and in this context it should be remembered that only one in four married women was working in 1964 – our principal's wife might have been diligently navigating through the minefield of early closing, or shortages, or merely of the routine challenge of popping down to the local high street, as most people still did rather than consolidating their shopping into one weekly trip to the supermarket, let alone the unheard-of joys of doing so online. Depending on taste and the presence of suitable kitchen equipment, there might be a few modest innovations in the couple's menu that night. As the social historian Dominic Sandbrook writes, 'Avocados, aubergines and courgettes were becoming increasingly familiar, while dinner-party guests were no longer surprised to be offered prawn cocktail or coq au vin from the hostess's new trolley.' (The guests themselves, if not previously familiar with the area, would have been armed with local directions along the lines of 'Third on the left past the diseased tree at the back of the pub ...' rather than those of today's personal-navigation industry.) Meat and two veg was still the staple diet, although the popular frozen Vesta curries and chow mein provided the first taste for many Britons of 'foreign grub'.

If the couple in question fancied a quiet night in, they may have switched on the radiogram or the television, the latter often a vast, fake wood device that doubled as a piece of furniture. On a typical weekday evening they could watch a two-channel line-up that ranged from *Coronation Street*, *All Our Yesterdays* and *Panorama* through to a few light-hearted American imports like *My Favorite Martian* or *The Lucy Show*, and a fifteen-minute main BBC news bulletin with a distinct touch of the *ancien régime* about it, both in terms of its booming, Soviet-style theme music and the almost impenetrably fruity accent of its presenter. By 1964 there were radio and TV programmes, magazines, shops, products and whole industries that bowed to the young, but apparently no one had yet brought this fact to the attention of the current affairs department of the nation's broadcaster.

Our mythical couple's home may have had the luxury of inbuilt heating, or just as likely they would have relied on a stone hot-water bottle or a Princess electric blanket to get through the long winter night. It wasn't unknown to wake up to find a layer of frost on the bedclothes, or icicles dangling on the inside of the windows in many middle-class British homes of the day. The standard way of making a bed was with layers of sheets and blankets, with an eiderdown on top, although thanks to the retailer Terence Conran, to whom we'll return, a few enterprising customers were soon experimenting with 'continental quilts', as duvets were then known, a flashy foreign interloper on the linens market.

We can perhaps leave our couple in peace at their bedroom door, although it's worth noting that the swinging conjugal etiquette widely associated with the Summer of Love and its aftermath may in fact have gotten off to a head start earlier in the decade. Eustace Chesser's seminal *Love Without Fear: A Plain Guide to Sex Technique for Every Married Adult*, retailing at six shillings, had sold an astonishing 3.2 million copies by July 1964, while the Marriage Guidance Council's recently published manual *How to Treat a Young Wife* contained the radical notion that women were no less libidinous than men, and that 'simultaneous orgasm is a highly desirable ideal.'

It's a truism, but one perhaps worth repeating, that British society as a whole was more sharply polarised then than it is now. For those passing the eleven-plus exam there was grammar school, with its prospect of university, the professions or the civil service. So a young man like our hero here might be commuting to and from his city-centre office and taking his wife for an occasional night out in the West End of London, or even on a flying overseas holiday, or he might be screwing caps on to bottles on a provincial assembly line for a take-home wage of two or three pounds a day, with a fortnight's seaside caravanning as the height of his recreational dreams. In either case, as Britons gradually went about their business on the cold Wednesday morning of 1 January 1964 they would almost certainly never have heard of Concorde, colour TV or pirate radio, of Habitat, home computers, *The Sun*, ATMs, *A Hard Day's Night*, *New York Times v. Sullivan*, indoor shopping centres, the Channel Tunnel, Milton Keynes, BBC2, *Match of the Day*, gay rights, Valium or the Viet Cong.

The swinging year lay before them.

I

WINTER

'WE ALL WENT TO BED WITH VICTOR'

On the stormy afternoon of Monday 9 December 1963, the day after a lightning strike had caused a Pan Am jet to explode over the American east coast with the loss of all eighty-one souls aboard, a 35-year-old man wearing a light sharkskin suit and dark glasses boarded the first-class cabin of a Boeing 707 operated by the same airline for the nine-hour flight from Chicago's O'Hare airport to London Heathrow. The passenger was a trim, youthful figure whose upturned nose and pinched, quizzical expression gave him a vaguely feral air – in one former lover's uncharitable phrase, like that of an 'evil mole' – along with a hint of schoolboy impishness. One close friend of the time described him as looking like a 'naughty kid who's just run away from ringing someone's doorbell', while another said that in light of the 'slightly overdone costumes and knowing leer permanently clamped on his face, you somehow always expected a row of naked ladies to suddenly appear and start dancing around behind him'.

This last image may not have been entirely fanciful, because the passenger's name was Victor Lownes, and he was on his way to London to open the city's first Playboy Club. If he had any misgivings about boarding a plane in the circumstances that prevailed that afternoon, he kept them from his two young companions, now remembered only as Mai and Tai, and ungallantly described as 'devoid of thought but so top-heavy you wondered they didn't fall over as they walked'. Lownes himself promptly bent down to kiss the ground when he landed safely at Heathrow shortly before midday on 10 December, not so much out of relief, he insisted, but in sheer gratitude at finding himself in the 'greatest city on earth'. As if to illustrate the fact, 'the sun came out just as we touched down over a whole country that seemed green and pleasant, wonderfully bright, and determined to have a good time'.

Lownes spent the remaining weeks of 1963 in a twenty-fifth-floor suite at London's newly opened Hilton on Park Lane, long remembering his delight in a 'red' city ('all those great phone booths and buses and postboxes') apparently teeming with 'bouncy, free-spirited types with longer hair and shorter skirts than the kids back home'. As a surface observation, this was probably true enough. But perhaps Lownes failed to similarly register the ranks of bus drivers, nurses, school janitors, dustmen and waiters who serviced the soon-to-be swinging city but couldn't themselves afford to live there, and were forced to cohabit with their parents or to find housing in the distant suburbs, commuting in on the most congested roads in Europe or else on the sadly reduced rail network. It's always tempting to cling to a cinematic image a particular city might present to us: you hop off the Greyhound bus in Los Angeles, and the cloud of exhaust clears to reveal you, smiling and arms thrown wide, ready to finally be discovered; or impeccably dressed Brits march past on Westminster Bridge, identical black brollies held at the furl, while Big Ben obligingly chimes overhead. 'Maybe I bought the idea of London,' Lownes would admit years later:

> The place wasn't just about bricks and mortar. It was about spirit. I was in love with the thought of dolly-birds sashaying up and down Kings Road, not with the delayed 7.25 train from Leatherhead with the blocked loo, chuntering past the corrugated retail units in the pouring rain. Both were real, but in my England it was always Saturday night, and it was always cool.

On 2 January 1964, Lownes placed an advertisement in *The Times*'s personal columns: 'American millionaire seeks a flat in the most fashionable part of London. Must be exclusive. Rents up to £100 a week.'

This, too, has a certain cinematic quality to it; as in a stylised Hollywood film, a gay young blade arrives in a promised land, ready to throw his money around, inviting the audience to vicariously share in the thrill of it all – and also in the protagonist's ultimate ruin.

In due course, Lownes found suitable accommodations at 3 Montpelier Square, opposite Harrods, whose rent fell comfortably within his budget at a weekly 75 guineas, or £1,250 in today's money. He never lost his sense of awed affection for England, where he lived for most of the remaining fifty-three years of his life. 'There were one or two speed bumps along the way,' he admitted to me – among them his financing of Roman Polanski's treatment of *Macbeth* that went disastrously over budget, and in time led Lownes to describe the film's celebrated director as an 'egomaniacal dwarf'; or for that matter the abrupt closure of the then loss-making Playboy Club in 1981 – 'but I still say that bliss it was to be alive in the early Sixties and to be in London was very heaven. And no, I never did take the 7.25 or any other train from Leatherhead.'

Of course, a wealthy American import essentially in the business of dressing pneumatic young women in a get-up of a snug-fitting corset teddy, collar, cuffs and a fluffy cottontail may not be entirely representative of the average resident of the United Kingdom in 1964, or for that matter any other year. But Lownes is still an interesting case study of assimilation into the British life of the day. He was born in Buffalo, New York, in 1928, into a privileged family with a lucrative interest in the Yale lock business. As a child he received an early education in the facts of life from a teenaged nanny who gave her young charge detailed accounts of her sexual liaisons along with his bedtime bath, a narrative she sometimes illustrated by exposing her breasts. At the age of 12, Victor accidentally shot and killed his best friend, an episode that resulted in his enrolment at a New Mexico military academy. From there he graduated to the University of Chicago, and eventually found employment with the family firm. 'I was promoted to manager within a few months,' Lownes would later note, 'due solely to hard work, conscientiousness and the fact that my grandfather owned the company.' At a party in 1954, he met Hugh Hefner, who had just launched *Playboy* magazine. Lownes came on board as marketing director, and was credited with overseeing a Viagra-like rise in the periodical's circulation figures. Among his contributions was the long-running campaign featuring the tagline 'What Sort of Man Reads *Playboy*?' At its peak, the answer was an astonishing 5.8 million subscribers a month. Lownes also steered *Playboy* into starting its own TV channel, and eventually to opening its namesake clubs all over the world. London seemed to him to be the centre of all that was young and fresh in late 1963, somewhere you could be whatever you wanted, and 'only squares called other people promiscuous, by which they really meant you were getting more sex than they were.' The fact that Britain had recently legalised casino gambling didn't hurt, either.

Twice married, with children, Lownes tended to eschew the traditional monogamous ideal. Stocks, the former girls' boarding school he bought for £107,000 in the Hertfordshire countryside, long retained a vestige of its previous role as a training camp for Playboy bunnies. Lownes furnished the fifteen bedrooms to reflect the lifestyle promoted by the magazine, and had the home's public areas fitted out with erotic Mogul statues, a private disco, and what was allegedly the largest jacuzzi in the world. 'We all went to bed with Victor,' admitted one former inmate. 'He used to have five girls a day, sometimes two at a time,' recalled another, 'Angie', who was 19 when she went to be trained at Stocks. 'I did think I'd make him a very good third wife, but when I was asked to move up to the attic, I knew it had gone pear-shaped.'

So perhaps Lownes falls some way short of the ideal male archetype scraping by in the Britain of 1964, with just enough left over on Friday night for the five-bob Smugglers Grill plate at the local Golden Egg followed by a stalls ticket to *Zorba the Greek*. But he was certainly one of those who now saw the English capital as the unchallenged style capital of the West, with a gaudy, youth-driven energy that made other European cities seem dowdy by comparison and to which he himself in a small degree contributed. As Lownes recalled, 'there was something in the air' in London, a mix of ancient and modern, where one could see a 'young bit in a miniskirt in the same frame as a couple of old City boys marching around in suits and bowler hats', already apparent by the time he excitedly bounded down the steps from his bumpy overnight flight from Chicago in December 1963.

★★★

There was a moment rich in significance for the future of the British press, and for public discourse as a whole, when, in March 1963, 51-year-old Randolph Churchill, only son of the nation's wartime premier, issued a flurry of writs for defamation against the recently launched satirical magazine *Private Eye*. As is so often the case in libel, the facts of the matter were both simple and a trifle ludicrous.

That February, the *Eye* had published a back-page strip commenting on the fact that Churchill had been lucky enough to win the commission to write his father's official biography. An apparently harmless joke was made of the fact that Randolph, like most eminent biographers, employed the services of a team of research assistants to help him compile the facts – along with the suggestion, made in similarly humorous vein, that certain events in the still-living Sir Winston's long and tumultuous life might not be presented in the finished book entirely in the same light in which they had been seen originally by his contemporaries.

It would be fair to say that Randolph Churchill did not react with the same sort of jocundity as that intended by *Private Eye*. In fact he was livid. Those who witnessed the author's fury on the subject would long marvel at the scene, speaking of it in hushed tones like old salts recalling a historic hurricane. 'Those utter *shits*,' he shouted down the phone to his wartime comrade Evelyn Waugh when coming to describe his journalistic antagonists, amidst a flow of other soldierly language so ripe that Waugh felt it best to hold the receiver away from his ear. Nor did Churchill's ire end there. On 11 February he fired off a sharp letter to the offending magazine, demanding an explanation of the 'points made in your cartoon'. Unfortunately, the editor of *Private Eye*, to whom Randolph's letter had been addressed, was unable to reply at once, since he was on holiday in Scotland. He returned to London to find that writs had been issued wholesale against all twelve members of the *Eye*'s staff – two of them actually addressed to fictional nicknames that appeared on the masthead – and that Churchill had retained the services of 49-year-old Peter Carter-Ruck, the man who became synonymous with libel law in Britain and who went on to enjoy a virtual season ticket to the High Court in his encounters with the *Eye*, where, with a certain inevitability, he was known by the slightly amended name of 'Peter Carter-Fuck'.

An opportunity of the sort provided by Churchill's brief was meat and drink to Ruck, in whose initial approach there was none of the gentlemanly reserve that characterised most other solicitors' correspondence of the time. Imperious in tone, his letter set a strict timeframe for the magazine's response to the 'most disgraceful opprobrium heaped upon our client's good name', or else invited them to settle their differences in court. (To further their chances of success, he had Churchill retain all the UK's available libel QCs to prevent them acting for the opposition, a practice since banned.) Faced with the prospect of financial ruin, *Private Eye* settled for £3,000 (around £45,000 today), the price of their publishing Churchill's letter of complaint splashed over a full page in the London *Evening Standard*, thus ensuring roughly twelve times as many people heard of the matter as saw the original cartoon, along with a grovelling apology for any unspecified remarks that might have impugned either the divinity of Sir Winston Churchill or the literary excellence of his son.

In due course, Carter-Ruck would go on to help define the whole concept of what constituted an acceptable attitude towards Britain's great and good, in the process doing for freedom of speech what Charles Manson did for struggling California singer-songwriters. Nothing was more likely to spoil a newspaper editor's morning than the couriered arrival of a letter bearing the dreaded lawyer's return address. Litigation 'waft[ed] the breath of life to me,' Carter-Ruck, one of those simultaneously comic and sinister figures familiar from the pages of Dickens, once confided. He would even, as a scorpion when aroused will supposedly sting itself, sue his own colleagues, when, for instance, in the early 1980s some of the partners in his firm rashly suggested he might retire. (On resolving that particular dispute to his advantage, Ruck had increased the sensation of pain by turning the signet ring on his right index finger inward, so that the jewels would bite deep into his former colleagues' flesh when they shook hands.) En route few prisoners were taken, and huge costs were incurred. Carter-Ruck would become almost as well known for his final bills as for his results. Among his most cherished possessions at the time of his death in 2003 were a Rolls-Royce Silver Shadow with the number plate L1BEL, along with a racing yacht he christened *Fair Judgement*.

It's worth mentioning Carter-Ruck here not only because he did so much to successfully exploit the draconian libel laws in England and Wales, but because these stood in such contrast to the standards established elsewhere in 1964. More specifically, there was the landmark judgement that March of *New York Times v. Sullivan* that still resonates today. The case arose from a paid advertisement in the USA's daily newspaper of record, headlined 'Heed Their Rising Voices', which among other things claimed that police forces around the country were attempting to derail America's civil rights struggle through acts of 'institutional racism and violence'. One Lester B. Sullivan, an elected official in Montgomery, Alabama, in charge of supervising that city's police, brought a suit against the paper on the grounds that inaccuracies in the ad had lowered his reputation. An all-white Alabama jury returned a verdict for Sullivan in the full amount demanded – half a million dollars – and the state's higher court affirmed this. At that stage, the *Times* appealed to the US Supreme Court, which issued a unanimous 9–0 decision in favour of the paper. The verdict resulted in three days of rioting in Alabama.

In the longer term, *New York Times v. Sullivan* established the principle of 'actual malice', which requires that public figures be held to a higher standard of truth than ordinary citizens before they can succeed in a defamation suit. In other words, in the United States – and also many other countries around the world – an aggrieved celebrity has to prove that a distasteful remark about him or her was not merely inaccurate, but was published with the advance knowledge that it was false, or at least with reckless disregard for the truth. As a result, from March 1964 onwards, high-profile litigants would increasingly favour the British court system, where the libel laws generally remain more congenial to the plaintiff. In time, this led to the peculiar spectacle of Lownes's sometime friend Roman Polanski, a Franco-Polish citizen, choosing to 'forum shop' by venting his displeasure at a large New York-based magazine by formally suing its more modest British edition, and even then doing so only by means of a videolink connection lest he himself be arrested on an outstanding warrant relating to his rape of a 13-year-old girl. It seemed to some a curious system that allowed a man like Polanski to be in the enviable position of being able to cherry-pick those parts of the judicial process that suited him, while ignoring those that didn't.

The fact remains that both in 1964, and throughout the Swinging Sixties and beyond, most British news outlets and their owners were painfully aware that the rules of engagement of the typical libel action had changed little since the days of Queen Victoria, and that the high price of defending such a suit, even when they might believe they had a good case, was like an expensive game of chicken. Under prevailing English law, the loser almost always had to pay the costs of the winner, as well as any damages awarded, which is why the UK press as a whole trod so warily in comparison to its foreign counterparts. If you were an actor or a politician or a business magnate in the England of 1964, and you read something in your morning paper to suggest that your carefully cultivated public persona might not be entirely consistent with your private conduct, you might well feel inclined to pick up the phone to Peter Carter-Ruck or one of his fellow practitioners in a way your equivalent elsewhere in the world wouldn't. The middle-aged Ruck himself retained the aspect of a 'civil, but when the time came, murderously assertive shark in the midst of a feeding frenzy', to quote Victor Lownes, although as *Private Eye* and many others like it would testify when watching Carter-Ruck in action, a shark might conceivably have had the edge in manners.

In January 1964, Tony Gill was a 23-year-old reporter on £1,400 a year at the Conservative-leaning *Daily Sketch*, under its superbly urbane editor Howard French. The paper was then selling close to a million copies a day, although sometimes the figure sloshed around like water in a bathtub, gaining or losing 100,000 or so in response to a particularly eye-catching headline or a new readers' spot-the-ball competition. 'Old French strutted about in his black suit, buttonhole, shoes highly polished,' Gill remembers. 'Handlebar moustache, clipped Sandhurst accent. Very military sort of cove.' What was more, 'everyone in the newsroom still wore a jacket and tie, everyone enjoyed a drink and everyone smoked.' The paper's few female employees were hired for their looks or willingness to 'put it about', regardless of any other skills. For Gill, daily life consisted of commuting in and out on the train from Essex – 'like the seventh circle of hell most days' – and laboriously scribbling copy in longhand which was then borne away by an office junior for the scrutiny of some unseen authority figure on the floor above, who might amend it with grammatical revisions or other more narrowly libel-preventive notations, before French himself, returning from his extended lunch at Soho's Gay Hussar restaurant, deigned to cast an imperious eye over the result.

One of the first stories Gill worked on in this fashion in 1964 was a press release from the US Surgeon General concerning the possible health consequences of tobacco use. It contained the shocking news that cigarette smoking was a probable cause of lung cancer, among several other diseases. There was a subsection in the report quoting a cross-section of consumer reactions, and on the whole these present a stark contrast to the public consensus on the subject today. The following week, a reporter from the BBC's current-events programme *Tonight*, hosted by the venerable Cliff Michelmore, went out on the streets of London to ask people there what they thought of it all.

One elderly man volunteered that he smoked between thirty and thirty-five cigarettes a day, and might have seemed, by our standards, notably sanguine on the subject. 'Quite honestly, I think that the end of one's life is probably more in the hands of almighty God, you know, than in my own hands or the hands of the tobacco manufacturers.' The *Tonight* reporter went on to ask a young woman whether, 'in light of the news out of America', the enjoyment she got from smoking was worth the risk. 'I think so, yes,' she replied evenly. 'If I'm going to die, I'm going to die, so I might as well enjoy life as it is now.'

Back in the *Sketch*'s grimy-walled Victorian offices in an alley off London's Fleet Street, Tony Gill remembers:

> French himself appearing one afternoon with the news that we would be launching one of our periodic 'investigations' into the perils of tobacco, although I have to say he wasn't exactly preaching to the converted because there was a constant haze of equal parts fag smoke and stale sweat around the newsroom, and by about four o'clock when the presses were ready to roll and everyone was crammed in there it got so thick you sometimes bumped into the furniture when you walked around.

Another story to come Gill's way in the early days of 1964 was a report that Leyland Motors, precursor to British Leyland, was due to sell 450 double-decker buses to Fidel Castro's hard-line Marxist regime in Cuba, in apparent defiance of the American-led trade embargo on the island where surface-to-air nuclear rockets had been stationed, pointing in Washington's direction, just over a year earlier. It was a case where hard-headed capitalism triumphed over fuzzy concepts of geopolitics or the so-called Atlantic special relationship. The deal was worth some £4 million to the beleaguered car and truck manufacturer, and the only note on the matter by the British Cabinet reads: 'The prime minister recorded his satisfaction with the terms of the arrangement.'

The US administration of Lyndon B. Johnson wasn't so persuaded, and during a phone conversation with his national security adviser McGeorge Bundy on 7 January, Johnson asked whether his slain predecessor in office, John F. Kennedy, had ever objected to the 'Limeys running around doing this kind of shit' in his meetings with Harold Macmillan. Bundy cleared his throat and replied:

Well, sir, I think you can say [Kennedy] raised it with them, because they would be in a position to say no formal objection was made, and the reason, I think, was that they would have come back to say, OK, you sell wheat to the Soviet Union, what the hell are you talking about?

After a suitable pause for reflection, Bundy continued:

We maintain that Cuba should be isolated because it's exporting subversion. The Brits would maintain that Cuba is no worse than the Soviet Union and that we greatly exaggerate this, and in their mind, they'd be right. I mean, that's their politics. The British man in the street thinks we've got a neurosis on Cuba.

'Right,' said Johnson, ending the conversation. Castro duly got his double-deckers.

There was another of those twists to the circular and seemingly eternal debate about Europe when, on 6 February 1964, the British and French governments agreed to build a physical link under the English Channel. The idea of a fixed passage between the two countries had first been mooted 162 years earlier, and in the event it would be another three decades before the 30-mile tunnel, originally estimated to cost £160 million, would be opened to the public with a final price tag of £9 billion, or some £17 billion today. 'It remains to be decided when and how best such an expense can be borne,' the UK transport secretary Ernest Marples warily informed Parliament. Tony Gill would remember a 'loud peal of laughter' greeting the announcement when it reached the *Daily Sketch* newsroom:

Behind the scenes most people in and out of politics thought the whole thing would never be built. They'd been talking about it literally since Napoleon's time. It was very much the Heathrow-expansion saga of its day. You'd get a plan, and there'd be protests, and then another plan and an inquiry, and then more protests and inquiries, each of them with its own set of rules and regulations, and motions about whether to 'note' or 'affirm' a past vote to 'regret' or 'consider' the latest objection, and all the time the final costs of this would be ticking over like a fruit machine, and most of us thought it would just be one of those projects that limp along forever before anyone actually sticks the first shovel in the ground.

Meanwhile, certain liberal and liberalising reforms around the world would come to affect British life, and to play a role in the making of 'the Sixties'. Some of these were of loftier origin than others. The years-long work of the Vatican Council, first convened in October 1962, transformed not only the liturgy and language of the Catholic Church, but took a first tentative step towards reconciliation with other Christian denominations, and for that matter with those of other faiths or no faith at all. Pope Paul VI noted in November 1964:

> The Church regards with sincere reverence those ways of conduct and of life, those precepts and teachings, which though differing in many aspects from the ones she holds, nonetheless often reflect a ray of that truth which enlightens all men.

Spotted: official recognition that there might be more than one way for human beings to contemplate their relationship with their maker.

Perhaps the Pope's announcement was only to formalise what was already becoming apparent. Traditional religious affiliation, whether Catholic, Protestant or otherwise, was declining steadily both in the UK and elsewhere. By January 1964 only about one in twelve adult Britons attended church on a regular basis. Fewer people were being married in church, fewer adolescents were being confirmed, and fewer than 50 per cent of babies were being baptised.

There were, however, at least glimmerings of the Vatican's new ideal of spiritual diversity at the grass-roots level. The first purpose-built Sikh gurdwara in Britain opened for business in Bradford on 29 March 1964, following that religion's more humble UK headquarters, established in an upstairs room of a terraced house in Shepherds Bush, west London. There were just seven registered Islamic mosques in the British Isles in 1964, although the Home Office reported that 'there are believed to be many places of Muslim worship that are not licensed, particularly in the industrial North.'

For all that, it might be fair to say that the nation as a whole still fell some way short of an ideal model of religious or racial inclusivity. The Pakistan-born cricketer Khalid 'Billy' Ibadulla then played as a professional for Warwickshire in the English county championship during the northern summer, and for Otago in New Zealand's Plunket Shield trophy in the winter. Although most people at the Midlands club went out of their way to make him feel welcome, not every member of the local community was as obliging. These were early days for the multicultural society, and many Britons, at all walks of life, avoided the shackles of excessive deference to what became known as political correctness. As it happened, there was one distressingly widespread illustration of the UK's still somewhat rudimentary concept of race relations: 'Paki-bashing', of which Birmingham saw its fair share around pub closing time most Saturday nights. Ibadulla himself was never directly targeted, but he attracted his full quota of muttered asides both on and off the cricket field. For some reason, a disproportionately high number of these seem to have come while playing away against Yorkshire. 'Chutney-breath' was one of the epithets to regularly greet Ibadulla when he appeared at the batting crease. Other terms of address were considerably less elevated than this.

★ ★ ★

It seemed that undreamt-of prosperity and consumption were a way of life – the American way of life – that lurked tantalisingly just across the Atlantic in 1964, in a vast, air-conditioned Neverland that most Britons still only experienced through the medium of film and television, rather than by making a long and expensive air journey. Of course, for all its material comforts, American society wasn't untouched by shadow. In February 1964, black and Puerto Rican groups boycotted the New York City public school system to protest the racial segregation still practised both there, and, in the words of one organiser, 'everywhere you turn in New York'. When 20-year-old Keith Richards of the Rolling Stones first set foot in the city that June, he remembered that 'nobody was talking about peace, love and flowers. The place was a fucking time-warp.' As the Stones strolled around Manhattan on a cool, drizzly evening, they found a town inhabited by funereally clad men with Eisenhower-era burr cuts, a pervasive musty stench of horse meat being sold from carts, and a backdrop of shabby high-rise apartment blocks that looked like central Berlin after a particularly heavy night in April 1945. The city's public water-fountains were still marked 'White' and 'Colored'. Even to a band of young musicians who had grown up in places like Dartford and Cheltenham, everything seemed strangely uptight. A few days later, in

Omaha, Richards casually poured himself a glass of whisky and coke backstage, and at that a gum-chewing policeman advised him that he was below the legal drinking age and to tip the contents down the sink forthwith. When Keith demurred, he looked up to find the man was pointing a gun at his head.

America was interesting territory for both the Stones and other British visitors, a place that 'did everything differently', as Richards was later to remark. There was a lot of noise and bustle, and a large number of people who made it their business to separate you from your money. I can speak from childhood experience in saying that American doctors, then as now, were somehow able to identify a range of baffling new diseases, as well as to charge impressively expensive amounts to treat them, for the most part unfamiliar to their British counterparts. You noticed how people employed a regretful yet at the same time animated tone when discussing their health, as if their most intimate ailments, distressing as they might be, were a positive joy to share with complete strangers. Americans always seemed to be obsessed with the state of their teeth and with the colour of people's skin. And of course there was the deepening morass of Vietnam to consider, where on 30 January 1964 a coup in Saigon ousted the curiously lethargic premier Duong Van Minh, known as Big Minh, and replaced him with a hard-line military junta. This last development set the scene for, if not made inevitable, the escalating armed confrontation with the communist regime in the north. Just four days later, President Johnson confided to a journalist:

There's one of three things we can do [about Vietnam]. One is run and let the dominoes start fallin' over, and God almighty what they said about us leaving China would just be warmin' up compared to what they'd say now. You can run or you can fight, as we are doin', or you can sit on your ass and agree to neutralize all of it. But nobody's gonna neutralize North Vietnam. That's totally impractical. So it really boils down to one of two decisions: gettin' out or gettin' in. We can't abandon it to the commies, as I see it. So I think old man De Gaulle [who was urging restraint] is puffin' through his hat.

REVOLUTION IN THE HEAD

In early 1964, the old, pre-war British establishment was still – just about – holding on, while a post-war generation was coming up behind fast. That the nation remained in two minds about the free-wheeling vernacular of the new 'beat' music, and for that matter about the tidal wave of youthful energy buffeting the cultural dam of the 1950s, can be seen from the progress that winter of the five provincial English boys calling themselves the Rolling Stones.

Late the previous autumn, the Stones had embarked on their first British national tour, when they appeared on the undercard to America's harmonising Everly Brothers – the latter, at least, with their shiny dinner jackets and strummed acoustic guitars, seemingly ill-suited to act as confederates of the lewd corrupters of the nation's youth. The homegrown element of the nightly bill, by contrast, achieved a near unanimity of critical derision. While other pop groups of the day might garner a dig from their local vicar, the Stones were panned by the Archbishop of Canterbury. 'Ugly Looks, Ugly Speech, Ugly Manners' was the verdict in one headline, thus sadly undermining the promise each of the band members had only recently made to do nothing that might lower their parents in the eyes of their suburban neighbours.

Twenty-year-old 'Mike' Jagger, as he then styled himself, late of the London School of Economics, was even now the focus of each night's presentation, spinning round at intervals to shake his bony posterior at the audience before camping his way through the group's thirty-minute stage repertoire. Jagger also minced, swayed, frisked and gambolled, all the while managing to look supremely bored, and there were long stretches in many songs when he did little else. This was a new development in terms of what defined an acceptable form of public entertainment. Indeed, there was something a bit unsettling about the Stones collectively, an act whose classic visuals were now fast falling into place. There was the little harlequinade of lip-pursing and bum-wiggling, for instance, that Jagger strutted out when not busy appraising the floor. There was the group's absurdly deadpan rhythm section. And, leering down at the front rows, there was the frock-coated Brian Jones, seeming less like a pop guitarist than some randy young Regency buck eyeing up the local talent, while the harsh cinema footlights did nothing to conceal the pallid cheeks and cratered pimples of Keith Richards, Jones's front-line colleague.

Above all, the group's progress that year demonstrates both the possibilities and the limitations of a budget-conscious British provincial package tour of the era. The deprivations included a poverty format that saw them paid just £35 (£525) for each of their sixty-one sold-out shows, of which the Stones pocketed roughly two pounds apiece; a succession of brilliantined house managers, on hand to act as a Greek chorus of disapproval, telling everyone to get their bloody hair cut; wolfed-down transport café meals; nondescript hotels with beds generally as uninviting as a cold park bench; and a provincial landscape so desolate that, as the band's travelling assistant Ian 'Stu' Stewart remarked, a compass of the sort he carried in his frayed Milletts jeans pocket was as important a tool as the roadie's ubiquitous gaffer tape. Of the band's internal dynamic, Stu noted, 'You really see the worst of someone when you're in the back of a van with your face stuck in their armpit all day' – an irrefutable truth.

The Stones were duly on hand to help launch a new weekly programme that soon became a rallying point for the latest and hottest tunes, with a strong fashion subplot: *Top of the Pops*, which first aired at 6.35 p.m. on New Year's Day 1964. The show was the brainchild of the 46-year-old BBC producer Johnnie Stewart, a graduate of the corporation's radio sound effects department and a somewhat unlikely godfather to the nation's 'now' mentality, who sold it to the higher-ups at Broadcasting House as a relatively cheap and harmless bit of fun with an unusually democratic format: the show would always end with that week's best-selling single, which was the only record to be repeated from the previous week. The broadcast would also always include the highest new entry to the Hit Parade and the fastest climber; nothing going down was permitted. Quality was not necessarily an issue. The record-buying public determined each show's content, and in a brilliant – if now dubious – move, Stewart also created a scantily clad female dance troupe to enhance the overall production, initially known as the Go-Jos and later as Pan's People, whose 'Babs' Lord would fondly remember the backstage ambience of 'the girls huddl[ed] in a grotty rehearsal room, where the old heater was belching black smoke and it was so cold you were wearing gloves'.

The first *Top of the Pops* was aired from a disused Wesleyan church, somehow a fitting symbol of the nation's shifting spiritual values, in Dickenson Road, Manchester, recently acquired by the BBC as a studio but still retaining much of its former ecclesiastical air. The groups themselves and their sprightly young audience were greeted by the superbly British sign nailed to the building's interior wall as a result of representations from the nearby Rainbow's End retirement home and miniature golf course: 'WORSHIPPERS ARE REQUESTED THAT THEY NOT CONTINUE TO SING OR AFFIRM LOUDLY WHEN LEAVING THE PREMISES FOLLOWING EVENSONG.'

The 37-year-old Jimmy Savile presented the first broadcast live, with a brief link back to his colleague Alan 'Fluff' Freeman – whose barrage of catchphrases, such as the celebrated 'not 'arf' were, once heard, if not to everyone's taste, rarely forgotten – to preview the following week's show. The host himself dressed theatrically badly in a sort of faux-Elvis sparkly tracksuit, with long, thinning dyed-blonde hair and enough chunky jewellery around his neck to ensure that salvage experts would have been required had he somehow drowned. Savile was fast on his way to becoming Britain's officially tolerated eccentric uncle, before eventually being outed as a serial sex predator and rapist.

The performers on hand for the first *Top of the Pops* transmission were called upon merely to mime to their designated hit, a challenge that some managed to bring off with more conviction than others. The line-up that night stands as a who's who of contemporary British music: Dusty Springfield, with her drowned blonde hair and smudged coal-black eyes, with 'I Only Want to Be With You'; the Stones, also in aspirational mood, with 'I Wanna Be Your Man'; the Dave Clark Five with 'Glad All Over'; the Hollies with 'Stay'; and the Swinging Blue Jeans with 'Hippy Hippy Shake', along with filmed inserts from Cliff Richard, Gene Pitney, and Freddie and the Dreamers – a sort of sound sculpture of classic early pop. Savile kept it brief in between numbers, yodelling out his own catchphrase, 'How's about that, then?', in his burlesque northern accent. It wouldn't have mattered had he been reciting the Muslim Brotherhood manifesto, because as the broadcast proceeded his words were increasingly lost in a cyclotron of hormonal abandon. Amid ear-splitting screams in the studio audience, the Beatles, no less, then climactically performed 'I Want to Hold Your Hand' – the fourth song that night to emphasise the singer's urgent romantic needs in its title, the week's number one and, with its plunging, dive-bomber bass, twin-octave vocals, and several other dazzling effects, a strong contender as the Big Bang moment of modern rock music.

The BBC had initially commissioned just six weekly episodes of *Top of the Pops*, but the run was promptly doubled and then extended indefinitely. The programme would rapidly become appointment television, with a regular Thursday night audience of 7 million viewers, a mixture of the thrusting new Britain and the grey years of war and rationing, or at least of the era when trade unions would come out on strike over the least dispute about the demarcation of labour. One of the show's most celebrated absurdities lay in its demand that the artists who performed each week had to re-record the backing track of their hit that same afternoon, when they might already have spent days or weeks in a studio creating the original version. In practice, bands often pretended to re-record the song, then used their existing tapes. Keith Richards confirmed:

> It happened to the Stones. We sat around and had a smoke, didn't do any [re-recording] at all, then used the studio version. It was bloody odd, Britain in those days – half of it was people getting high and wanting to spike the country's water supply, and the other half was a lot of farts straight out of the army telling you to get a haircut and learn to play 'Moon River'.

Both at the old Wesleyan church and out on the road, the first quarter of 1964 was a time of some little ferment in the life of the Stones. Late in March, they set a one-night attendance record (netting them £218 10s) in the heady atmosphere of the Plaza Ballroom, Guildford. Fans had been queuing up in the rain since nine that morning. 'Most kids [would] never go for indifference,' the band's 20-year-old manager Andrew Oldham had repeatedly impressed on his charges, but outright contempt would work every time. So when the Stones eventually slouched on stage at Guildford an hour and a quarter late, they neither apologised nor acknowledged the crowd, nor for that matter made much overt display of pleasure to be there. After glaring around the room for a moment or two, Keith Richards then counted the band in for the siren-like intro of Chuck Berry's 'Talkin' 'Bout You'. The place immediately erupted. Mike Jagger was in prime motivational form throughout. 'Now we'd like to do "Roll Over Beethoven", that famous song written by the Beatles,' he announced, in a rare lull between numbers. The crowd said nothing. 'You're thicker than I thought,' Jagger remarked. 'It's another one by Chuck Berry.' Abandoning the insolent half-smile that serves as the mask of the bright but insecure, Brian Jones threw back his head and laughed maniacally, and Charlie Watts did a ba-*boom* roll of the drums. The chafing from the stage only roused the crowd to greater transports of delight. As the curtain fell there was another full-scale riot in progress, ended by the traditional means of hurriedly playing the national anthem over the hall's public address system: the two Britains, as it were, in juxtaposition. The show closed with Brian Jones being pulled to the floor by several young girls, an experience he seemed not to actively dislike.

In short order the Stones went up in Ian Stewart's powerfully fetid minivan to the newly opened Cubi-Klub in Rochdale, Lancashire. Before long the place looked like a Hieronymus Bosch painting of hell, with waves of girls swarming across the footlights to clutch even at members of the support act. Police refused to let the Stones go on, and instead gave them a high-speed escort down the A58 to Manchester. Two nights later at a northern music hall, an elderly lady pianist, Miss Olivia Dunn, warmed up the room with a selection of bygone show tunes. When the Stones appeared, the crowd quickly forgot all the admonitions about staying in their seats, stood up as one, and rushed down to the front, trampling Miss Dunn and her piano underfoot.

Later that week the Majestic Ballroom, Birkenhead, was rocking to a lusty chant of 'Mick!' (as he was becoming known) and 'Brian!' that had already soared up to the pain threshold long before the Stones themselves appeared. When Keith Richards then opened proceedings with the guitar chop of Buddy Holly's 'Not Fade Away', there were suddenly '500 kids running towards us – it was like D-Day,' he told me, still fondly remembering the melee thirteen years later. Abandoning their instruments, the band members hurriedly left the stage, coming under a rain of assorted wooden chair legs, freshly shed underwear and other debris as they did so. Peeking out from behind the velvet curtain, they watched as Stu was left to pad lugubriously around the stage, muttering 'Excuse me' as he went, to retrieve their equipment as best he could. After Oldham intervened, the Stones were paid their full fee – now £315 15s – for their roughly ten-second performance. The *Daily Express* considered the affair 'Shocking!' and the Stones themselves a 'cause of growing concern.' By March 1964 they weren't just a pop group, they were news.

★ ★ ★

'If you pretend to be wicked, you'll get rich.' This was Andrew Oldham's considered managerial advice to Mick Jagger, who had hitherto been pondering a career in the diplomatic service, or possibly as a provincial schoolteacher like his father and grandfather before him. And even in 1964, there were times, Jagger later admitted, when he came to rue his decision to align himself with Britain's most notorious pop group as an alternative. That the nation as a whole hadn't yet succumbed to the Stones' charms could be seen on a wet night that spring when the band played a show in front of twenty-three customers, counting the landlord, in a London pub, which was depressing enough even before the volume on everyone's instruments suddenly went down to half power owing to a wildcat strike by local electricity workers. There had then been a distressing incident following a suburban engagement later that week, when Keith Richards was leaving the premises pursued by a small but animated posse of young girls. Ian Stewart had swiftly assessed the situation and backed his van up to the stage door of the club. Keith reached for the van's door handle, but this came off in his hand, leaving him at the mercy of his admirers. 'Very bitter about it, he was, too,' Stu recalled.

A trainee London office clerk named Cecilia Nixon caught some of the essential drama of the era:

> It was all very primal stuff, and there was a definite us-versus-them feeling in the air in 1964. I remember the local paper was up in arms about the "potential provided by the cover of darkness in cinemas for acts of moral lewdness" between teenagers. Those were the exact words. You heard people standing in shops or waiting for the bus say that even *Top of the Pops* was an encouragement to would-be sex maniacs. "They're all at it, you know." Well of course they were – starting with the middle-aged perverts who were running it.
>
> The Stones were already pretty incredible on stage by that point. There was the beat, and there was the drama of the singer hopping around with his maracas, scowling at you, between the two evil-looking guitarists. Basic, basic stuff. You saw boys fighting. Girls touching themselves in inappropriate places, legs akimbo. The stench almost knocked you backwards. I remember walking in to my first concert as this very prim young lady, and by the time they stopped playing I was pogoing up and down and I couldn't stop myself screaming. *That's* what I mean by primal.

On Monday 3 February, the Beatles concluded their only fitfully successful French tour – audiences had proved deaf to all but the band's
Motown cover songs – by visiting the American embassy in Paris to
obtain their H-2 work permits, which were strictly contingent on there
being 'no unemployed US persons capable of performing the duties
specified.' This was a reasonably safe bet. Four days later, the group
were aboard Pan Am flight 101, bound for New York. At 1.20 p.m. local
time, the band's plane – the *Clipper Defiance* – landed in a light snow-
storm at the recently christened John F. Kennedy airport. Everyone
sat and waited. No British band had ever before seriously cracked the
mass American market, and even a big homegrown name like Cliff
Richard had bombed on his one US tour. There was no chit-chat
among the four young musicians on their arrival that afternoon, just
increasing nervous anticipation and repeated whispers from up front
that a big crowd was there to meet them. Finally the cabin door swung
open, admitting a blast of arctic air, and even the Beatles gaped:
4,000 screaming, banner-waving fans were packed onto the adjacent
Arrivals building balcony.

The author Tom Wolfe, then on assignment for the *New York
Herald-Tribune*, told me of what followed:

> Here came hundreds of boys, high-school kids, pounding past me with
> their combs out, and they were frantically combing their hair forward
> as they ran, so it would fall over their foreheads like the Beatles' ... I'll
> never forget that scene. That was symbolic of a big change; the last
> vestige of adult control of music *vanished* at that instant.

On the Sunday evening of 9 February, amid scenes akin to *Mission:
Impossible*, a group of young men with matching Beatles wigs set off in
a decoy car from New York's Plaza Hotel, while the real Moptops were
spirited out the back door and driven at wild speed half a mile down
Broadway to the 728-seat Studio 50 in midtown Manhattan. They
were there at the behest of a small, jowly man, habitually dressed like a
funeral director, whom they'd encountered quite by chance when passing him at a brisk trot in the Heathrow departure lounge one morning
late the previous October. The man's name was Ed Sullivan, and for
the past fifteen years he'd hosted a top-rated Sunday night variety hour

on coast-to-coast American television. For most of that time, 'Uncle Ed's' show had consisted of the most familiar, family-oriented fare, with one or two mild concessions to youth: back in 1956, he'd introduced the viewing public to the 'singing truck driver' Elvis Presley, whom the cameras showed only from the waist up. Like most adult Americans, the 62-year-old Sullivan had never previously heard of the Beatles. He did, however, recognise mass hysteria when he saw it, and after being 'physically kapowed' by the hordes of pre-teen girls rushing past him that autumn morning at Heathrow, he rapidly sought out the band's manager to talk about having the boys on his show.

As luck would have it, the Beatles' arrival at Sullivan's theatre three months later coincided with something of a youth-led consumer boom in the United States. In the wake of sweeping tax cuts that January, President Johnson's economic experts pronounced themselves full of optimism about the nation's overall financial health. Walter Heller, head of the Council of Fiscal Advisers, told his boss that the economy was 'showing new vitality and promise', with unemployment rates 'about invisible' and 'no inflation in sight'. One way or another, it seemed there was more money circulating in almost all walks of American life than even a year or two earlier during the halcyon days of the Kennedy administration. Greater disposable income, and the consequent retail boom, not only in practical household products like washing machines and cars but also in such youth-themed accessories as record players, transistor radios and boutique clothes, offered a chance to return to something like normal life after an extended period of collective mourning for the late president. All this combined to help create the conditions for a sudden release of pent-up youthful energy at the time the Beatles found themselves waiting nervously that cold February night at Sullivan's theatre, where their host clanked around his dressing room trying to memorise all their names. Perhaps rashly, Brian Epstein chose that same moment to walk in and announce, 'I'd like to know the exact wording of your introduction.'

First Sullivan reddened. Then he said, 'I'd like *you* to fuck off.'

When the time came, around eight that night, Ed kept it short: '*Lezz 'n gennlemun, the Beatles. Let's bring 'em on!*'

The decibel level of ensuing screams and cracking seat fixtures comfortably exceeded that of the music, which 'might as well have been us farting', as John Lennon later noted. A lady from upstate Hartsdale, New York, with the striking name of Debbie Drooz, was in the audience that night as a 14-year-old schoolgirl. 'They'd warned us not to get out of our seats when the Beatles appeared,' she remembers. 'I probably lasted about ten seconds longer than the other kids in my row. It was crazy. One girl next to me kept yelling "Paul! Paul!" at the top of her lungs, as if McCartney was literally treading on her corns.' When John and Paul then stepped forward to the mike for the 'Wh-ooh' chorus of 'She Loves You', which they sang in falsetto, both shook their pudding-bowl hair in unison. At that precise moment the dominant noise in the studio changed from one of sustained applause to one of frenzied shrieking. At the end, the four band members gave a stiff, theatrical bow, quickly drove back to the Plaza, rang some girls, had a few drinks and laughed about how they'd played out of tune. The reviews were still terrific. The Beatles got a Trendex rating of 73.5 million viewers, then easily the largest in US television history.

★ ★ ★

It was with a sense of liberation, nonetheless, that Paul McCartney returned to his enviable home life as a permanent guest in the former parlourmaid's room of a five-storey Georgian house in Wimpole Street, central London. His steady girlfriend, 17-year-old Jane Asher, lived there with her music-loving parents, who made the broadminded suggestion that their daughter's famous partner move in with them. As well as being 'a bit of posh', as the upstairs tenant called it, the place had the bonus of being a *salon*: Jane was a working actress who was busy that winter filming *The Masque of the Red Death* and guest-starring in *The Saint*, while writing pop reviews, opening village fetes and generally being the It Girl of 1964. Her sister Clare was also in showbiz, appearing on the radio soap opera *Mrs. Dale's Diary*. Their brother Peter, a bespectacled 19-year-old with red hair that he combed forward in a Beatle cut, formed an Everlys-style pop duo with his schoolfriend Gordon Waller. That spring they had a number-one hit with 'World Without Love', a tune Paul had furnished for them. The children's mother, Margaret, was a professor of oboe at London's Guildhall School, and always thought their houseguest had the makings of a perfectly good musician if only he would take lessons. Presiding over the household was the brilliant and voluble figure of Dr Richard Asher, artist, collector, world-renowned consultant in blood and mental diseases (himself bipolar), co-discoverer of

Munchausen's syndrome, best-selling author of *Nerves Explained* and of a scholarly paper on mass hysteria – the greatest single cause of which in much of the Western world now happened to be resident in a room directly above Dr Asher's study, furnished by a small, iron-framed bed, an upright piano, two Cocteau sketches, and a hand-drawn sign over the door saying 'Paul's Place'.

On 2 March, McCartney and his colleagues, having hurriedly joined Equity, the actors' union, earlier that morning, assembled at London's Marylebone station to begin filming *A Hard Day's Night*. The original idea was to turn out a cheesy Elvis-style romp and matching album to capitalise on all the fuss before the whole thing ended just as quickly as it had begun, as everyone still assumed it would. Paul himself, who showed distinct signs of intelligence beneath the bangs, then brought in the Welsh-born Alun Owen, who was fast making a name for himself as one of the young playwrights on ITV's Sunday night 'kitchen sink' drama anthology *Armchair Theatre*, with the sharp-witted Dick Lester, of *Goon Show* fame, to direct. The resulting studio deal, even after haggling, was far below even the modest norms of a 1964 feature-length British film. *A Hard Day's Night* would be shot for £180,000, of which the band was paid a flat fee of £21,000, or roughly what a Vin Diesel spends today on lunch. But it was enough. Cavorting around various locations in London and the south east over the next six weeks, the Beatles made that rare thing: a day-in-the-life story that was fresh, funny, and with an infectiously snappy beat.

In time, the band's success on both record and film achieved the seemingly impossible in making Merseyside fashionable, and Brian Epstein was busy grooming a stable of supporting acts. Having been an impoverished backwater, somewhere the 1930s Depression had set in like a chill Atlantic fog and lifted again just in time for the Luftwaffe, Liverpool suddenly seemed set to become the cultural centre of gravity in western Europe. Every theatrical bill and poster was designed so that, after the Fab Four, came the 'top rising stars in the pop firmament': Gerry and the Pacemakers, Billy J. Kramer and Cilla Black, to name just the most prominent. This was astronomy according to Eppy, who relied on Lennon and McCartney to provide everyone with hits. There was even a thriving fortnightly music paper called *Mersey Beat* to celebrate the area's renaissance. It was edited by a former classmate of Lennon's called Bill Harry, and by January 1964 it was selling roughly 80,000 copies an issue. When *A Hard Day's*

Night hit British cinema screens in July it was followed by a shoal of satellite films, plays and television programmes typically set in gritty, working-class communities, with accents and language to match. The sense of suspended time that had hung over much of Britain in the early 1960s, where many businessmen really did wear bowler hats and carry a copy of *The Times* rolled up under their arm, and the typical BBC newsreader's voice was so plummy you could barely understand what he (it was always a man) was saying – a world seemingly sealed in aspic since the war – truly seemed to have run its course.

In the event, there was a colourful display of British adolescent life, whipped up into one of those periodic, Fleet Street-inspired moral panics, seen at various English seaside resorts that late winter and early spring. This was the Mods and Rockers phenomenon: essentially two conflicting youth cults distinguished by their contrasting fashion and musical tastes. The Mod movement favoured sharp suits and Vespa or Lambretta motor scooters, with a preference for British blues-rooted bands like the Yardbirds, the Small Faces and the Who. By contrast, the telltale signs of the Rocker were his black leather jacket and pompadour hairdo, and a fondness for the primitive strains of Eddie Cochran, Gene Vincent and Bo Diddley.

The exact statistics are elusive, but there were enough active members of each faction, and sufficient mutual animosity between them, for spirited fights to break out among the rival groups even in the chilly weekends of late March 1964, when more than one previously sedate yachtsman's haven came to resemble the setting for one of those Roger Corman films where the decent folk are suddenly invaded by Hells Angels. In time even the cobbled lanes of Margate in Kent rang to the sound of teenagers pursuing each other with bike chains and broken milk bottles in order to resolve the points that lay between them.

Commenting on the ensuing fracas that came up for his attention among the petty larcenies and traffic offences that were the more normal staple of his court, Dr George Simpson, chairman of Margate magistrates, remarked: 'It is not likely that the air of this town has ever been fouled by the hordes of hooligans, male and female, such as we have seen this week,' surely an unassailable truth. 'These long-haired, mentally unstable, petty little hoodlums,' Dr Simpson continued, warming to his theme, 'these sawdust Caesars who can only find courage like rats hunting in packs, came to our lovely Margate with the avowed intent of interfering with the peaceful life and property of our inhabitants.'

Dr Simpson then jailed eight men aged between 18 and 21 for three months each, and imposed fines totalling £1,900 (£28,500 today) on thirty-six other defendants. It seemed to some of the nation's moral guardians that a culture of rampant vandalism and hooliganism, rather than of self-effacing service to Queen and country, was now the distinguishing characteristic of Britain's youth, and many agonised media debates involving bishops, Cabinet ministers, charity organisers, chairs of local government committees, senior police officers and sundry academics and headmasters followed as a result. That there might be some sort of new juvenile delinquency abroad in the land, indifferent to the traditions or welfare of the past generation, seemed to gain ground in spectacular fashion when an 18-year-old brought down a heavy wine decanter on the head of the former chairman of the Labour party, George Brinham, with fatal results, although the assailant claimed that this was less a case of protest against Brinham's continued support of a British independent nuclear deterrent, as was widely reported at the time, and more one of his rebuffing an unwanted homosexual advance.

Meanwhile, there were curious scenes that winter in the small, privately owned port of Greenore, in Carlingford Lough, a mile or so to the southern side of the border between the two Irelands. At intervals in February and March, the locals noticed that their village seemed to be unaccountably full of strangers who spent their days working on an elderly, 700-ton former Scandinavian passenger ferry named the *Frederica* which lay tied up in a nearby slip, and in time came to acquire a battery of mysterious electronic equipment topped off by a 180-foot-high radio mast. Other men and women with suspicious continental accents were seen going about the town, buying up the entire stock, such as it was, of O'Flaherty's Disc and Dat record shop, while still others laid on impressive quantities of baked beans, bottled water, paracetamol and Guinness. The local pubs, of which there were many, soon hummed with speculation about spies, or possibly some sinister connection to the various Irish nationalist groups who, under the banner of the IRA, continued to demand the reunification – by force if need be – of the island.

The air of intrigue surrounding the old hulk in their midst deepened later in March, when the residents of Greenore found that their television reception was being interrupted by nocturnal transmissions apparently coming from the *Frederica*. One particular Friday night the chorus of Chuck Berry's 'Let It Rock' was interpolated gigantically into an otherwise sombre segment of the BBC's main news bulletin about the week's military coup in Gabon. Later that month it was noticed that Greenore's red and green harbour lights had begun flashing on and off in a strobe-like effect in time to a loudly amplified broadcast of the Beatles' 'All My Loving', a clear breach of the prevailing navigation safety regulations. It was all very odd. One stormy evening towards the end of March the ship simply slipped away into the Irish Sea, having previously told the UK's Maritime Compliance Agency of its intention to sail to southern Spain. The agency may well have been perplexed when a day or two later the vessel instead steered east into the English Channel, proceeded along the south coast, then turned north again before eventually anchoring in international waters off the port of Felixstowe in Suffolk. On the Saturday night of 27 March, the ship made her first trial broadcast as Radio Caroline, a name chosen in honour of the 6-year-old daughter of the late President Kennedy, before going live on air at noon the following day. Initially a cult largely restricted to listeners in East Anglia and the south of England, by July 1964 the station's manager could boast in the *Daily Mail* of having an audience larger than that of the all-powerful BBC. By later in the autumn the Home Office was sufficiently disturbed by the seafaring intruder on the nation's carefully monitored public airwaves to issue an official report on the matter: 'The "addicts" of this pirate enterprise are predominantly young people,' it noted, perhaps unnecessarily. 'Half of them are under 30 years of age. Addiction to Caroline is uncommon amongst 30–50 year-olds, and very rare indeed amongst those over 50.' Putting the best face possible on this affront to the BBC's Light Programme's broadcast monopoly of popular music, the report concluded:

> The 'image' of Caroline is of a 'lively', 'cheerful', 'friendly' service, but the same adjectives are also frequently applied to the Light Programme which, unlike Caroline, is also commended for being 'varied'. The important point is that friendly feelings towards Caroline do not necessarily imply unfriendly ones towards the BBC. Few of the general public want Caroline to stop – most of them are simply indifferent to its fate, whereas most would be 'sorry' to see the end of the Corporation.

The moving force behind Radio Caroline was a 23-year-old Irish nightclub owner turned pop impresario named Ronan O'Rahilly. He had been born in Dublin, the third of five children of a local manufacturing and shipping tycoon (who also happened to own the port in Greenore), and the grandson of an Irish Volunteer Force fighter who was one of those killed by English soldiers during the 1916 Easter Rising. Perhaps the whole Radio Caroline enterprise was some form of deeply ingrained if unstated O'Rahilly family revenge against the British establishment. Perhaps, too, there was an element of neo-hippy idealism to a project essentially dedicated to bringing the subversive new music to the masses. Or perhaps, finally, there was a touch of self-interest as well as of high-minded opposition to the BBC's closed shop. O'Rahilly had a controlling stake in the young blues singer Georgie Fame, but struggled to get his records played on the Light Programme. Convinced that there was an untapped market for Fame and others similarly ignored by mainstream radio, he made the audacious move to literally launch his own station. In short order, O'Rahilly hired a cadre of disc jockeys from British ballrooms and pop stations in the United States and Canada, told them to play only records the average parent would hate, and tried to instruct them in his slightly dotty theory of 'loving awareness', which entailed much free-spiritedness and hugging, along with the only optional wearing of clothes. In some ways he was the Kerry Packer figure of his time: a born entrepreneur, half visionary, half hard-headed pragmatist, and in either case quite happy to stuff it to the establishment.

Shortly before noon on Sunday 28 March, O'Rahilly, in a neat blue suit and tie, sandy hair flopping lightly on his forehead, sat nervously fidgeting with a bulky Zenith radio while a dozen journalists looked on, with varying degrees of amusement or impatience, in the saloon bar of the Cheshire Cheese pub just off Fleet Street, close to where most of them still had their offices. The press had been invited there to hear the first fruits of the Irishman's somewhat improbable tale about having his own floating broadcast studio. But no matter how much O'Rahilly twiddled the dial on the receiving radio, all he could pick up in the smoke-filled pub that Easter lunchtime was static and a few snatches of the Bishop of London's sermon from nearby St Paul's Cathedral. Some of the scribes packed up and went home, convinced that the story was all blarney. Tony Gill of the *Sketch* was one of those who stayed, if only because O'Rahilly had thoughtfully opened a slate at the bar for everyone's refreshments. Despite the hospitality, 'it wasn't going too well,' Gill remembers:

> After a lot more farting around with the radio, Ronan, who by now had had a few jars himself, sidled up to me and muttered, 'I don't know what the fock is happening.' Maybe the ship had sunk, or maybe the Coast Guard had boarded her. There was a lot of 'zany' young guys on board, he said, in charge of running the equipment, and maybe there'd been a technical glitch of some sort.
>
> After a lot more in this vein, finally O'Rahilly suggested that we all go outside to see if he could get a better signal by waving the radio around in the air. By now the idea that we were about to witness a great revolution in British broadcasting – as Ronan had promised we would – had become ludicrous. It was about as hi-tech as a couple of kids trying to see if they can talk to each other through two tin cans with a bit of string attached. You could see the other guys smirking a bit, but in the end they all went along with it. They didn't really seem to care. They probably thought there was a good silly-bugger story there for Monday morning's paper. Besides, they were drunk as well. Anyway, we all trooped out onto the freezing cold corner of Fleet Street, O'Rahilly holding the set aloft over his head like a religious icon, all the while still merrily twiddling away. Anyone who happened to have walked by and seen us would have thought we were bonkers, but suddenly, standing there in that grey Sunday afternoon drizzle, the radio came to life.

'This is Radio Caroline on 199 metres, your all-day music station,' a disc jockey who introduced himself as 'Rhymin'' Simon Dee said. Next, with a certain aptness, came the Rolling Stones's 'Not Fade Away', which was dedicated to O'Rahilly. Soon after that, Gill and the rest of the reporters drifted off back to their offices. They had their story.

Those faint but distinct strains of the Stones performing their version of the venerable Buddy Holly hit were the sound of revolution superbly controlled, and another milestone down the road of the British teenager's perennial campaign to distance their tastes from those of their parents. By the summer months of 1964 Caroline's audience, estimated at around 5 million, was both vast and somehow still exclusive-feeling, something like a secret club where you could commune in the dark with your favourite pop stars in the company of those 'zany' personalities, several of whom became celebrities in their own right: Tony Blackburn,

Dave Lee Travis, 'Emperor' Rosko, Tommy Vance and the evocatively named Spangles Muldoon, each working two weeks on, one week off for an annual salary of £1,300 plus room, board and what for many became a generous quota of sex with the female staff. By early August, O'Rahilly had a second ship operating off Frinton-on-Sea in Essex, while the original took up anchorage near the Isle of Man. The two stations had a reported 8 million daily listeners between them, and the whole vexing matter of radio piracy was being debated in Parliament. Asked what he intended to do to close down these illicit transmissions 'so injurious to the moral health of the country, especially our younger people', the Postmaster General, an ex-army officer named Reginald Bevins who had a pronounced independent streak, could reply only: 'I have received a very considerable number of representations about the activities of Radio Caroline, and I am taking the views of such groups into account.'

Before he could definitively rule in the matter, however, Bevins had lost his parliamentary seat, and declared he wanted no further truck with Conservatism until the 'entire upper-class echelon which clings to the old ways of life, still obsessed with the war' had been swept away. Among his last acts in office was to grant a licence to Manx Radio in August 1964, another significant step in loosening the cold grip of the BBC on the nation's public entertainment. Ronan O'Rahilly's whimsical initiative with the repurposed Danish ferry was thus the direct forerunner to the sprawling farrago of the UK's public-broadcasting network, with its roughly 600 licensed radio stations and 480-plus free-to-air or subscription TV channels we enjoy today.

TOFFS BEHAVING BADLY

One of Reginald Bevins's complaints about the Britain he helped govern in 1964 was that the sort of principled ideologue of his formative years in the 1930s, appalled by fascism and entranced by the possibilities of economic redistribution and a fairer, more egalitarian society, seemed to have been replaced by a 'lot of graspers solely interested in making money'. To his regret, most people at the time he served in Cabinet were concerned less with the great issues of the day and more with simply being entertained. 'Britain in the early 1960s was still a deeply divided place,' Bevins later noted, 'its government in the hands of an elderly Scotch earl who spoke in the clipped tones of one addressing the under-housemaid, and where real power lay in the hands of a tiny elite, not all of whom set the nation a shining moral example.' Indeed, in 1964 the behaviour of certain members of the British establishment, as commentators had come to call the mechanism through which power was exercised in the country, might well have caused comment at a Roman orgy.

The Queen herself, already in the twelfth year of her long reign, and as always personally irreproachable, now stood as the focal point of a court of frock-coated attendants and military officers draped in gold braid and medals who somehow looked increasingly Ruritanian in a post-Suez environment characterised by swingeing defence cuts at every level below the strictly ceremonial. This was a Britain where the monarchy kept around 150,000 precious artworks 'in trust' on behalf of the nation, received some £800,000 (£12 million today) per annum as part of a 400-year-old system for providing financial support to the royal household, paid no income tax, enjoyed the services of a Page of the Backstairs and a Yeoman of the Pantry, as well as of a fully staffed oceangoing yacht, and, despite the formal end to the practice in 1958, still welcomed if not ritually 'received' debutantes at a court, incalculable as any oriental sultanate, whose concentric layers of flunkies owed their very existence to heredity. Perhaps the best way to see it all is merely to say that in casting the drama of monarchy by birth, the British constitution rendered the participants mere actors in an unusually resilient and well-scripted soap opera.

On 11 March 1964, the *London Gazette*, itself in its 300th consecutive year of publication, led with the headline:

EXTRAORDINARY

Published by Authority

Registered as a Newspaper

WEDNESDAY, 11TH MARCH 1964

Whitehall, 10 March 1964

This evening at twenty minutes after eight o'clock Her Majesty THE QUEEN was safely delivered of a Prince at Buckingham Palace.

His Royal Highness the Duke of Edinburgh was present.

Her Majesty and the Infant Prince are both well.

This was none other than the future Edward, Earl of Wessex, whose early life – Gordonstoun, Cambridge and the Royal Marines – trod a broadly conventional path at least up until the moment he discovered showbusiness in the 1980s. There were, it's true, one or two concessions to the times in the specific circumstances of the new prince's delivery. Edward's three elder siblings had all arrived while the Queen was reportedly put into a state of 'twilight sleep' during labour, in which a morphine solution is pumped through a heavy rubber mask clamped over the expectant mother's mouth, and the baby itself then extracted using forceps. By March 1964, the 37-year-old monarch understandably opted for a more natural procedure, without, it was thought, excessive medication. Again one relies on hearsay, but apparently the new mother chose to breastfeed her infant son rather than delegate the task to the traditional wet nurse. And perhaps more important than the technical obstetric details, there was the fact that the 42-year-old Prince Philip became the first royal father in modern history to personally witness the arrival of one of his children, thus playing something of a trailblazing role in British family life of the 1960s.

Just seven weeks later, a mile or so across the park at Kensington Palace, the Queen's 33-year-old sister Margaret gave birth to her second child, today's Lady Sarah Chatto. While perfectly effusive, there was perhaps less of the celebratory cannon fire and church bells tone to the coverage of the event. By that stage Princess Margaret's marriage to the dapper and sexually omnivorous photographer Antony Armstrong-Jones, Lord Snowdon, was thought both more fractious, and, it was whispered, more morally freewheeling than customary in royal circles. Indeed, in some ways the Snowdons became the ideal cipher for an age that was rapidly promoting style over status but had by no means renounced inherited privilege. Anyone asked to spend an evening at No. 1A Clock Court, the couple's twenty-four-room official residence, could look forward to an occasion that mixed light-hearted and often surprisingly ribald entertainment with the princess's own unvarying insistence that her royal status demanded the utmost respect regardless of circumstance or behaviour. Even such hardened socialites as Noël Coward admiringly recorded an affair at Kensington Palace as 'louche but charming', confiding in his diary that when his hostess had sat down at the piano to perform one of his own songs, 'PM is surprisingly good. She has an impeccable ear, her playing is simple but she has perfect rhythm, and her method of singing is really very droll.'

The novelist Angela Huth and her then-husband the travel writer and restaurateur Quentin Crewe, a friend of Snowdon from their days together at *Queen* magazine, moved in what was called the Princess Margaret set. After being invited to lunch at Kensington Palace, Huth thought to return the favour by asking the royal couple to one of her own famously lively parties:

> We always had the people of that day – the Rolling Stones, George Melly, the Tynans – so we thought they might enjoy it. I rang up Princess Margaret and asked her if she'd like to come, and she said she'd love to. I remember [the publisher] Anthony Blond being very drunk, [the singer] Sandie Shaw standing there with bare feet as usual, Mrs. Tynan lying under the piano, and Shirley MacLaine holding hands with [the novelist] Edna O'Brien. Princess Margaret absolutely adored it, and they stayed until seven a.m. From then on we were tremendously good friends.

Not all of the Snowdons' nights out were quite as elevated as this one. To quote the *Guardian*:

> Princess Margaret and her husband broke new ground socially, making friendships, or at least acquaintance, with all the usual Sixties names: Nureyev, Peter Sellers, Vidal Sassoon, Mary Quant, and the more flaky, including John Bindon, a minor actor of East End sensitivities famed most for an interesting trick involving beer glasses with handles and a private part of his anatomy.

Since literally thousands of magazine articles, several full-length books and at least one film have been devoted to the subject, perhaps it's best to be brief when it comes to the matter of Princess Margaret's lapses from the strict conventions of mid 1960s royal protocol, rarely if ever broadcast at the time but achieving a wide circulation in later years. To give just three of the many examples available: there was the night when Margaret was seated opposite the teenaged but already widely photographed Twiggy at a London charity event. At the time the crop-haired young model was rapidly making a name for herself as an androgynous fashion icon for British youth on the cover of scores of magazines. But Princess Margaret clearly rose above such considerations of merely transitory fame. After an hour of frosty silence, the princess abruptly turned towards her fellow guest and asked, 'Who are you?'

'I'm Lesley Hornby, ma'am,' Twiggy replied. 'But people call me Twiggy.'

'How unfortunate,' said Margaret, ostentatiously turning to face in a different direction for the remainder of the meal.

Or there was the troubling matter of Robin Douglas-Home, a married, jazz-loving Scottish laird (and nephew of the sitting prime minister), with whom Margaret discreetly stepped out in 1964. This was not thought to be the first such intrigue for either party. In fact, Douglas-Home might be said almost to have made a career of disporting himself with high-born European ladies, having previously seen something of the young Princess Margaretha, the great-granddaughter of the ancient King of Sweden. *Time* magazine caught some of the spirit of this liaison when it wrote:

> It all began when the willowy 22-year-old royal princess went to London to brush up her English ... One night she and some friends dropped in at the Casanova Club, one of the upholstered haunts of the Princess Margaret set. There, playing a lively piano, was none other than Douglas-Home [the jazz lover, not the PM], a close friend of that young cutup the Duke of Kent, and frequent escort of the Duke's sister Princess Alexandra. Soon Home was taking Margaretha to dinner; once, dressed as Little Jack Horner, he escorted Margaretha, fetchingly clad as Little Red Riding Hood, to a ball sponsored by Princess Margaret. In due course he wrote to the former's mother Princess Sibylla, asking for Margaretha's hand. Margaretha abruptly returned to her palace in Stockholm.

At that stage Douglas-Home proceeded to marry the fashion model Sandra Paul, who ultimately divorced him after he began to explore the limits of his wedding vows by openly dallying with the Queen's younger sister. The most poignant thing he reportedly ever said to her was, 'Without your love I am delivered to the misery of boredom.' The impact of that line was deepened by the 1968 suicide of Douglas-Home, who swallowed a cocktail of alcohol and barbiturates at his home in Sussex, not long after Princess Margaret had put an end to their affair. He left behind a tape-recorded message in which he said,

'There comes a time when one reaches the conclusion that continuing to live is pointless.' He never spoke to the press, nor tried to make money from Margaret's love letters to him, despite being deeply in debt from gambling losses at the time of his death.

Or there was the time, improbable as it sounds, when the princess arrived unannounced one evening in March 1964 in the Thameside saloon bar of the Prospect of Whitby pub, redolent of an East End history of thieves, sailors and stevedores, having decided to pop in from 'Up West' for a night out. The *Sketch*'s Tony Gill said of this:

> One heard that Her Highness, though expecting, had concluded her evening by ingesting the product of half of Bolivia's cash crop up the royal hooter, before jigging an animated version of the sailor's hornpipe up and down the sawdust floor. Today there'd be a video with about 80 million hits on YouTube. But it was 1964, there was still an Edwardian veto on exposing society hijinks, and no one said a word.

The lean and hirsute 'Tony' Snowdon, with his preferred wardrobe of hip-hugging slacks, rollneck sweaters and suede shoes, was thought not to actively relish his stultifying life at court with its litany of endless provincial hospital visits and factory openings, during which he had to walk always several paces behind his wife. One observer wrote: 'He was part of the royal family and yet not royal, routinely sneered at and ignored by the servants who were resentful of his ambiguous position within the household.' But Snowdon did at least help usher in one lasting if cosmetic change to British life, more or less single-handedly inventing the modern idea of the fashionable professional photographer. 'No longer is the mere snapper of pictures a type of glorified plumber, answering to the beck and call of rich clients,' the journalist and future Tory Cabinet minister Jonathan Aitken explained:

> Almost overnight lensmen became invested with glamour and prestige. Advertisers grew more conscious of their talents and more generous with their cheques; the newspaper and magazine industry extended handsome verbal and photographic patronage; debutants fought for jobs as photographers' receptionists; Oxbridge graduates, Old Etonians and young peers of the realm flocked to join their ranks; and the bandwagon of fashion was well and truly rolling.

The *Sunday Times* colour supplement ran with much the same theme in its cover story of 10 May 1964:

> The London idea of style in the Sixties has been adjusted to a certain way of looking, which is to some extent the creation of three young men, all from the East End. These are the fashion photographers Brian Duffy, Terence Donovan, David Bailey. Between them, they make more than £100,000 a year, and they are usually accompanied by some of the most beautiful models in the world. They appear to lead enviable lives.

Much the same could be said for their raffish colleague Tony Snowdon and his royal-rebel wife, whose mutual appearances in England during the winter months became more sparing than those spent under the bluer skies of their South Pacific or Caribbean retreats. The art critic Sacheverell Sitwell claimed that the glamorous pair even dyed their hair to match, 'the colour of peach' complementing their holiday tans. Their style was described as 'hip plush', and their intimate relations as intense: 'She certainly didn't go short in that area,' said one observer. 'If it moves, he'll have it,' was the verdict on Snowdon by another friend who preferred anonymity.

The couple's exchange of vitriol and mutual promiscuity became the stuff of legend. Princess Margaret would walk into her husband's studio, only to be told, 'Never come in here without knocking!' At parties he would cut her off in mid-flow. 'Shut up and let someone intelligent talk, you bitch,' was one reported injunction. An infamous note from husband to wife apparently read, 'You look like a Jewish manicurist and I hate you.' At a ball at which Snowdon spent too long dancing with an attractive guest, Princess Margaret steamed up under full sail to ask the woman if she were enjoying herself. 'Very much so, ma'am,' she replied, at which point the princess's eyes had acquired a Clint Eastwood squint and she said, 'That's enough, then, for one evening, run along home.' With his gift for wordplay, John Lennon expressed a view some people had of the royal pair when he dubbed them 'Priceless Margarine' and 'Bony Armstrove'.

★ ★ ★

In 1964, the same Edwardian reticence when commenting on royal or society indecorum also applied elsewhere in the Queen's extended family. There was, for instance, the matter of the monarch's two 'hidden' cousins, Nerissa and Katherine Bowes-Lyon. Born respectively in 1919 and 1926, they were the daughters of Jock Bowes-Lyon, a cricket-playing stockbroker, the future Queen Mother's brother, and his wife Fenella. The sisters struggled with several learning difficulties, and following the death of their father in 1930 they were placed in care at the starkly named Redhill Asylum for Idiots in south London. Both women were listed in the 1964 edition of *Burke's Peerage* as having died in 1940, when in fact they were then living in a small dormitory with barred windows and chamber pots under the beds, and enduring all the other privations of an institutionalised life essentially unchanged since the reign of Queen Victoria. Poignantly, both were apparently well aware of their noble lineage: when royal events were shown on television, they would curtsey to the screen. Three other sisters who were the Queen's second cousins were confined in the same home. It was a terrible regime, and a cruel example of the indifference of a certain kind of bureaucracy.

No formal diagnosis was ever made, or at least none was published, but the women's condition was thought to have been hereditary, and acquired from their common maternal grandfather, Charles Trefusis, 21st Baron Clinton, whose own parents had been first cousins. 'Nobody outside the charmed circle knew about the "Princesses in the Tower"' says Tony Gill, 'and in those days the public didn't really want to hear anything bad about the royals, let alone about mental illness.'

But others did. Anne Tennant, *Tatler*'s debutante of the year in 1950, was at one time engaged to Johnnie Althorp, later father to Princess Diana. The Althorps objected to the match on the grounds of 'mad blood', a reference to her Trefusis ancestry, and the fixture was scratched. Nerissa Bowes-Lyon herself died aged 66 in 1986, and was buried in a grave marked only with a plastic name tag and a serial number. Katherine stayed on in the Redhill hospital until 1997, when it closed amid abuse claims, and then lived in another home in Surrey. She died aged 87 in 2014.

We've noted the multifaceted affair going under the umbrella name the Profumo Scandal that tied together sex, class, drugs, race and spies in a sort of greatest-hits package of classic ingredients, and which continued to enliven both the nation's newspaper headlines and many ordinary family dinner tables throughout 1964. Profumo himself soon volunteered his services as a penitent at the Toynbee Hall settlement, a charitable trust which helps support the most indigent residents of the East End of London. It's a minor curiosity that Princess Margaret had been enjoying her night out at the Prospect of Whitby that March while just a mile or so away her one-time society friend, the ex-Secretary of State for War, was first clocking on for his duties scrubbing the Toynbee Hall lavatories. Profumo never returned to politics. His latter-day career was entirely laudable, even if his unregenerate former self was thought to lie dormant but not entirely extinct. When promoted to a clerical position at Toynbee Hall, it was noticed that he kept in his desk a supply of ballpoint pens each adorned with a picture of a naked woman that floated up and down in an oil-filled translucent tube. Nearly a quarter of a century later, the distinguished British author Juliet Nicolson, then in her mid-30s, found herself alone for a moment in a country house garden with the 75-year-old Profumo, whereupon he suddenly took the opportunity to pinch her bottom. The historian Richard Davenport-Hines neatly sums up the fallout from the original scandal: 'Authority, however disinterested, well-qualified and experienced, was increasingly greeted with suspicion rather than trust.'

As it happened, there was to be widespread public and press interest in a broadly similar case of a fallen elite that late winter of 1964. This was the lingering aftermath of the Argyll v. Argyll divorce case that had provided such guiltily enjoyable entertainment the previous year. Eighteen months after the original petition, the duchess now returned to court to prevent her ex-husband from putting his name to a newspaper article said to comment unfavourably on her 'personal affairs [and] confidences communicated to the defendant during his marriage to the plaintiff and not hitherto made public property'. As usual on these occasions, the duchess's attempts to defend her privacy only had the effect of publicising the matters in question to a global audience several times larger than the 80,000 or so readers of the duke's original story.

By the time of her divorce in March 1963, the 51-year-old Duchess of Argyll, the former Margaret Whigham, had for some years divided her time between her husband's ancestral estate in Scotland and a 13-bedroom house near the American embassy on Upper Grosvenor Street in London. 'She lit up the room,' it has been fairly said of her. Born into wealth, after an upbringing largely spent in New York, where she was relieved of her virginity at 15 by the actor David Niven, Margaret had been launched on society as a glamorous if somewhat stony-faced pre-war debutante. In 1951 she married Ian Campbell, the 11th Duke of Argyll, but their happiness was short-lived. As the High Court judge hearing their divorce was to note, with evident distaste, the duchess was 'a highly sexed woman who [had] ceased to be content with normal sexual activities, and started to indulge in disgusting exploits to gratify a debased erotic appetite'. It is somehow difficult to read such evocative words without wishing to know more about them.

Speaking under ground rules of anonymity, several people familiar with the Argylls' domestic arrangements have suggested that Margaret had, for instance, at one time in the past bedded a visiting young American congressman and fellow free spirit, the future President Kennedy. Kennedy later advised his friend Hugh Fraser that the duchess had possessed 'the greatest ass [he'd] ever seen on a woman' – no small accolade – and that as a result of this feature she had been one of the few people of his acquaintance who could 'make an entrance by leaving a room'. It's a striking image, and while it should be stressed that there is no evidence for any such affair in the publicly released files, it wouldn't be entirely inconsistent with the known facts. John Kennedy had an acknowledged weakness for a certain kind of British bohemian-aristocratic type, and Margaret in turn seems to have been uninhibited in her selection of lovers. When in due course her husband the duke came to consider the matter of possible co-respondents in his divorce proceedings against his wife, he found he was somewhat spoilt for choice. He and his advisers eventually narrowed the list down to eighty-eight, of whom four were named on the petition.

Other than the simulated moral outrage it provoked in Fleet Street – matched only by the volume of additional copies it sold for them – the Argyll divorce case had two significant long-term results. Whether or not Kennedy had played some personal role in the prologue to the affair, we know that, as president, he took a keen interest in the day-to-day reports of the proceedings, which came to include a saga of wholesale adultery that might later have caused tuts of disapproval among the attendees of one of Cynthia Payne's more wanton functions at her Streatham brothel. Later that spring, Kennedy took the trouble to place a phone call on the subject to his friend David Ormsby-Gore, the British ambassador to the United States, but less formally a boon companion of the visiting young American in what he called 'places of low entertainment' in late 1930s London. What particularly drew the president to the Argylls' story, Gore reported privately, was above all 'the duchess's habit of wearing nothing but her pearls at the moment of coitus'.

But while Kennedy may have enjoyed the more salacious details of both the Argyll and Profumo affairs, he was wary enough of their political consequences to ensure that his official visit to Harold Macmillan in June 1963 take place at Birch Grove, the PM's family home in West Sussex, rather than in the febrile atmosphere of Westminster. A certain coolness descended on the Atlantic special relationship as a result of these tangential matters – characterised by Macmillan as 'events, dear boy' – that survived the abrupt departure of both heads of government that autumn and extended into the more robust early Johnson era of 1964. The latter's idea of a successful diplomatic démarche was an encounter with the courtly Sir Alec Douglas-Home, whom LBJ described as 'all over me ... He was ready to go in the barn and milk my cows, if only he could find the teats,' among other colourful epigrams that perhaps betrayed the president's formative years on the farm in Texas. Even the more urbane Kennedy had previously seen fit to inform Macmillan of his reservations about the Anglo-American team sent to negotiate a nuclear test ban deal with the Soviets in Moscow: 'The one question which might prevent accord would appear to be the handling of the wider non-aggression pact issue. The communiqué language suggested by your man seems to me to go too far.' Among other things, Kennedy wanted the words 'proliferation' and 'intercourse' removed from the text, because, he told Ambassador Gore with a straight face, 'these might provoke thoughts of Lady Argyll and her circle'.

The other long-term result of the Argylls' marital rift was the shining of a light on Britain's archaic family and divorce laws. The legislation as it stood in 1964 generally required evidence of some specific 'carnal offence' before a marriage could be dissolved, which led to a thriving trade in illicit weekends spent in seaside lodgings, interrupted, by prior arrangement, by a hired detective with a camera, thus providing the necessary proof of the conjugal lapse the courts desired. The overarching principle was that marriage was not so much a contract between two individuals as it was between the individuals and the state. As an institution, it served the greater good of society, rather than such hazy concepts as the personal happiness or fulfilment of the married couple. As a result of the Argyll case, the maverick Labour MP Leo Abse, a tireless champion of the individual's right to regulate their own affairs (even if rather curiously later campaigning for the rock singer Alice Cooper to be banned from the UK on the grounds that Cooper was 'peddling the smut of the concentration camp'), introduced legislation to permit fault-free divorce after seven years of separation, regardless of other factors. It was unsuccessful, but at least seemed to help focus minds on the issue. In due course, a blue-riband Church Commission proposed accepting 'irretrievable marital breakdown' as sufficient grounds for dissolution, rather than 'perpetuat[ing] the existing emphasis upon attributing guilt and blame'. The Divorce Reform Act followed in 1969.

The Argyll case also foreshadowed certain less salubrious aspects of our courtship environment. There was the duchess's 'slut shaming', for instance, among the other unappreciative terms applied to women who violate traditional norms of behaviour relating to sexuality. For that matter, the modern fondness for revenge porn might be glimpsed in the duke's decision to parade in evidence a series of thirteen photographs depicting his wife, naked save for her ubiquitous pearls, in two separate close encounters with men, framed so that they were headless but widely supposed to have been the actor Douglas Fairbanks Jr and the Tory MP Duncan Sandys, who in 1964 happened to be the Secretary of State for the Colonies as well as the recently divorced husband of Winston Churchill's daughter Diana.

EVENTS, DEAR BOY

Two criminal cases, one real, one fictional, held a firm grip on the British public's imagination in the winter of 1964. The first was the Great Train Robbery of August 1963, which came to trial early in the new year at the assizes in Aylesbury, Buckinghamshire, about 8 miles from the scene of the crime. The proceedings lasted fifty-one days, and caused something of a sensation not only for their final verdict and sentencing of the accused, but in the scenes of abandon that typically greeted the comings and goings of the defendants at the otherwise staid two-storey Georgian courthouse with its classical façade symmetrically divided by a humble vertical black drainpipe.

As Fleet Street's representatives arrived each morning for their pre-trial libations in Aylesbury's nearby market square, something like a mob orgy could be seen on the courthouse's well-worn front steps, and those of the adjacent council building used as an annex. Local shoppers would jostle with busloads of the curious or obsessed, driven in from London or other parts, many of whom paraded through the streets in support of the accused. The *Sketch* was apparently in two minds about this early display of the sort of decadent voyeurism of later high-profile criminal cases.

'Throughout the [trial] people have flocked to the Assizes building in droves, the majority being female,' the paper reported. 'Trinkets and light refreshments are sold as at a village fete, and the babel of the vendors is heard on every side. Souvenir train-sets commanded a brisk sale.' Five years later, there would be similar shouts of 'Good old Bruce!' and other endearments as one of the latter-day defendants arrived at the same building – 'another striking case of our strange compassion for the criminal class,' the *Sketch* tutted.

Bruce Reynolds, then aged 31, was one of fifteen men who halted the Glasgow to London night express in the early hours of 8 August 1963 about 35 miles short of its destination, broke into a Royal Mail coach and, in a swift if not quite perfectly executed operation – as the train's driver Jack Mills grappled with one of the robbers he was struck on the head by another with a cosh – departed with £2,631,684 (roughly £40 million today) in used banknotes. A tall, etiolated figure whose dark eyes swam around behind thick bifocal glasses, Reynolds did not come from a stereotypically deprived background, even if his later career followed a classic petty criminal trajectory. He was an only child, brought up in London, whose father worked as a union organiser at the Ford car plant in Dagenham and whose mother was a nurse. The latter's early death marked a turning point in young Bruce's fortunes. Reynolds's father married a woman with no obvious affection for her stepson, and in time the 9-year-old boy was evacuated to Suffolk on the outbreak of war.

Reynolds left school at 14, essentially unqualified. Rejected by the navy because of his poor eyesight, he took a job with a bicycle fitter in Clapham, south London. It was while employed there that he met a young colleague known only as Cobby, a slick-haired hoodlum with a folding razor habitually tucked in the pocket of his drainpipe coat, who introduced him to petty crime. Reynolds knew nothing about burglary at the time he pulled off his first job, but he learned quickly. Breaking into shops and factories soon gave way to a more ambitious plan to assemble his own gang and hijack a security van at Heathrow airport. Reynolds and his associates walked away with £62,000 as a result, an impressive enough haul in its own way if significantly less than the half a million they had expected. That same year, the gang managed to rob a mail train at Swindon. This also proved something of a fiasco, and they came away with only £700. But trains were now in Reynolds's mind, and his life became a rollercoaster of greater or lesser such jobs, from which he would periodically alight only for another stretch in prison. 'It didn't bother me in the least,' he later said of his occasional terms as a guest of Her Majesty. 'I was mixing with a sophisticated crowd [who] all had glamorous women and flashy houses on the outside, and I had some excellent mentors. I got my first car – a Triumph TR2 – and then an Aston Martin, and I was having suits made in Savile Row.'

The iconic robbery itself wasn't without ingenuity, and it was this factor, rather than the final outcome, that perhaps did most to establish Reynolds and his crew as so many latter-day Dick Turpins, whose spirit of enterprise many ordinary Britons found they could respect if not actively admire. The express was stopped in the dead of night by tampering with the signals. When the train came to a halt, a team of balaclava-clad robbers swiftly emerged from the undergrowth to run up from the trackside and jump into the cab of the locomotive. The gang's replacement driver's effectiveness was limited by his inability to operate that particular model of engine, but they improvised by rousing the semi-conscious Jack Mills and forcing him back to the controls to move the carriage a half-mile further down the line where they planned to relieve it of the money. There was no police officer or security guard on board to protect the goods. 'This was an oversight,' a Home Office report later acknowledged, 'but there were no grounds to anticipate the crime ... It appeared to be a perfectly routine journey.'

In due course, the robbers removed 120 sacks containing 2.5 tons of cash, which they transported to a waiting truck and two Land Rovers by forming a human chain. The whole procedure lasted about thirty minutes. It remains a matter of opinion whether Reynolds and his accomplices were in fact criminal masterminds, or displayed something closer to the sort of comic ineptitude of a Woody Allen heist caper. It has to be said they made several errors, the most disastrous of which was to warn the train's staff not to move or try and raise the alarm for a precisely stated thirty minutes. This suggested to the investigating detective, Jack Slipper of the Yard, that the gang's local hideout must lie within a half-hour drive of the crime scene. Sure enough, the police dragnet soon closed in on a remote farmhouse that lay between the Aylesbury Vale villages of Oakley and Brill. The robbers had already moved on, but they left behind their fingerprints. The firm was gradually rounded up, and on 20 January 1964 ten of those involved went on trial. On the whole, the ensuing press coverage was more censorious of the accused than was much of the public reaction. Perhaps as a nation we have a sentimental streak towards the sort of diamond geezers supposedly seen in the Aylesbury dock, who became widely familiar in the country at large by their nicknames – Roy 'Weasel' James, Lennie 'Fingers' Field and 'Big Jim' Hussey, among others. The presiding judge, the austere Mr Justice Edmund Davies, evidently had no such romantic illusions, reminding the jury in his summing up that the driver Jack Mills had been struck over the head with such ferocity that he would never be able to work again. 'Let us clear out of the way any notions of daredevilry,' the judge said. 'This is nothing less than a sordid crime of violence inspired by vast greed.'

The 34-year-old Ronnie Biggs, one of the accused, expressed his views on this summation in unusual fashion. Shifting his weight from side to side from his cramped seat in the dock, he let rip with not so much a conventional fart as a sustained intestinal oratorio. It seemed to take on a life of its own and to change in pitch and volume halfway through. All eyes turned to the defendant, but, displaying a certain gift for deadpan comedy, the guilty party did not bat an eyelid and simply waited for proceedings to resume. The archetypal chancer, Biggs subsequently absconded from Wandsworth Prison and spent thirty-six years on the run, much of it hiding in plain sight with a series of female companions in Rio de Janeiro. Reynolds himself initially eluded capture but was eventually arrested, rather more prosaically, in Torquay and jailed for twenty-five years.

Mr Justice Davies's original sentences were handed down on 15 April 1964. They were not noted for their leniency. Six of the guilty men were given the going rate for the first wave of Train Robbers of thirty years apiece; three more were sent down for between twenty and twenty-five years; and one defendant, a bent solicitor, got off with three years. A number of these terms were later reduced on appeal. 'They are intended to have a punitive effect,' the presiding judge had added at Aylesbury, perhaps needlessly. In the Commons, the prime minister took the opportunity to announce that the government was to undertake a fundamental review of the British judicial system, and, seeming to tie the Train Robbery to the ongoing Mods and Rockers outrages, the Labour MP Marcus Lipton asked the home secretary to strengthen the laws against hooliganism and violent crimes. 'Recent events have shown that members of the judiciary are not afraid of imposing sharp sentences,' Lipton noted, with evident approval. 'Those who perpetrate such atrocities in our midst must not be permitted to benefit from their wickedness.'

This would not seem to have been a particular problem in the case of the Great Train Robbers. Admittedly Ronnie Biggs, the lowly 'tea boy' of the team, despite his later folk-hero status, teased the British legal system to distraction after being discovered living with his pregnant girlfriend on a Rio beach, but eventually voluntarily returned to face the music, served eight years, suffered a series of strokes and heart attacks, and died in a north London hospice at the age of 84. 'Buster' Edwards, the man believed to have wielded the cosh used to hit the unfortunate Jack Mills ('He just fell backwards onto my hand, didn't he?' Edwards once informed me), fled to Mexico after the robbery but also gave himself up in 1966; he served nine years, emerged to set up a flower stall outside Waterloo station, and was found hanged in a London lock-up garage in 1994 at the age of 63. Like Biggs, Charlie Wilson also escaped from a British jail, only to be recaptured in Canada; he spent another decade behind bars and then moved to Spain, where he was shot and killed by a hitman on a bicycle. Even Bruce Reynolds, who gloried in the nickname 'Napoleon', ended his days on income support in a modest Croydon bedsit. None of the old firm wound up conspicuously wealthy. In 1978, some of them seemed to taunt the establishment a second time by negotiating a publisher's advance for a book in which they concocted a story that Otto Skorzeny, the SS commando who rescued Benito Mussolini from wartime captivity, had financed the 1963 robbery. This might have come as news to Skorzeny himself, who conveniently had died three years earlier. There are parts of the original crime that might almost have made an Ealing comedy, with someone like Terry-Thomas or Alastair Sim in the lead role and Ian Carmichael as the amiably inept police chief giving chase. It stands as an affair that's about equal parts enterprise, adventure, brutality and farce – a peculiarly British confection.

Meanwhile, the flawed hero and psychotic villains at the core of Ian Fleming's novel *You Only Live Twice*, published in March 1964, were attracting almost as much attention as the men in the dock for the Great Train Robbery. The book was the eleventh instalment in Fleming's James Bond series, and the last one released in his lifetime. That August, the author went out to play a late afternoon round of golf with friends, then sat down to dinner and collapsed with a heart attack shortly afterwards. Impeccably mannered, at least with strangers, to the end, Fleming's last words were spoken to the crew of the ambulance taking him to hospital: 'I am terribly sorry to trouble you chaps. I don't know how you get along so fast with the traffic on the roads these days.' He was just 56 at the time of his death.

The plot of *You Only Live Twice* sees Bond at something of a midlife crisis, perhaps modelled on Fleming himself, with the author's own note of world-weariness, dry humour and enjoyable streak of malice. The novel is the last in the so-called Blofeld Trilogy, and starts where *On Her Majesty's Secret Service* leaves off, with Bond mourning the loss of his young wife the Contessa Teresa di Vicenzo, or 'Tracy' as he prefers to call her, whom we're reminded was mown down by his criminal nemesis Ernst Stavro Blofeld and his matronly sidekick Irma Bunt. (Fleming was always good with names.) At his wits' end, M, the head of MI6, a role the actor Bernard Lee was fast making his own in the early Bond films, decides that the only way to snap his agent out of his torpor is to send him on an improbable diplomatic mission to Japan. His contact there is M's local counterpart Tiger Tanaka, who agrees to do business if Bond will assassinate one of his enemies: an enigmatic Swiss botanist named Dr Guntram Shatterhand who, as such persons do in Bond's world, has recently taken up residence in a volcanic castle where he lures unsuspecting victims into his garden of death to commit suicide. If Bond can kill this man, Tanaka will hand over a Russian decoder in his possession.

Time passes, and there's a generous amount of exegesis about oriental culture and a rumination on the decline of British overseas prestige, with the 1963 defection of the double agent Kim Philby as a real-life backdrop. After examining photographs of Shatterhand and his wife, Bond, by now pretending to be a mute Japanese coalminer named Taro, determines that the couple are actually Tracy's murderers, the criminal tag team of Blofeld and Bunt, giving the novel its central revenge theme. The book's exotic locale had an obvious appeal for a British public in many cases still in two minds about Japan, less than twenty years after the end of the war, perhaps compensating for some of the longueurs of a plot which in its early stages can seem as perfunctory as watching a traffic light change. At the end, by contrast, the book's action is rushed out in throwaway fashion: Blofeld decides Bond may not be a voiceless local miner after all, and takes him captive. There's some subsequent unpleasantness involving a near-execution, followed by a climactic duel between the book's main two protagonists. Bond eventually strangles Blofeld with his bare hands, thus avenging his late wife, and then blows up the castle. Upon escaping, he suffers a head injury, leaving him enfeebled once more, living now as a native fisherman with a sultry new companion named, implausibly enough, Kissy Suzuki, while the rest of the world believes him dead. Bond's obituary appears in *The Times*, a poignant harbinger of Fleming's own notices just five months after the book's publication.

You Only Live Twice, a relatively minor Bond novel that has always found greater favour with the general reader than the critics, commanded 70,000 pre-orders in the UK, and sold some 4 million copies worldwide within a year. The book did indeed get a second life as a blockbuster feature film in 1967. By that time, Bond had become such a lucrative commodity that the producers felt able to spend £3.8 million (around £55 million today) bringing Fleming's story to the screen, nearly as much as the budgets of the first four films in the franchise combined. Bearing only a passing resemblance to the source material, the movie might be best remembered today for Donald Pleasence's insinuating turn as the bald, scar-faced Blofeld stroking his albino cat, and the theme song, handled by Nancy Sinatra after her father had declined the honour. The film's screenwriter Roald Dahl was to remark that the original novel was 'Fleming's worst book, with no plot in it which would even make a movie to speak of', comparing it to an extended Asian travelogue 'with tits thrown in'. Literary competence, however, was not the quality most admired by the book's reading public. Escapist fantasy was, and for that Bond, Blofeld, Bunt, Shatterhand and Kissy provided potent symbols.

Among 1964's other best-selling books in the West were J.G. Ballard's *The Terminal Beach*, John Braine's *The Jealous God*, Saul Bellow's *Herzog*, Agatha Christie's *A Caribbean Mystery*, Len Deighton's *Funeral in Berlin*, Iris Murdoch's *The Italian Girl*, Leon Uris's *Armageddon*, Gore Vidal's *Julian*, Edgar Rice Burroughs's posthumous *Tarzan and the Madman*, and the seventh episode of Anthony Powell's 'Dance' sequence, *The Valley of Bones*. Even so, it wasn't all a case of literature having succumbed overnight to a fit of hopelessly populist fare, with its telltale signs of linear narration, credible dialogue and convincing internal logic. The Nobel Prize that year went to 59-year-old Jean-Paul Sartre, despite his attempts to refuse it by saying that 'a writer should not allow himself to be turned into an institution' (ten years later, he sent the Nobel committee a request for the prize money, but was himself refused). Sartre's most recent publication was a five-part memoir, aptly called *The Words*, in which he discussed, at some length, his belief in life consisting of 'the experience of the indeterminate character of existence in anguish'. No one can doubt Sartre's wide-ranging engagement with the political and cultural issues of the day, or his perhaps still-topical faith in the moral superiority of the Soviet system. But as a page-turner, his autobiography's merits were limited.

CANCER ON THE CHEAP

Harold Macmillan's abrupt exit the previous October – he was thought to be suffering from cancer, but in the event lived for almost another quarter of a century – had once again seen those on all sides of the political spectrum tiptoe warily through the minefield of the British class system. There was a touch of drama mingled with a generous amount of farce to the actual handover of power. Macmillan underwent successful surgery at King Edward VII's Hospital in London, and later admitted that it had been something of a struggle to deal with the official papers still dutifully brought to his bedside. 'The public events of these days are quite beyond me,' he was left to ruefully note in his diary. The Queen and the Queen Mother had rung the hospital four times to enquire about him, he added, 'but it has been a bad [time], and I can't understand what they are saying'.

When the Tories assembled that week at Blackpool for their annual party conference, the leading contenders as Macmillan's successor were 'Rab' Butler, his long-serving deputy; Lord Hailsham, fresh from exasperating his US counterparts at the Moscow test ban talks; and Reginald Maudling, the chancellor, at 46 representing youth. Three days later, Maudling had been ruled out after delivering a monotonously flat speech to the party faithful, Hailsham was sunk by openly campaigning for himself in a manner widely thought vulgar, or, in *The Times*'s withering phrase, 'indulging in those excesses more worthy of an American convention', among them bottle-feeding his infant child for the benefit of the TV cameras; and Butler, the heir-apparent, self-destructed by going to the opposite extreme and seeming not to care one way or another. Out of the vacuum emerged the almost impressively archaic figure of Lord Home, the foreign secretary, who among other things happened to have been Neville Chamberlain's principal assistant at the time of Munich.

Having come to office in January 1957 following a series of Tory back-room manoeuvres, Macmillan left it again in similar fashion nearly seven years later. On the morning of 18 October 1963, the Queen took the unprecedented step of going to her prime minister's hospital bed in order to accept his resignation. Macmillan received her wearing his pyjama bottoms and a white silk shirt, which he partly covered with a well-darned grey V-necked sweater. The overall effect was said to be more comic than dignified. The heavily sedated premier advised his monarch to send for Douglas-Home, which she duly did. Thirty minutes later, a man in brown overalls appeared in the outgoing PM's hospital room to remove his special scrambler link to the RAF's 'V-Force' bomber command responsible for the country's independent nuclear stockpile, at once a symbolic and tangible end to the trappings of high office. The passage of power was especially swift in those days, with little pretence of any leisurely American-style transition. Macmillan left his hospital room without even a single secretary at his disposal. 'It seems strange,' he wrote, 'no longer to be able to ring the bell for a young lady at any time, day or night.' Having never learnt to drive a car, he had to rely on his wife Dorothy to get him around, 'and [she] was not to be whistled up at a moment's notice,' he added wistfully.

Douglas-Home's accession to Downing Street was not universally welcomed even within the ranks of his own party. Some objected on what could be called philosophical grounds, believing that the Conservatives had taken a step backwards with his appointment, and that they needed to modernise themselves before someone else did so for them by hauling the old guard away in tumbrils. Enoch Powell, the health minister, complained that Macmillan had 'bounced' the Queen into accepting his nominee, noting that Caligula's appointment of his horse as a consul had been a piece of prudent statesmanship by comparison, while Iain Macleod, the brilliant if sometimes tetchy party chairman, was on grounds well beyond this when writing a caustic article in the *Spectator* published early in 1964. Macleod's essential thesis was that the leadership contest had been less one of a democratic consultation befitting the 1960s and more that of a toffs' magic circle (almost entirely composed of Old Etonians) closing ranks in like-minded alliance. The fallout of the whole affair was the first item of business at the Cabinet meeting of 17 January 1964:

> The Foreign Secretary: All ministers should refrain from commenting on Macleod's article. I am taking this opportunity to call for a pledge of loyalty to the leader.
>
> The Prime Minister: I thank you one and all. We must concentrate now on winning the election. That is paramount.

Britain had last gone to the polls in October 1959, when the Conservatives were returned to office with a majority over all other parties of 100 seats. It was as much as anything a personal triumph for Macmillan, who noted in the privacy of his diary that 'telegrams of congratulation are pouring in, from Eisenhower, Debré, Adenauer etc, down to the humblest folk'. But by January 1964 the humblest folk were proving restless in the wake of Philby and Profumo, and the Douglas-Home administration, relentlessly attacked by the likes of the *Daily Mirror* for its apparent economic muddles and excessive dependency on Washington, was rightly concerned about its prospects at the election due to be held nine months later:

> The Prime Minister: I spoke to [the West German chancellor] Erhard. Many subjects were raised. I said we were interested in Western European political unity, but can't afford another rebuff in joining the Community. Therefore we should play it slow until the election. Erhard agreed.

And elsewhere in the same meeting, on the contentious matter of Britain's shrinking national rail network:

> The Prime Minister: We must deal with [the cuts] in services we want delayed. We must have a respectable reason.

The Lord Privy Seal: We might say that no popular resort lines will be closed until after the holidays this year.

The Prime Minister: Yes.

The Lord Chancellor: But one can't exempt a whole category. And some holiday lines are already [scheduled] to close.

The Secretary of State for Industry: Even so, say that no decision will be given until after the holidays.

And later still:

The Lord Privy Seal: The government is simply drifting. Our support is disheartened. A clear electoral theme is required. Perhaps something [on] the economy ... an Export Council.

All democratic governments naturally have an eye on the next election. But in the case of the Conservatives in 1964 it was a tacit and often explicit factor behind almost everything ministers said or did as the clock remorselessly ticked down to October.

In what was either a whiff of that faint air of bumbling characteristic of the British ruling elite, or possibly just an endearing show of self-effacement, however richly deserved, Douglas-Home himself made no pretence to fiscal expertise. He once noted that his problems in office were of two sorts: 'the political ones are insoluble and the economic ones are incomprehensible.' On another occasion he remarked, with no apparent attempt at levity, 'When I have to read Treasury documents I have to have a box of matches and start moving them into position to simplify and illustrate the points to myself.'

Perhaps his government's singular initiative in the financial field was the 1964 Resale Prices Act, intended to prevent manufacturers and suppliers from fixing the cost at which their goods were sold to the retailer, and thus on to the ordinary shopper. The industry secretary and future prime minister Ted Heath introduced the legislation to Parliament as much in its broader social terms as its narrow commercial ones:

I hope that the influence of the changes we are proposing will spread far beyond their legal scope. They should help to change the whole climate of our national life, and enable us to get away from the atmosphere in industry and commerce in which sometimes keen competition is thought to be hardly respectable ... The private citizen and the nation as a whole have paid a heavy price for such comfortable complacency. We intend to create a much sharper environment.

It remains debatable how much Heath's vision of a bracing new competitive economic culture did to benefit the average British consumer. The nation's annual inflation rate as measured by the retail price index was 2.02 per cent in 1963, 3.28 per cent in 1964 and 4.77 per cent in 1965. On top of that, the gap between the wealthy regions of London and the South East and the former industrial hubs further north grew even wider. By December 1964, only the greater London area and its surrounding counties reached the national average wealth per capita. The rest of the country fell far behind, with the typical householder in the North East enjoying just over 60 per cent of the spending power of his or her counterpart in Surrey or Kent. When President Kennedy's former special assistant Arthur Schlesinger found himself in the Newcastle suburb of Wallsend while on a private visit to the UK in March 1964, he wrote that local residents endured conditions that had 'changed little since Charles Dickens's day', although even that chronicler of Victorian slum life 'might have been shocked by the washroom facilities at our so-called hotel – I won't enlarge'. Heath may have been a sincere idealist in extolling the new spirit of competition abroad when it came to vying for the individual consumer's money. But *Private Eye* characteristically punctured some of the calculation and humbug of the era in its cover cartoon commenting on the latest NHS funding crisis: 'Now even cancer is cut price.'

The dark winter months were at least enlivened by the antics of what the Kinks would memorably come to call the dedicated follower of fashion, or the gilded circle of the music and showbusiness scene as a whole. One especially bleak Monday morning in early February, the 38-year-old actor Peter Sellers opened his copy of the *Sketch* to see an alluring photograph of the Swedish starlet Britt Ekland, who was 21, pouting back at him. Realising that they were both staying at the Dorchester Hotel in London, Sellers sent his valet down the corridor to present his employer's compliments. By then it was about 10 o'clock in the morning, and Ekland happened to be in the bath. 'I wrapped a towel round me and rushed to open the door,' she remembers. 'This very proper Englishman in a black suit said, "I am Mr Sellers's personal gentleman." Would I like to go to his suite?'

In something of a whirlwind romance, Sellers rang Ekland two days after their first date, she recalls: 'Peter said, "I have told the press that we're going to get hitched."' He followed this announcement up by sending her every bloom in the Dorchester's flower shop and a dachshund puppy named Pepper, before taking her to dinner at the Ritz. The couple were duly married in the more modest setting of Guildford Register Office on 19 February, nine days after they had first met. It was all 'very passionate', Ekland later recalled. She was 'deliriously happy', 'madly in love' and apparently also soon to be a big star. Calling in at the Dorchester, one paper remarked breathlessly that Ekland had 'held her cup whilst at tea like a lady', and was therefore destined for success in her adopted country.

But even then there were warning signs ahead. Two days after the Guildford ceremony, Sellers flew to California for a film and sent his young wife a 'crazy' six-page letter obsessing that she might be unfaithful, and adding that he wanted to have 'violent' sex with her. It was signed with twenty-five kisses. Sellers soon persuaded Ekland to join him in Hollywood, brushing off her commitment to shoot the period drama *Guns at Batasi*, where she was due to star alongside the likes of Richard Attenborough and Flora Robson, at Pinewood. 'I was young, in love and I acquiesced,' she said. Later that week, Sellers had the first of a series of heart attacks, after taking the sexual stimulant amyl nitrate. He found himself briefly on life support, while Ekland was fired by the studio for breach of contract. The dog Pepper was somehow lost in all the excitement.

In some ways, this was the logical curtain-raiser to the affair between 38-year-old Richard Burton and Elizabeth Taylor, who was 32, both of them then fresh from filming a slightly eccentric romantic comedy called *The V.I.P.s* about a group of beautiful people stuck in the terminal at Heathrow because of fog. The real-life couple enjoyed a courtship that was almost quaintly slow compared with that between Sellers and Ekland. They had first met at a party in 1952, where Burton's reputation as a womaniser preceded him. 'I'm not going to be another notch on his belt,' the young actress later wrote, having already embarked on a matrimonial career that proved long and colourful, if not untouched by shadow.

Aged 24, Taylor married her third husband, the film producer Mike Todd, and spoke about retiring with him to live in Connecticut. Tragically, after just fourteen months with his wife, he died in a plane crash, and she was a widow at 26. Her good friend Debbie Reynolds came to comfort her, and Taylor in turn stole her husband, Eddie Fisher. But this was just the prelude to her renewing her acquaintance with Burton on the extended shoot of the film *Cleopatra*, which proceeded in Hollywood, London, Rome and the Egyptian desert at intervals between September 1960 and March 1963, at an eventual cost of $46 million (£700 million today), with Taylor getting a flat $1 million fee and ten per cent of the gross profits for her services. This time around, she and Burton were instantly smitten with each other ('I get an orgasm just listening to that voice of his,' she reported), despite both being married, Taylor now for the fourth time. *Life* would go on to call *Cleopatra* the 'most talked about movie ever made', thanks to both its price tag and the scandal surrounding its co-stars. It was also the number one box office film in the United States throughout the latter part of 1963, before being dethroned by *The V.I.P.s*.

In one of his early love letters, suggesting their relationship might even then have passed from the strictly professional, Burton wrote, 'I lust after your smell ... and your round belly and the exquisite softness of the inside of your thighs and your baby-bottom and your giving lips and the half-hostile look in your eyes when you're deep in rut with your little Welsh stallion.' Their existing marriages terminated, the couple tied the knot on 15 March 1964 in a ceremony at the Ritz-Carlton Hotel in Montreal, about 300 miles from where Burton was appearing in a stage production of *Hamlet* in Toronto. The choice of venue was necessary as both partners had Mexican divorces that at that stage were recognised as valid in the Canadian province of Quebec, but not in neighbouring Ontario. According to a published account in a book aptly entitled *Furious Love*, 'As the limousine picked up speed, leaving the Montreal hotel, Elizabeth smiled sweetly and waved to the adoring crowd like royalty – all the while silently mouthing the words "Fuck you – and you – and you, dear!"' It would be the first of the couple's two marriages, the second coming in Botswana in 1975, with two hippos as witnesses. Both ended in divorce.

Back in London, Victor Lownes was putting down the first three months' deposit to lease the ten-storey apartment block at 45 Park

Lane, just down the street from the Dorchester in the heart of Mayfair, that housed the city's first Playboy Club. The modernist tower was envisioned as a multi-entertainment complex. On passing through the discreet Curzon Street entrance, the customer, or keyholder as they were known, would arrive at a reception desk carved of meat-pink marble, with a lounge and well-stocked Playmate Bar beyond. The Living Room restaurant and discotheque were on the first floor. On the second floor, the VIP Room hosted fine dining and dancing. The Playboy Playroom restaurant and stage were found on the third floor, followed by the *pièce de résistance*: the fourth-floor Penthouse Casino. There would be a certain amount of speculation over the years concerning the exact function of the floors above that, which among other things seem to have contained a number of serviced apartments for such visiting celebrities as Rudolf Nureyev, Roman Polanski and Sammy Davis Jr. Lownes himself went about acquiring the new club's most visible asset, the Playboy Bunnies, one of whom, named Serena Williams, remembers, 'We were auditioned in day-long shifts, and then given weeks of training. It was intense. And it wasn't just the size of a girl's bust or the shape of her body, it was very much about her face and personality, her countenance overall.'

The spirit of the club was represented by an elaborate style book presented to each successful Bunny candidate (only one in forty, it was said, of all applicants) on her graduation. This far-reaching manual contained rules on everything from the correct way to walk from A to B, to the protocol to dealing with any unwanted romantic advances. Drinks were served using the patented 'Bunny Dip', an athletic back-bend, just short of a limbo, which allowed the young waitress to slide glasses from tray to table without exposing undue cleavage. 'Den Mothers' gave instructions and maintained discipline, issuing fines to the young women for misdemeanours ranging from slow service to bad posture. 'It was a respectable and luxurious venue,' Lownes would insist. 'The Bunnies weren't nude, they were girls in costumes. And the punters weren't just people handing over money. It wasn't a trust-fund Johnnies, inherited thing. We were open to anyone, and everyone wanted to be part of us.'

Lownes himself enjoyed the use of one of the building's fully sound-proofed upstairs flats, and press photographs of the era frequently caught him with a pneumatic young companion on either arm and a boyishly happy leer on his face. A button on a console beside his bed controlled the apartment's concert-quality music system, and by pressing a second button a painting of two nude women rose to reveal a hidden colour TV set. Lownes also had a chauffeur-driven Rolls at his disposal and, should he wish to exercise the American side of his personality, use of the club's two silver Cadillacs. 'It was very easy being me,' he noted.

Somehow it doesn't seem entirely illogical to pass from Lownes to the furore surrounding the 1964 reissue of John Cleland's eighteenth-century novel *Memoirs of a Woman of Leisure*, or, as it was more popularly known, *Fanny Hill*, a work sometimes considered the first example of English prose pornography. The book's most striking scene perhaps comes when the titular heroine remarks to a suitor at the moment of congress: 'I felt pretty sensibly that it was not going in by the right door but knocking desperately at the wrong one, and I told him of it. "Pooh", said he, "my dear, any port in a storm".' Or, on a slightly more metaphysical level: 'All my foundation in virtue was no other than a total ignorance of vice.' The book, which was illustrated by some early twentieth-century images of Fanny in poses of extreme relaxation ('dressed in clothes of the most meagre sort, or in none at all', to quote the official complaint), caught the eye of a vigilant beat policeman when he passed by the window of the Magic Shop in London's Tottenham Court Road one dark winter night. A plain-clothes colleague subsequently called at the shop, bought a copy of the book, and in due course brought it to the attention of the Bow Street magistrate Sir Robert Blundell, who issued a search warrant. The police then returned to Tottenham Court Road and seized all 171 copies of the offending book, charging the Magic Shop's owner Ralph Gold under the Obscene Publications Act.

It may seem odd that a 216-year-old novel should have sent the country's legal system into a moral panic at roughly the same time that the Rolling Stones were busy leaving behind them a trail of wrecked theatres and slashed cinema seats in the wake of their latest tour, or that the full majesty of the Quarterly Sessions of the Bow Street Magistrates should be required to parse the book's sometimes flowery Georgian terminology, with its catalogue of askew petticoats and heaving orbs, and the 'throbbing engine' handled with professional finesse by Fanny before finding the 'blissful spot', and culminating in the 'effusion' of pleasure. Sir Robert and his colleagues duly found for the prosecution, formally banning the book from British shops; it would reappear, uncensored, in 1970. The leader writer in the *Sunday Telegraph* was not entirely unhappy with the result. 'It would surely be odd,' he noted, 'for a society pledged to monogamous marriage to allow any citizen with a few shillings in his pocket to buy *Fanny Hill*.'

The 60-year-old society photographer and designer Cecil Beaton was one of those who thought the whole trial a nonsense, writing about the 'grotesque' judge in the case, with his 'Renaissance-type hair, leering, suety face and potato nose' emerging from court each afternoon after all the talk about lesbians and flagellation. As a younger man, Beaton had had his share of relationships with women, including Greta Garbo, but had since settled down with his male friend Kin Hoitsma, an American-born teacher, in their palatial Queen Anne home at Broadchalke in Wiltshire. Sitting in the train going between Waterloo and Salisbury, he would sometimes look out on a sign by the line advertising 'Brides!', sigh, and say, 'There but for the grace of God go I.'

★ ★ ★

In early 1964, Peter Sellers remained an institution in the tabloid gossip columns, which at least in those days was just as he liked it. Apart from his wedding and his health, and a penchant for conspicuous consumption in the form of chunky jewellery and other high-end accessories second only to that associated with the Burton–Taylor merger, there was the release that January of his starring vehicle *Dr Strangelove*. While shooting the film at Pinewood, Sellers had sometimes thrown dinner parties for his New York-born director Stanley Kubrick and his fellow cast members at his timbered manor house at Chippenfield in Hertfordshire. The actor George C. Scott would remember arriving one night and 'Pete greet[ing] his guests at the baronial front door, cigar in mouth, enquir[ing] in a broad accent, "Well, man, how d'ya like the pad?"' Sellers had fitted the home with an impressive array of gadgets which dimmed lights, raised or lowered pieces of angular furniture from the floor and swivelled desks and bookcases around like a revolving door in a Charlie Chan movie, and a sound system that pumped out the strains of the John Coltrane Quartet and Thelonious Monk. *Strangelove* itself opened to the familiar mixed reviews, until gradually coming to be accepted as the consensus political satire of its day. Sellers's going rate for the project was the same as Taylor's on *Cleopatra*: $1 million, plus a wealth of perks that included a permanently reserved suite for his use at the Dorchester Hotel, with all that ensued as a result.

Kubrick himself, then aged 35, soon decided to settle in England, buying a large Georgian house not unlike Sellers's in the Hertfordshire countryside. The director briefly flew back to New York in February 1964, narrowly missing the Beatles en route, to meet with Roger Caras, the Columbia Pictures executive assigned to *Strangelove*. Caras politely enquired over drinks at Trader Vic's what he was thinking of doing next, and Kubrick leant forward conspirationally and said, 'Don't laugh, but I'm fascinated with the possibility of extra-terrestrials,' which was the first time anyone heard him mention the project that became *2001: A Space Odyssey*.

These symptoms of a fresh and invigorating spirit of cinematic adventure – it was also the season of *Zulu*, *The Night of the Iguana* and the socially conscious *Black Like Me* – were matched by the unmistakable signs of a generational clash stirring elsewhere in the lively arts. Apart from the Beatles and the Stones, there was the quartet from the West London suburbs who early in 1964 decided to change their name from the Detours and, after kicking around alternatives like 'the Group' and 'the Hair', finally hit on the Who. The band's fortunes took a significant step forward that April when a ginger-haired 17-year-old part-time musician and full-time sales clerk at British Gypsum, based around the corner from the Playboy Club in Park Lane, proposed himself as their new drummer. His name was Keith Moon, and he passed the subsequent perfunctory audition.

Moon was not the originator of the classic Who sound, but at least he was its midwife. Shortly after his arrival, the band cut a single, called, in an attempt to appeal to a Mod audience, 'Zoot Suit'. It did nothing. The Fontana label then released the song's B-side, 'I'm the Face'. It too did nothing. Finally, the group's songwriter Pete Townshend locked himself in his bedroom for a weekend spent listening nonstop to Bob Dylan, Charlie Mingus and John Lee Hooker, among others, and, trying to summarise the way the music made him feel, wrote the line 'I Can't Explain'. That gave him his song's title. For the tune itself, Townshend fell back on emulating the Kinks' latest hit 'All Day and All of the Night'. The result was at least a modest Top 40 success, although it was the Who's live performances that whipped up their audiences into a semblance of Beatlemania with a touch of *Clockwork Orange*-like ultraviolence thrown in. The band's singer

Roger Daltrey started wielding his microphone lead like a lasso on stage, Moon threw drumsticks in the air and caught them again mid-beat, while Townshend, then essentially a stick with a nose attached to it, mimed machine-gunning the crowd, leapt in the air, and brought his right arm crashing down on his guitar strings as if violently yanking the cord on a chainsaw. As the Who's biographer Mark Wilkerson remarks, they were 'a hard-nosed band who reflected the feelings of thousands of pissed-off adolescents at the time'.

Some of this same pent-up youthful angst might also have been expended at British football matches, which on the whole had a less cosmopolitan and perhaps even more aggressively tribal quality to them than today. As the historian Tony Judt notes, 'No one who attended games in those days between England and Germany, for example, or for that matter Germany and the Netherlands (much less Poland and Russia) would have been under any illusion about the Treaty of Rome and "ever-closer union".' The obvious reference point was the Second World War, and at least some of the fixtures pitting British club or national sides against European opposition were vicarious, emotionally charged reruns of the nation's military history. In 1964 it was still highly unusual for a British football supporter to see a foreign-born import in his home team, and in some cases even out-of-town transplants were the subject of unfavourable comment on the terraces. The most expensive move in league history to date was that of the return of Denis Law from Torino to Manchester United for the fabulous sum of £115,000, or £1.7 million today. There was an average attendance of 18,434 at each First Division match in 1964, low by modern standards but often enlivened by the crowd's creative adaptation of the lyrics of popular Top 40 songs, and readiness to put the boot in to the opposition fans. Liverpool swept all before them in the race for the league title. Jimmy Greaves netted 35 goals in 41 appearances for Spurs to finish as the division's top scorer, while a 17-year-old called George Best was in his first season alongside Denis Law at Old Trafford.

For its part, English cricket was in one of its cyclical crises of reappraisal, having only recently abolished the sport's hallowed 'gentleman' and 'player' status and simultaneously introduced the game's first domestic limited-overs competition, the Gillette Cup. Sussex won the first two annual trophies, which saw Lord's transformed into a reasonable facsimile of Wembley, complete with rattles and horns and a blaze of flags, along with singing, cheers and even a few jeers. Although the

English game wasn't yet the fluorescent-clad jamboree it later became, a definite note of adventure could be glimpsed in such developments as the appointment of the raffish Ted Dexter as the nation's Test captain, and that of the former Middlesex skipper Walter Robins (like Dexter, the maverick all-rounder of his day) as chairman of selectors. Robins began his tenure by issuing an ultimatum to England's 300 professional cricketers. *Wisden* summarised: 'Play aggressively at all times; otherwise you will not be chosen for your country.' Despite these strictures, the England side that toured India in early 1964 drew all five of its Test matches there. The truth is that traditional, 'red ball' cricket was gradually slipping to a niche position in mass entertainment terms, thus triggering a debate about the structure and purpose of the domestic game still largely unresolved sixty years later.

Scotland and Wales shared the Five Nations' rugby union championship played in early 1964. Despite trouncing England in front of 50,000 fans at Twickenham, Ireland took last place. Football, cricket and rugby, in both codes, still comprised the holy trinity of organised team sports, although others preferred the charms of more solitary pursuits like angling, horse-riding, cycling, snooker, darts and golf. The 118th Grand National was run at Aintree on 21 March and narrowly won by the American-owned Team Spirit, ridden by Willie Robinson, which came in at odds of 18-1. There was a tragic footnote to the day when a light plane crashed into a cabbage patch near the course, killing the popular journalist Nancy Spain, her life partner the *She* magazine editor Joan Laurie and three other passengers on their way to watch the race. Spain, who was 46 at the time of her death, was something of a professional controversialist as opposed to a mere recorder of dry facts. The *Daily Express* had promoted her as 'Vulgar ... unscrupulous ... the woman you can't ignore', while the *News of the World* made a perhaps unwitting reference to her private life when it trumpeted: 'She's gay, she's provocative, and she's going places!' Anyone familiar with the early twenty-first-century TV series *Brass Eye*, with its cast of self-regarding but in their way fearless investigative reporters, need only think of one of those same characters in pearls and a flared trouser suit to get some of the flavour. Evelyn Waugh, who had twice successfully sued Spain for libel, called her a 'peddler of malicious infelicities'. By contrast, Noël Coward wrote on her death, 'it [was] cruel that all gaiety, intelligence and vitality should be snuffed out, when so many bores and horrors are left living.'

Four thousand miles away in Miami Beach, 22-year-old Cassius Clay sensationally defied predictions to deprive 33-year-old Sonny Liston of his world heavyweight boxing title that month after Liston had failed to answer the bell for the seventh round. In the ensuing pandemonium, Clay skipped to the ropes, his eyes bulging from their sockets, and shouted at the sportswriters below: 'Eat your words!' In one of those iconic moments that transcend their sport, he then continued his dancing tour of the ring, all the while – in a departure from the traditional, grunted post-fight platitudes – bellowing, 'I shook up the world!', 'I'm the prettiest thing that ever lived!' and 'I'm the greatest!'

Two days later, Clay let it be known that he would henceforth answer only to Cassius X, before going on to adopt the name by which the world knows him today: Muhammad Ali.

II

SPRING

THE WILD ONES

The gap between Britain's older, Depression-scarred and war-ravaged population and the younger, pampered one coming up behind it could hardly have been better expressed than by the scenes taking place at the Scala Theatre, in London's Charlotte Street, in the early afternoon of 1 April 1964. It was almost as if one generation were playing an April Fool's trick on another one. Outside, you had the building itself, established in 1772, with its fussily ornate façade, carved marble columns and grand entrance steps all making it the last word in Palladian opulence, if nowadays looking a little frayed around the edges. Something about the Scala's sheer bulk and curved, cream-coloured front wall dotted by small, circular windows suggested a great ocean liner moored in the street. There were other unmistakable signs that the venue was a British institution of the most solid and conventional sort, somewhere people might go to enjoy a family night out watching a musical like *Oliver!* or *Brigadoon*, or to take in a Christmas panto. One way or another, it was a reassuringly decorous place, with its uniformed commissionaires, brownish but still elegant cut-glass chandeliers, velvet pile carpeting and faded playbills displayed in glass cabinets in the foyer. Everything outside the auditorium itself was antiquated, respectable, and, in certain visible places, just slightly shabby.

Inside, there were the Beatles, completing work on *A Hard Day's Night*. The shooting script for the film's climactic scene, surely one of 1964's emblematic moments, both for the band themselves and for the flood of youthful energy it helped to release, reads:

INTERIOR: THEATRE AUDITORIUM

We see the audience of girls streaming in and settling down in their places for the show. There is the usual business of getting ready, and we see SHOTS of the girls' faces, then JOHN, PAUL, RINGO and GEORGE looking at them. At last, on cue from the floor manager the BOYS start their act to the audience's screams. During the number we constantly CUT away to the house with various shots of the girls. They are ecstatic.

This rather bland precis of events was perhaps to understate the orgiastic response of the 350 young audience members present that afternoon, many of them displaying the two extremes of self-expression and inhibition by alternately screaming and stuffing handkerchiefs into their mouths, and a few even clambering across the footlights to clutch at their idols, who were content to yell back into the din for twenty minutes before exiting the theatre by way of a fire escape and an unmarked delivery van which, in scenes reminiscent of an early comedy, took off down Charlotte Street, made a screeching turn and disappeared in the general direction of Tottenham Court Road, all the while backfiring loudly, with some of the fans in hot pursuit. One way or another, it seemed the Beatles had woken a sleeping generation. And whatever you think of the ultimate results that followed, they also passed on the torch: an electrician's mate from Bromley named Dave Jones, later relaunched as Bowie, and the 12-year-old Gordon Sumner (aka Sting) were among the legions converted by *A Hard Day's Night*, while the teenaged Phil Collins, then in his first year at a West London stage school, was actually on hand as one of the few male extras in the Scala audience, paid the union scale of £3 2*s* for a six-hour shift, significantly less than his future daily rate as the nation's beloved singer-songwriter and sometime drummer for Genesis.

The world would later hear a good deal about the pre-eminence of science and technology, and how this would sweep away the old taboos and superstitions, liberating us from much of the drudgery associated with chores such as the ordeal of properly written longhand correspondence, if not from the ravages of a global pandemic. The first editorial of *The Sun*, launched in September 1964, seemed to offer itself up as a newspaper for the Space Age:

> We welcome the era of automation, electronics, computers. We will campaign for the rapid modernisation of Britain regardless of the vested interests of management or workers ...
>
> For all the millions of people with lively minds and fresh ambitions, the *Sun* will stimulate the new thinking, hoping to produce among our readers the leaders of tomorrow, knowing that they are more likely to emerge from a college of advanced technology than from Eton or Harrow.

Sixty years on, it remains a moot point how far this bright new prospectus of Britain's egalitarian future has come to pass. But it's undeniably true that at the time of *The Sun*'s launch there were developments in mechanisation and technology that led some to imagine the country in terms of a reborn nation fairly pulsing with dynamic vigour, or at least one where the car and the television had changed millions of Britons' daily habits, and where the set-piece visit to the supermarket was fast replacing the obligation to pop down to a local shop that as often as not trafficked solely in string, toffee apples and copies of *Radio Times*.

One of the great high-end innovations of the day, still unknown to the general public, but not to the number-crunchers at the Ministry of Aviation or their colleagues in the Treasury, was a futuristically sleek aircraft in the early stages of its construction in a somewhat dilapidated row of hangars next to a golf course in the Bristol suburb of Filton. The plane under development was then named Concord, and the programme's cost, shared with the French, was estimated at £70 million, or roughly £1.2 billion in our terms. Thanks to the usual overruns, the final price tag was about ten times this figure. The plane's eventual roll-out displayed the fundamental extremes of so much of British life, the brilliance of the basic concept matched by the almost embarrassed reaction to its triumphant debut. As the then Labour aviation minister Tony Benn said:

The original plan was that both the French and English Concordes would be spelled thus, with an 'e'. But Harold Macmillan had been insulted by Charles de Gaulle on a visit. De Gaulle had said he had a cold and couldn't see him. So Macmillan came back and removed the 'e' from the end. I decided to put it back again. We had to have the same name for the same aircraft, and besides, it was reversing an insult to the French, which I wasn't in favour of.

'I went to Filton for the first test flight of the British model,' Benn continued:

The French had had a huge rollout, with great panache, but typically for Britain we just treated Concorde as another plane. The first flight was hilarious. It was just like a village cricket match. There was Sir George Edwards, the chairman of British Aircraft Corporation, in his pork-pie hat, pacing up and down waiting for the flight to start and muttering, 'It's these chaps in the backroom who are causing the delay – lot of poppycock.' Finally, Brian Trubshaw, the test pilot, came out, and people waved at him as if he was going in to bat. 'Good old Trubby!', that kind of thing. But when Trubby came out and got into the plane and it boomed into the air, the vibration was so great I felt I was being filleted. It was as if the flesh was falling off my backbone.

Another of those peculiarly British marriages of the sublime and slightly haphazard came on 20 April 1964, with the launch of BBC 2. This followed on the report of a blue-chip committee under the chairmanship of the glass magnate Sir Harry Pilkington, which in June 1962 had recommended that there be a 'thorough reappraisal' of the upstart ITV network, with tougher rules about advertising. By contrast, the BBC – 'the principal instrument of broadcasting in the United Kingdom' – was to be 'authorised forthwith to provide a second programme, and this new channel should at all times disseminate material with depth and substance, of cultural and spiritual value to the nation'. In essence, the general idea was that BBC 2 would exist slightly above the humdrum level of the established free-to-air television channels. Its role was to 'entertain' and to 'uplift', Sir Harry added, if not necessarily in that order of priority.

It's not known what, if anything, the Pilkington committee made of the subsequent series of BBC 1 animated adverts to promote its fledgling sister channel, which consisted of a cartoon featuring 'Hullabaloo' the kangaroo and 'Custard' her joey. In January 1964, the network began to broadcast short films made externally by companies such as Shell and BP, which served to enable engineers to test reception but soon themselves became cult viewing. Sir Hugh Greene, the Corporation's go-ahead 53-year-old director-general, stressed that he wanted the new channel's programme makers to 'reflect the attitudes of the 1960s', while restating the Reithian ideal of 'propagating all that is best in every department of human knowledge, endeavour and achievement ... A sense of pride in the excellence of British arts and technology is obviously paramount'.

Alas, the actual launch of BBC 2 fell some way short of these lofty standards. Set to kick off at 7.20 that balmy spring evening with a routine by the comedy troupe The Alberts, then a performance of Cole Porter's *Kiss Me, Kate* and – that rare phenomenon – a Soviet stand-up comedian, Arkady Raikin, followed by a climactic firework display live from Southend Pier, the schedule did not quite go as planned.

'Most of Fleet Street, half the Cabinet and a fair sprinkling of old-fashioned twits in brigade ties were summoned to a great viewing party at [Television Centre in] White City,' Tony Gill remembers:

What a night. There were BBC dolly-birds handing round drinks and goody-bags. The booze was soon flowing, and I seem to recall more than one old boy's hand straying on the girls' derrieres. All very jolly. We were told that there was even a live kangaroo in the building, and that this would join us bang at 7.20 p.m. to celebrate the off. Talk about drama. There was a telly in the room along with a great big ticking clock on the wall, and with thirty seconds to go everyone started counting down, just like on New Year's Eve. Five, four, three, two, one. And then: bugger all. We stared at the blank screen. Not a flicker. You could have heard a pin drop. 'A moment of farce had intruded on the year's great televisual drama' I wrote for the next day's paper. And then after a bit more silence, the next thing you heard was old Mike Peacock, the head of BBC 2, yelling at someone on the phone: 'Get it effing sorted!' and 'Now!' That sort of thing. Then Mike banged the receiver down again and walked over to us. 'Well,' he said quietly. 'That's it. We're completely stuffed, gentlemen.'

With a certain synchronicity, it later emerged that the new channel was beset by not one but two separate technical issues that evening. A massive fire had broken out around 6.30 p.m. at Battersea Power Station and, at the same time, a fault occurred in a 70,000-volt cable carrying electricity south from the Midlands to a relay station at Iver in Buckinghamshire, plunging much of London and the home counties into darkness. BBC 2's first-night presenter Gerald Priestland did, however, still intermittently have power at his disposal in the small studio at Alexandra Palace from where he was supposed to bid everyone a cheery hello and then introduce the Alberts. Sitting behind a plain wooden desk with typewriter and telephone, he duly appeared, blinking rapidly into the camera as if himself part of some surrealist comedy sketch with Pinteresque undertones. Still unaware of the technical glitch, Priestland began reading his welcoming script, even though for the first minute or so no one could hear him. Then a man in a dark suit suddenly appeared at his shoulder and handed him a note with the information that only a small number of people could see him, and nobody at all could hear a word he was saying. Priestland again blinked rapidly at this report, and then stared fixedly at the camera. By now he was sweating profusely. A minute can seem a long time in live broadcasting. Then the phone on his desk rang. Apparently no one was at the other end. It rang again. This time Priestland listened for a moment, put the phone down, and, at last fully audible, announced that he would start his introduction again in one minute. Now it really was like a proto-Monty Python sketch. A few seconds later, the screen abruptly went blank once more, and a poorly printed card appeared, saying: 'BBC 2 will start shortly.'

It never did. Quarter of an hour later, Priestland reappeared, mumbled a few words of apology, and then looked back in desperation towards the man in the dark suit. 'Anything else?' he enquired. There was nothing else. After a while, the typed card returned on screen, and the whole ghastly business was called off shortly after 9 p.m. Back at Television Centre, Tony Gill remembered, 'the lights had flickered on and off, though luckily the booze kept flowing at full force, and after a bit everyone went back downstairs to the street led by this old bloke holding a torch. It was like the Blitz all over again.' Gill heard later that the kangaroo had got stuck in the lift and 'went berserk, punching its handler', although this last detail has proved hard to corroborate. BBC 2 tried again the following evening. The luckless Priestland was given the night off, and the new presenter Denis Tuohy didn't directly refer to the original fiasco, although at the end of his stint he silently produced a flickering candle and blew it out. Perhaps the whole episode was good publicity, because the new channel was soon enjoying figures of between 2.7 and 3.2 million viewers nightly, which was eminently respectable in view of the fact that only 8 million householders owned television sets able to receive it in the first place. There were then 15,884,679 TV licences in the UK, at a basic cost of £4 per subscriber, or £62 in today's money.

★ ★ ★

On Tuesday 21 April, 46-year-old Keith Joseph, then going under the somewhat ungainly title of Minister for Housing and Local Government and Welsh Affairs, told his Cabinet colleagues of an exciting new report just completed by his office.

'There are expected to be at least a million more people living in South East England by 1981,' Joseph opened. 'Such an increase will present formidable problems for what is already the most congested part of the United Kingdom.' Part of this recent surge in population was attributable to what Joseph called 'unprecedented levels of immigration', and part to a surprising fact brought to his attention by the UK's Registrar General.

'The annual number of live births in the nation rose sharply at the end of the war to a peak of 881,000 in 1947,' Joseph explained to his colleagues:

> The Registrar, in making his initial demographic projections for planning purposes, assumed that there would then be a sharp fall from this peak ... The annual number of such births did in fact fall more or less as expected in the early 'fifties and reached a nadir of 668,000 in 1955. From then onwards, however, a wholly unexpected rise took place, which continues today. In 1962, the last year for which figures are available, the number was 897,000, the highest for any post-war year to date. The total net migration in England and Wales that same year was 287,000.

'This unexpected increase will have a significant effect on land use planning,' Joseph concluded:

The Registrar's population projection in 1948, on which the first round of local authorities' development plans was based, supposed a civilian population of England and Wales in 1971 of 45.28 million, a natural increase of about 2 million during the two decades 1951–71. But between 1951 and 1961 the increase in England and Wales, only marginally influenced by net inward immigration from overseas, came to just under two million, or virtually the entire 20-year projected gain in only the first ten. In other words, the volume of natural growth in Britain during the decade 1951–61 proved almost twice as large as had originally been expected, with significant results for the new and existing metropolitan centres.

In truth, urban 'planning' in the UK had long been a somewhat haphazard affair, subject to wildly varying estimates, if not rank guesswork, about future demographic trends, with no discernible strategy to integrate housing, services, jobs or transport. As one historian notes, 'The goal was simply to clear slums and accommodate growing populations, quickly and cheaply.' Between 1964 and 1974, 384 prefabricated tower blocks, many in the brutalist style of the era, appeared on the London skyline, one of which, Newham's Ronan Point, promptly collapsed again, and another, the Metro Central Heights complex in Walworth, became famous not for its architectural beauty but for the 'sick building' syndrome which caused the thousands of Department of Health staff working there (though not the ordinary rent-paying tenants) to be hurriedly relocated to alternative premises across the street. There had been plans in the early 1960s for a great new network of orbital and ring roads around London, with much the same intent as the wide avenues proposed by Christopher Wren some 300 years earlier, but they had come to nothing. What did change was the growth of satellite towns such as Milton Keynes, then taking shape just across the recently opened M1 motorway from Newport Pagnell in Buckinghamshire, if lacking any of that latter town's raw energy, vital nightlife and racy promise. Visiting this testament to his one-time ministerial enthusiasm in the 1970s, Keith Joseph was forced to conclude that the place reminded him of nothing so much as some woebegone wartime spot like Coventry or Liverpool after a hammering from the Luftwaffe.

It might be fairer to say that the sympathetic conservative visitor to Milton Keynes, and to many dormitory towns like it, finds much to enjoy, even if struck by the absence of old buildings. The place as a whole continues to polarise opinion. Milton Keynes's supporters point to the large number of business start-ups, some of them successful, and its above average economic performance in general. Set against this, one former president of the Royal Town Planning Institute portrays the city as 'bland, rigid, sterile and totally boring', with a preponderance of concrete slabs, roundabouts and expressionist statues as its sole points of distinction.

On much the same note, 29 May 1964 saw the opening by the Duke of Edinburgh of that monument to provincial pride in reinforced concrete, the Birmingham Bull Ring. Inspired by American indoor malls, the Bull Ring promised 'coatless shopping' in a climate-controlled maze of corridors kept at 'late-spring level.' Birmingham was not alone in developing a brave new city centre look for the 1960s. The author Geoffrey Moorhouse spoke elegiacally of the 'triumphant renewal' of the south Yorkshire of the day. 'As you look down on Sheffield now from the Pennine rim,' he wrote, 'you see new tower blocks shimmering like beacons upon the small peaks of the city, escarpments of masonry following the contours around the bowl of land.' Or put another way, a series of rainswept high-rises looming up like gallows straight out of the local dales.

In the same week that Prince Philip strolled with a somewhat clenched smile up and down the antiseptic hallways of the new Birmingham shopping centre, a 32-year-old entrepreneur opened his first era-defining shop in London's Fulham Road. The retailer in question was named Terence Conran, and his design and housewares outlet was Habitat. Perhaps it would be going too far, but not, perhaps, going in entirely the wrong direction to compare Conran's cultural influence over the years to Andy Warhol's; he made design fun and accessible. After the drab war years, the brightly coloured, brilliantly packaged Habitat soon became a flagship of hip, officially declaring your granny's traditional three-piece suite 'grotty' and 'far too boring' a concept. Instead, customers would be buying a basic, cotton-covered Larnaca sofa with a couple of related beanbags. Before long, other, similarly enterprising retailers competed to introduce the UK to such exotic commodities as fresh fruit and shops that stayed open until after five in the afternoon. John Stephen and Mary Quant were showing that you didn't need to go to Savile Row or Bond Street for fashionable tailoring; in time, out went old fogies in sensible suits, in came with-it young professionals in flares and miniskirts. Meanwhile, by a lucky bit of timing, the rapid availability of the female contraceptive pill – first introduced on the NHS in 1961 for married women only, and for general consumption five years later – happened to coincide with the arrival of that other defining symbol of swinging bedroom etiquette: the duvet.

Terence Conran grew up in the 1940s 'nouveau poor', as he put it. His South African-born father Gerard was an importer of gum copal, a substance used to make paint and varnish, not an overpopulated field in Britain at that time. Aged 13, Terence suffered a burst appendix, which forced him to stay home for six months. 'It was then that I got my first workshop going,' he recalled, adding that his mother Christina had encouraged him to build things – dollhouse furniture and the like. After public school came London's Central College of Art, which Conran left in 1949 only to emerge into a post-war England that was all spam fritters and ration books. Four years later, he opened his first restaurant, the only half-jokingly named Soup Kitchen, near London's Charing Cross, followed in time by Habitat, with its distinctive mix of modern (airy, grey-carpeted shop floors, with pop music swirling from the rafters) and vintage (hardbacked cane chairs, and rows of Spode pottery and rural copper-bottomed pots and pans). The original Habitat shop had a whitewashed interior wall and a false ceiling with spotlights, for a vaguely theatrical effect. 'Atmosphere' was all-important; it came not just from the goods on display but from the young, primarily female shop assistants, the cool music, and even from the smells emanating from the kitchen department generated by packets of 'Provençal herbs, pungent and aromatic', which seemed to complement the 'pastoral flowery mugs in soft browns and blues, enamelled in innumerable colours', to quote the shop's first catalogue, perhaps somewhat purple itself. In short, shopping at Habitat was an experience, not necessarily an ordeal. As one early reviewer explained, 'Terence Conran's vision combines the informality of the boutique with the abundance of the warehouse.'

Conran himself, by then on his third wife (having parted from his second, Shirley, the future bestselling author, after she caught him in flagrante with his secretary), would of course go on to be fabulously successful, opening more than fifty restaurants, putting his name to a shelf-ful of books, regenerating the Shad Thames area of London around Tower Bridge with his eponymous Design Museum, and, with a certain inevitability, also attracting his share of detractors along the way. 'Ambitious, mean, kind, greedy, frustrated, emotional, tiresome, intolerant, shy, fat' – those descriptions were courtesy of Conran himself. Sir Roy Strong, the dandified former guru of the Victoria and Albert Museum, portrayed him as a bullying egomaniac with one good idea: Habitat. Even the Design Museum's first MD, Stephen Bayley, called Conran a 'self-mythologising bastard'. And those were just some of the kinder critics, who admired his obvious presentational flair. Perhaps it would simply be fair to say that Conran, who died in 2020, combined a certain visionary concept of British high street retailing with a hard-headed business acumen that might just as easily have seen him swap his preferred pastel shirt and floral tie for the heavy black frock coat and watch fob of the Dickensian industrial tycoon. He was not always an easy man to work for. Conran once left a piece of crumpled paper on the desk of a senior colleague, with the scribbled note: 'I found this in the bin and want to know why it has not been reused.' He literally did count the pennies, both at work and at home. Conran himself once admitted: 'I don't like waste. I try to tell everyone how much photocopies cost, and I encourage them to switch the lights out. I don't like to throw away anything that can be used. Perhaps people confuse that with meanness.'

There were other signs in the spring of 1964 that Britain's consumer culture might be undergoing one of its cyclical revolutions, whether due to a hip new post-war generation assuming the controls of fashion, film and music, or perhaps to the dawning awareness of a few sharp retailers like Conran that it was the relatively prosperous younger breed who could increasingly afford things like French cuisine, Italian shoes and homegrown modish hair styling. There was also the significant fact that compulsory national service had been phased out for British males born after 1 October 1939, at once a symbolic and literal lifting of the restrictions on adolescent life, producing a crop of young men with little exposure to, and often no interest in, the previous era's culture of communal service, let alone of the military ideals of conformity, tidiness and punctuality, which bulked so large in the consciousness of those who came just before them. If you wanted to put a human face on the difference, you needed to look no further than the Rolling Stones: Bill Wyman did two years in uniform; Keith Richards didn't.

Whether as a result of some inchoate need for 'self-expression', or just obeying the rule demanding that each generation offend the one immediately before it, public displays of flesh and sexuality now also became more common, and it was partly as a result that a 57-year-old Bank of England director's wife named Helen Brook opened the first of her Advisory Centres in 1964. Brook did not approve of promiscuity, nor did she care for abortion. Her primary interest was the strictly pragmatic one of offering free and confidential advice on sex and contraception to young people, in an attempt to reduce the number of 'illegitimate' births. It was all part of a larger scheme of things, Brook later explained. 'I felt that until women were free of the fear of unwanted pregnancy, they would not be able to take up the equal opportunity of work.'

Fashion continued to be a vital generational and social identification marker, with a profusion of colourful if often oddly militaristic outfits tending to the androgynous and deliberately unsuited to anyone over 30. For the slightly more adventurous, there were also the sparingly cut dresses and, in due course, hot pants, PVC raincoats and sleek bob haircuts associated with Mary Quant and her business partner Archie McNair. Contrary to popular legend, Quant invented neither the miniskirt nor coloured patterned tights, but did create something more important. She triggered a new era in style, one in which fashion was for any modern young working girl rather than just for society debs. Anyone could wear a Quant mini, if they had the legs. In keeping with the emphasis on display, and more particularly with female freedom of expression (not least when this simultaneously appealed to male appetites), 1964 also saw the launch of the 'monokini' swimsuit, essentially a brief, close-fitting bottom and two thin straps that made a halter around the neck, with the wearer's breasts generally left to fend for themselves. Many of the monokini's early customers found themselves arrested for indecency, and for this and perhaps more prosaic climatic reasons it remained something of a novelty item in the Britain of 1964. Certainly there were few of the daring topless numbers to be seen on Brighton beach over the chilly Whitsun bank holiday of 17–18 May, when rival gangs of Mods and Rockers again assembled to throw deckchairs at one another and generally offend decent opinion, as expressed by the front-page headline in Tony Gill's *Daily Sketch*: 'The Wild Ones of Whitsun Went Even Wilder Yesterday!' the paper announced. 'Attacks on police! Vandalism! Violent clashes!' it shouted, along with as much feigned outrage as befitted a paper where scandal and prurient smut coexisted with the moral indignation of a Victorian temperance league campaigner.

ALL THE LONELY PEOPLE

Just as it's wrong to portray young people in Britain as suddenly in thrall to a nonstop priapic bender of skimpy beachwear and general licentiousness, it's worth remembering that the nation as a whole still remained beholden to an almost surreal raft of checks on private behaviour and freedom of speech introduced in the First or Second World Wars and never withdrawn. One of the most obvious was the enabling clause of the 1914 Defence of the Realm Act, limiting the hours that pubs could sell alcohol, which was gradually relaxed some seventy years after the Kaiser's troops had run up the white flag, but not fully repealed until 2003. Similarly, the last of the emergency Defence Regulations rushed through parliament in August 1939, giving the government sweeping powers to regulate private industry and impose price controls on goods and services, left the statute book only in December 1964. Even these petty restrictions on day-to-day British life might have seemed compellingly vital to the nation's welfare in the 1960s compared with the continued entitlement of the Lord Chamberlain's office to censor or ban any public entertainment, a prerogative first granted it by the Licensing Act of 1737 and still actively in force 227 years later. As a result, there would be a prolonged row over Edward Bond's play *Saved*. Its scene of a baby being murdered at the hands of teenaged delinquents, and its subversive use of words such as 'arse', 'crap' and 'shag', were officially deemed 'a revolting exercise in coarseness'. Even a heavily edited version of the play, staged at the Royal Court theatre in London, which turned itself into a private club to avoid a ban, was met with cries of 'shame' and 'sick' in the audience, and punctuated by the bullet-crack of hastily vacated seats.

The vice-like grip of the state on the employment and welfare, and all too often on the morals and opinions, of its citizens was matched by a number of private sector initiatives that ultimately went on to transform many ordinary peoples' lives. For instance, the computer. In 1964, this was still generally a vast, family refrigerator-shaped device, full of flashing lights and rapidly spinning and reversing spools of magnetic tape, as opposed to something you casually extracted from your pocket every few moments. If you wanted to know, say, the current GDP of Ghana or merely to reserve a hotel room for a business trip, you tended to do so by respectively consulting an encyclopedia and making a phone call with a formal letter of confirmation to follow. But a few enterprising companies like DEC and Olivetti were already developing futuristic-looking transistorised boxes attached to a keyboard that could be installed on an ordinary office worker's desk in a suitably air-conditioned room, the first step towards the essentially solitary work environment we enjoy today, boasting some of the characteristics of a modern PC. The Olivetti P101, launched in 1964, might seem hopelessly crude by our standards. It could perform rapid if basic mathematical calculations, printing its results onto a roll of paper like that of an old-fashioned cash register, but was incapable of higher thought. It was also priced at $3,200, or about $48,000 (£60,000) in today's money. But it was a definite signpost to the information superhighway, and to the computer as an inseparable part of human life. No fewer than 47,000 models were sold in the twelve months after it made its debut at that year's New York World's Fair.

On a more immediate note, a 31-year-old British engineer named Adrian Ashfield, working at the Decca Research facility in Brixton, south London, came up with the idea of a card system to 'securely identify a user, and control the dispensing of goods and services upon insertion into an appropriate sensing mechanism', to quote the official Patent Office licence, number 959,713, of June 1964. Ashfield's side project developed into the nation's first ATM, or cash machine, installed in the wall of the Barclays Bank in Enfield, north London (chosen as a suitably obscure location in the event of failure), and unveiled by Reg Varney of *On The Buses* fame in 1967. It's thought there are now some 3.25 million ATMs in the world, roughly 60,000 of them in the UK. Disillusioned with life in 1970s Britain, Ashfield eventually emigrated to New Jersey, where he died in 2019, largely forgotten by the wider world, at the age of 85.

A second British engineer, named Greville Wynne, was more prominently in the news in 1964. Born in Shropshire, he'd served in the army before going into business for himself selling industrial parts to a variety of government agencies and private customers throughout Eastern Europe. As a result, he was recruited as a bagman by MI6, in time making contact with the disaffected Soviet GRU officer Oleg

Penkovsky and smuggling secret intelligence back to London, as later enacted in the Benedict Cumberbatch film *The Courier*. Wynne, using the somewhat unimaginative alias of Greville Veen, was duly waiting for Penkovsky to appear for a meeting one day at the time of the Cuban Missile Crisis in October 1962 when, as he recalled, 'Four men suddenly appeared as if by magic. They were all short and thick-set and wore trilby hats at the same angle. One of them said quietly, "Mr Veen?" and I said, "Yes, that is my name".'

Wynne was then hit over the head and knocked out, bundled into a car and taken to prison in Moscow. A day or two later, his guards led him down the corridor as Penkovsky approached in handcuffs from the opposite direction, so that both could see the other had been arrested. The pair went on trial in 1963, and Wynne was sentenced to eight years' hard labour. Penkovsky was not so fortunate. He was either immediately shot or, in some accounts, strapped to a stretcher in a crematorium and burnt alive. On 22 April 1964, Wynne was exchanged at a checkpoint in Berlin for the Russian spy Konon Molody, better known in Britain, where he stole naval intelligence during most of the 1950s, as Gordon Lonsdale. Wynne later wrote a best-selling memoir about his experiences, although historians have tended to cast doubt on some of the book's specific detail. His own ghostwriter later remarked that 'Greville was a brave patriot who deserved not to be taken entirely seriously.' Perhaps he had merely suffered intolerable mental stress in the course of his eighteen months as a guest of the Soviet state. Like Adrian Ashfield, he never quite reconciled to daily life in Britain. Wynne struggled with depression and alcoholism, never received the military pension he felt he was entitled to, and died in London in February 1990, aged 70.

★ ★ ★

So many fans had now abandoned England's traditional summer pastime, county cricket, that the authorities at Lord's had recently seen fit to introduce a first knockout competition, on the sensational, and far from universally welcomed, basis that a single match might be completed in under three days. This was the previously noted Gillette Cup. A 'cheap and cheerful sideline,' as *The Times* put it, this vulgar necessity was nonetheless a popular commercial success. There was no stopping it now. Some of the tabloid press ran stories about hopelessly outmoded toffs in striped blazers, anachronistic rules and conventions, traditional matches where there had been more players on the field than there were spectators in the stands, and in general applauding the new spirit of enterprise represented by Gillette. 'This triumphant sporting experiment may not have been cricket to the purists, but by golly it's just the stuff the doctor ordered,' wrote the widely read Peter Wilson in the *Daily Mirror*.

Like cricket, domestic football also suffered from falling attendances. In 1953–54, the English league clubs had sold just over 40 million seats, but a decade later the total had fallen to less than 27 million, an unsustainable 33 percent drop in those paying at the turnstiles. Part of the problem was due to changing consumer habits as a whole; there were more leisure options to choose from, and the mass popularity of the television meant that a young man or woman no longer had to stand on a rainswept concrete terrace at 3 o'clock on a Saturday afternoon in order to demonstrate their loyalty to their team. And part was narrowly practical. It's sometimes easy to forget how different things were in British public entertainment just fifty or sixty years ago. The fee-paying customer often took their life in their hands merely to attend a football match, which apart from the very real potential for violence meant enduring catering and toilet facilities often redolent of a particularly unattractive North Korean prison.

The football establishment's response, much like their counterparts in cricket, was simply to add more matches. Like the Gillette trophy, the League Cup, introduced in 1961, was meant to combine the blood-and-thunder atmosphere of the traditional professional game with a few modest innovations such as midweek evening ties played under floodlights. Not everyone was impressed. In another thundering editorial, *The Times* wrote:

> Where a drastic reduction is required in an attempt to raise quality, no doubt quantity and a further spread of mediocrity will be the dose. Where some of wider horizons think in terms of a European League for the future, our masters' only proposal is to implement this useless Football League Cup ... It gets the players, the clubs and the public nowhere.

The average attendance across the Cup was just 11,246 in 1963–64, which was in line with the typical gate for the Second Division. When the time came, Leicester City, captained by 21-year-old Mike

Stringfellow, won the two-legged final, played on 15 and 22 April 1964; a total of 47,681 fans each paid around 6s (30p, or £4.50 today) to see the matches in which Leicester beat their midland rivals Stoke City 4–3 on aggregate. On both occasions, seventeen of the twenty-two players on the park were English-born, and the other five were Scottish. Each member of the winning team was paid a flat £40 for his services, although the Leicester goalie Gordon Banks, already the holder of eight of his eventual seventy-three England caps, was on a special superstar deal, and took home the startling wage of £52 10s a match, with a £20 bonus for helping win the cup.

The two teams contesting the FA Cup Final, held at Wembley on 2 May 1964, were both somehow redolent of a time when English football was a mud-spattered affair played by men wearing baggy, knee-length shorts hoofing around a leather ball that could double in weight over the course of a wet ninety minutes: Preston North End, founded in 1880, and West Ham United, who began life as Thames Ironworks in 1895 before assuming their modern identity five years later. I was present that day at Wembley as a child, and remember the absence of any absurd rules restricting things like drinking, smoking or fighting. In fact, these activities were rather encouraged.

There was some attractive action on the field that spring afternoon, not least from Preston's 17-year-old wunderkind Howard Kendall, then the youngest player ever to appear in a Wembley cup final. For their part, West Ham had Bobby Moore, their captain, in the middle and Geoff Hurst up front, both soon to help define a year and even a decade with their respective roles in the next World Cup. This being 1964, there was also a fair amount of robust give and take on the park, as well as some uninhibited comment in the crowd, although a respect-ful hush fell over the proceedings when Preston's evocatively named Nobby Lawton kneed Hurst in the back when the latter was haring towards goal. Hurst went out like a light, a collision the defender later insisted was a terrible accident caused by his opponent accelerating backwards towards him (much like Buster Edwards recalling the curi-ous episode of the spontaneously collapsing engine driver on the night of the Train Robbery), telling reporters that 'Geoff [had] just keeled over' for some unfathomable reason. To be fair to Lawton, he was an unusually cultivated player for the most part, and had once even fought back from a case of double pneumonia bad enough to have caused him to lose the use of his legs for a time.

Many of the non-committed, like our own party, were cheering for second-division Preston to defy logic and bring home the cup that day. They were a model club of their kind, run on a shoestring, with an agreeably ramshackle home ground and the enterprising former player Jimmy Milne as manager. It was all end-to-end stuff at Wembley, and Preston twice held the lead until a Ronnie Boyce header won it 3–2 for West Ham in stoppage time. No one invaded the pitch, nor showed any particular emotion at the end. Boyce himself pulled up his socks and strolled off, his face deadpan, looking for all the world as if he was returning from a gentle knockabout on the training park. A few teammates offered a handshake, and Johnny Byrne went so far as a gentle pat on the back. But that was it for any unseemly display of euphoria. Bobby Moore, genial as ever, went across to console the teenaged Howard Kendall, before the teams headed up to be handed their medals by 'Earl Harewood, president of Leeds United, graciously representing Her Majesty the Queen', as the announcer told us. All eleven of the West Ham players were Englishmen, ten of them born in London or Essex. A ticket to the terraces that day cost £1 2s 6d and a match programme was a shilling – £17 and 80p, respectively, in today's money. There were a total of six arrests in the 93,000 crowd for public disorder offences. The winning players each got a £30 bonus, and there was a modest team dinner a few nights later at a West End hotel. It was the first of three annual visits to the Wembley royal box for West Ham's 23-year-old captain, who also found time to play accomplished cricket for the Essex second team in the summer. Bobby Moore, it's true, may not have been the most engaged player on the pitch. He was not acquainted with every blade of grass, unlike West Ham's ubiquitous John Bond (fondly nicknamed 'Muffin' because of his ability to kick like a mule). He didn't do covering or man-marking or closing down. He didn't actually move that often. But when he did, it was invariably to telling effect, distributing the ball to all parts as smoothly as hot butter sliding across a pan. Moore's rationing of effort was an art form; you could clearly see in 1964 the slick operator who would hold the Jules Rimet trophy aloft for the nation two years later.

After the Cup Final, the principal back-page news in the British press was successively Wimbledon, where the singles' champions were Australia's Roy Emerson and Maria Bueno of Brazil; the Open Championship at St Andrew's, which the American Tony Lema won by five strokes, in the event proving his only major title before he and his wife died in a light-plane crash two years later; and the British Grand Prix, which Jim Clark (later killed in a Formula Two race) narrowly won over Graham Hill, who himself died in tragically similar circumstances to the Lema family when he crashed his twin-engine plane while on a night approach to Elstree Aerodrome in thick fog in November 1975.

In traditional cricket, the headline news was the arrival in Britain of Bobby Simpson's Australians to play a series of five Tests, twenty-six other first-class matches and the grand total of no one-day internationals or similarly frenetic floodlit slogs. As noted, England's captain that summer was 29-year-old Ted Dexter, late of Radley College and Cambridge. In his own way, the aquiline-nosed Dexter, with his faint but discernible air of boredom at it all, was a classic representative model of the social divisions of British life. The son of a former Royal Artillery officer turned Lloyds underwriter, he was born in Milan, and returned to England just in time to ensure he would be known as a 'filthy Eyetie', among other unappreciative terms, throughout his early schooldays.

Dexter dedicated himself to cricket at Radley, where he acquired the nickname 'Lord Ted' for his insouciant attitude. Following national service, he went up to university, captained the side at Lord's, signed as an amateur for Sussex, and made his England debut in 1958 before flying out as a late replacement on that winter's tour of Australia, where his cravat sparked predictable derision, and was leading his country just three years later. England's Yorkshire-born spin bowler Jim Laker was not impressed by the last-minute addition to the side Down Under. 'Just why the selectors wanted Dexter sent out, rather than one of half a dozen more deserving players, I shall never know,' he wrote. 'I can only assume they fancied a touch of the gay abandon.'

Coming in to bowl at a particularly tense moment in a Test at Sydney, Laker once froze in his delivery stride when out of the corner of his eye he saw Dexter – as ever so impeccably groomed that his colleagues sometimes half-expected him to break into a chorus of 'I Feel Pretty' in the dressing room – airily practicing his golf swing on the square leg boundary. Something about this struck the bowler as not only ill-advised in the context of the match, but also 'all too typical of the public-school attitude that assumes cricket is all a bit of a lark', and a contributory factor to the feeling that sport, like so much else in British life, was really a matter of a tiny elite at one end and a large residue of what amounted to useful servants at the other.

One morning in June 1965, Dexter decided to treat himself to a day out in his new metallic-blue Jaguar at Newbury racecourse. On his way back to London, the car ran out of petrol. Rather than wait for assistance, England's captain elected to push the vehicle down a hill to a spot where he thought there might be a garage. Unfortunately, he lost control and it ended up pinning him to the gates of a champagne distribution warehouse, breaking his right leg. It was a serious injury, although, mixed in with the widespread expressions of concern, there was also a certain amount of dark humour, precisely because the whole affair, with its bill of fare of the races, the Jag and the champagne, seemed to be the sort of thing that happened to Dexter rather than to normal cricketers. He had then just turned 30, and other than a brief, unhappy comeback in 1968 his Test career was effectively over.

For all that, only the most partisan spirit would write Dexter off as a stereotypical toff of the old school, attending Henley and other jollities when not swanning around the field at Lord's, for whom it was distinctly bad form ever to be thought to be trying. For one thing, he was the genuine article as a cricketer. An almost audible shudder of excitement swept the ground whenever Dexter strode to the crease. He was rarely boring, and never intimidated. Some of his most memorable innings came against the ferocious West Indies bowling attack, including a brutal 70 in the remarkable Lord's Test in 1963, where with one ball to go all four results were still possible. Twelve months earlier, against Pakistan at the Oval, Dexter had scored 172 in a record-breaking stand of 248 with Colin Cowdrey. Few men have hit the ball harder, and when in the mood he could destroy any bowling line-up in the world. In later years, Dexter variously turned his hand to a range of interests that included flying, writing, broadcasting, modelling, politics, and running a successful public relations firm, while owning both horses and a string of greyhounds. There was a glorious moment in a television interview given in his seventies when asked if he had any remaining ambitions in life, and he replied emphatically: 'Yes. Climb Everest.' Jack Nicklaus once remarked that Dexter could have been a top professional golfer but for the fact that he was too busy for all the 'non-playing crap' that goes with it. A brief foray as chairman of England's cricket selectors proved a rare failure, although even here he left his mark, arriving for meetings at Lord's on his powerful Norton motorbike before peeling off his leathers to reveal a beautifully tailored City suit. Cricket was rarely dull when Dexter was around.

'While everyone knows that Englishmen are sent to public schools because that is the only place where they can learn good manners,' the author Rebecca West once noted, 'it unfortunately happens that the manners they learn there are recognised as good only by people who have been to the same sort of school, and often appear very bad to everyone else.' This aphorism may well have been true, at least on one level, in Dexter's case. Among other peccadillos, he was sometimes thought just a touch too keen on certain *ancien régime* cricketing mannerisms such as his habit of wearing an Edwardian-era Harlequin cap, or of employing his languid drawl to address his subordinate players while in the field as 'My good man', while avoiding their company entirely at all other times. Then there was the fact that he regularly brought a portable television to the dressing room to follow the progress of a horse in which he had a vested interest, and once declared a Sussex innings closed while at Brighton Racecourse. Earlier in his career, Dexter had found himself in Copenhagen one weekend immediately before being due to represent his county in a first-class match beginning at Hove the following Tuesday. In his own words, 'I was fascinated by an adorable Danish girl, so I stayed and sent a coloured postcard to Sussex saying I was sorry, but I could not play for them as arranged.' The cricket world did not know him as Lord Ted for nothing.

For all that, Dexter was also an outstanding example of the contradictory values of the 1960s, for some a golden era of class-busting egalitarianism founded on unprecedented affluence and fuelled by mind-expanding drugs, for others the primary cause of our present-day social malaise. 'One was always conscious the times were changing,' he once told me, 'and strutting around as if to the manor born wasn't necessarily the best way to win friends and influence people.' Sensitive to this fact even at the time, Dexter did not always care to play up his privileged background. When asked by an Australian radio interviewer in 1964 where he'd gone to school, England's cricket captain replied, in a studiously non-fruity accent, 'Oh, some place out by Oxford', as though it might have just been the local comprehensive. Over time, Dexter worked hard to remove that thin film of superiority that seemed to separate him from lesser mortals, and which in later years he attributed not so much to any sense of aristocratic entitlement as to his own crippling shyness. 'I just shudder now at what some people must have thought of me,' he said.

Dexter was also painfully sensitive to the notion that it had all come too easily for him, that he had simply been wafted down from Olympus, as it were, into the upper echelons of an English society, where he had few obligations beyond gliding around the nearest games field, quaffing port and oppressing the proletariat. He was particularly incensed at the allegation contained in an otherwise admiring biography of him published in 1995 that his youthful spell in the London insurance trade had come about through influence rather than hard work on his part, and kept up a lively correspondence on the subject until the end of his life more than a quarter of a century later. In his retirement years, Dexter chose to live not on the French Riviera or in one of the more fashionable quarters of London, both of which he haunted at one time, but in a modest home in suburban Wolverhampton, where he acted as a volunteer teacher at the local primary school. Taking his life as a whole, it might be fair to conclude that he was never quite a stereotypical upper-class idler; that as England captain he wasn't the sort of leader content just to follow the manual with little or no variation; and that his absolute refusal to accept handed-down truths, whether on the field or elsewhere, remained the one constant factor in his character. In short, he was an energetic, impatient, romantic sort with a low tolerance for the mundane details of life and a sharp nose for the direction the social wind was blowing. Ted Dexter was not only an emblematic, but also a representative figure of the 1960s.

Nor could it be concluded, from the list of names overseeing English cricket in 1964, that Dexter was alone in displaying an occasional imperious flourish. There was the presidency of the MCC, for instance, which changed hands that summer from the patriarchal George 'Gubby' Allen, late of Eton and Cambridge, to the 75-year-old tea baron Richard Twining, himself a product of Eton and Oxford, who had graced a few games for Middlesex at about the time of the Great War, or the club's long-serving secretary Stewart 'Billy' Griffith, known far and wide as 'Colonel' in deference to his role as the former commander of a unit of the Glider Pilot Regiment. Just fourteen months earlier, the MCC, or de facto England, side had returned from a gruelling away series to Australia during which they were managed by none other than the 16th Duke of Norfolk, Earl Marshal of England, an estimable figure in many ways if not necessarily one suited to the day-to-day demands of running a major international sports tour of the 1960s. As noted, the chairman of the national selectors was Walter

Robins, late of Cambridge, of whom his friend the cricket writer E.W. 'Jim' Swanton once said: 'Most of us grow mellower, I suppose, with age, but poor Walter became if anything less so; in retrospect those early days of the 1960s must have seen the first onset of the hardening of the brain arteries which proved fatal towards the end of the decade.' The inimitable Yorkshire and England bowler 'Fiery' Fred Trueman recalled that Robins was in the habit of arriving in the home dressing room where, with all the finesse of a gas-main explosion, he would publicly castigate his team's captain and any other players whose performance he thought deficient. 'I literally kicked his arse out the door one time,' Trueman assured me.

In terms of the actual cricket: the summer's first Test match at Nottingham's Trent Bridge ground was drawn, largely thanks to rain, and the second, at Lord's, went much the same way. The latter was a representative English summer sporting occasion in its way. There was a mile-long line of cabs and cars stretching around St John's Wood on the first of the scheduled five days' play, with many of the intending customers dressed as if for a garden party, passing through the ancient turnstiles at what seemed to be the rate of about one a minute, the ground itself *en fête*, decked out with hanging baskets splashed in red, yellow, purple, and the flags above the pavilion snapping in the fresh northerly breeze. Looking down from the top of the tiered mound stand on the first morning, rather as though in the dress circle of a vast theatre, the field as a whole was a vivid emerald green with one or two biscuit-coloured patches on either side of the covers, with banks of shiny white benches and a pleasantly leafy backdrop. In general the whole place was flatter and airier than it is now, although with two utilitarian black cooling towers soaring up on the road outside the main Grace Gates.

Unfortunately, it was also persistently wet. A full house of 27,000 spectators sat good-naturedly watching the umpires trudge to and fro on one of their unhurried hourly inspections of the Lord's playing area, and the ground staff listlessly push a mop across the outfield. There was no play at all on the first two days, and the only highlight after that was an accomplished if somewhat measured century by England's John Edrich, very much in the Dunkirk spirit, and a six by the Australian tailender Graham McKenzie that sailed over the roof and bounced into St John's Wood Road, where it struck a 55-year-old pedestrian named Richard Horton on the bridge of his nose, breaking his glasses.

On the third day, a letter appeared in *The Times* from a Mr Keith Falkner, complaining about the facilities at Lord's:

> It was ludicrous to all of us watching despondently yesterday to see the falling rain run off the playing area, by hosepipe, to the very parts of the ground which need drying. It is an elementary thought that the water could have been drained off instead of being left to saturate the turf. In future, may this be considered for the benefit of thousands of us for whom the Lord's Test is the one event which takes precedence over all else?

It was one of those times that make you wonder how the English could ever have come up with a national sport with a minimum requirement of at least halfway dry weather. There were no refunds for the disappointed spectators, and no reports of any public order disturbances. In any other country, or among the devotees of any other game, there would have been a riot. My uncle was visiting us from California, and, watching it on television, remarked, 'A baseball crowd would have burnt the place down.'

By 1964, a few enterprising professional cricket and football clubs were at least beginning to cultivate a thin veneer of cosmopolitanism by signing their first overseas players. There was no such pretence to sophistication in the world of professional snooker. The sport's so-called International Championship was revived after a seven-year hiatus in April 1964 with a match between the Devon-born John Pulman, who was 40, and 50-year-old Fred Davis of Derbyshire, held in the early Victorian Burroughes Hall in central London. It, too, in its way, was a quintessentially English occasion: the players were each paid 40 guineas (about £680 today) for their services, with a further cheque for £65 to the champion, the ambient smell in the hall was one of Watneys and stale Woodbines, and nobody bothered too much with any fire or safety regulations. 'I'm a sloppy old bugger,' Pulman, the eventual winner, genially informed the *Sketch*, his sellotaped glasses and randomly brushed hair suggesting that this lack of vanity was a product of indifference. In general he was one of those slightly chaotic sporting figures, not infrequently hailing from the West Country, whom the British sometimes take to themselves. Pulman had initially trained for the match at the home of his friend Bill Lampard, a confectioner from Bristol who installed a billiard room for his use above his shop, but this arrangement had ended after Pulman was discovered in bed one day with his host's wife. The player's career never again quite recovered its 1960s lustre. Pulman was eventually declared bankrupt with debts of £5,916, and moved into a modest hotel in Bromley, Kent, dying after a fall down stairs on Christmas Day in 1998, at the age of 75.

Then there was the swashbuckling Ted Dexter figure of the jet-propelled racing world, Donald Campbell. Campbell, born in 1921, was the son of the record-breaking racer Malcolm Campbell (1885–1948), and inherited his father's raw courage, flamboyant manner and tendency to exaggerate. The younger Campbell was essentially a Regency figure born out of his time, with an exotic home life to match. He was also intensely superstitious. No speed attempt could be made without the accompanying talisman Mr Whoppit, his red felt-jacketed teddy bear. Campbell so hated the colour green that his team manager Evan Green had to go by the name Evan Turquoise. He also believed that nothing good ever happened on a Friday, that the dead could communicate from beyond the grave and that it was invariably fatal to wish or be wished good luck. On 17 July 1964, on a track at South Australia's Lake Eyre that was still wet from recent floods, Campbell set a new land speed record of 403.10mph. Five months later, he went on to break the record on water, travelling at 276.30mph in his jet-engined hydroplane *Bluebird K7*, also in Australia, becoming the first and so far only man to hold both records in the same year.

Donald Campbell died on 4 January 1967 while racing a modified K7 at 320mph – a rate that, if sustained, would have seen him cross from New York to Southampton in just nine hours – over the choppy surface of Coniston Water in Cumbria. At the end the boat lifted from the water, took off at a 90° angle, somersaulted and plunged back into the lake nose first, then cartwheeled before briefly coming to rest and sinking. While playing cards the previous night, Campbell had drawn the queen and ace of spades, the 'death hand', and calmly told his partners at the table that he had a fearful premonition that he was going to 'get the chop'. His last words recorded over his radio intercom were, 'I can't see much ... The water's very bad indeed ... I'm galloping over the top ... Getting a lot of bloody row in here ... Everything's green ... Hello, the bow's up ... I've gone!', passing away 'like an English gentleman', as one obituary put it. Campbell had often remarked that in death a skipper should stay with his craft. But in May 2001 divers finally located human remains near the wreck of the *Bluebird* and brought them to the surface. Campbell's funeral ceremony was held on 12 September, more than thirty-four years after his death, but was overshadowed in the media by the coverage of the 9/11 attacks in the United States.

While not quite sport in the narrow sense of the word, there was a striking example in April 1964 of the British gift for not always taking politicians as seriously as they might like, and also perhaps of the true grandee's characteristic grace under pressure. The story first appeared in Lord Hailsham's diaries, published after his death in 2001.

'An odd tale of 1964, never revealed,' he wrote:

Alec Douglas-Home (then prime minister) was staying in Scotland with John and Priscilla Tweedsmuir, who had no room for Alec's private bodyguard. The latter went to the nearest town and John and Priscilla left Alec for a time alone in the house. Knock at the door. Door answered by PM in person.

Deputation of left-wing students from Aberdeen University. Said they were going to kidnap Alec. He, 'I suppose you realise if you do, the Conservatives will win the next election by 200 or 300?' They were serious. He then asked and received permission to pack a few things and was given ten minutes grace. After that they were offered and accepted beer. John and Priscilla returned and the kidnap plot abandoned. The bodyguard swore Alec to secrecy as his job would have been in peril.

With the best will in the world, it's somehow hard to see even a humble member of the US Senate, whose denizens would probably wear togas if they felt they could get away with it, let alone the chief executive himself, in the same straits. It may be that Douglas-Home, despite or because of his air of languid detachment, was one of the few senior politicians of the era free of the self-aggrandising pomposity that characterises the world's second oldest profession. 'Britain is not a serious country,' President Johnson was moved to remark later in 1964 to his adviser George Ball (bemoaning British reluctance to commit troops to Vietnam). Although one might reasonably in turn ask how truly serious America herself was, or is, given her witless and tendentious public life, and her extraordinary delusion that those elected to political office in Washington might in some way be worthy of public deference merely by virtue of their status, as opposed to anything they might actually do or say to advance the common good.

AUNTY'S TEA PARTY

One part of the small change of adolescent revolt in 1964 was the cinema. British films as a whole were full of young people, and increasingly appealed to them as their core audience and market. At one level, this meant products like *French Dressing*, the first feature directed by a 36-year-old hitherto studiously upmarket documentary-maker called Ken Russell. Loosely in the school of Jacques Tati, and set in the fictional rundown beachfront resort of Gormleigh-on-Sea (shot in real-life Herne Bay), it at least proved moderately popular with its teenaged audiences if not always the grown-up press. The *New Statesman* critic described it as a 'seaside rainswept comedy of some charm and freshness', which qualified as a rave compared with some of the other notices. Russell himself later wrote of the experience:

> A script by a couple of West End revue writers didn't jell [*sic*] with the images concocted by an arty director from TV, making his first film ... There are a few good gags, but there's only so much comedy you can wring out of extras in top hats making fools of themselves on a beach with buckets and spades and Hula-Hoops.

Despairing of the thematic clichés and laboured jingoism of most established British cinema, Russell was one of those quintessentially Sixties figures who set out to reinvent the genre, even if this sometimes meant having to wait for the necessary funds to realise his vision. His next project, by way of contrast to *French Dressing*, was a severely spartan hour-long documentary on the late Hungarian composer Béla Bartók. Later that year, Russell wrote a three-page treatment for an adaptation of Anthony Burgess's novel *A Clockwork Orange*, which was to have starred the Rolling Stones. One of the film's first episodes was intended to show the young band members enjoying a communal drink of LSD-laced milk, then strolling around London vandalising shops and randomly assaulting pedestrians before going on from there to get a bit raunchy in a gang rape scene. Even the Stones turned Russell down.

At a slightly more exalted level than the likes of *French Dressing*, there was the aforementioned *A Hard Day's Night*, the *Casablanca* of pop musicals and arguably the founding event of Sixties youth culture in Britain, where it received a royal premiere at the London Pavilion on 6 July 1964. Many arts critics came to scoff, but were forced to admit that the picture was 'fresh' and 'irreverent', with 'daring camerawork, fast cuts and breezy improvisation', and in all 'a catalytic blast of propaganda not only for the Fab Four but for the much vaunted "younger generation"'. Later that night, there was a small party back at the Dorchester Hotel, just the band, their immediate entourage (but no wives or girlfriends) and Princess Margaret. Later still, their roadie Mal Evans opened the door of the private room where everyone had gathered to usher in a conga line of scantily clad women, who briskly fanned out, sat in people's laps and lit cigarettes. 'Help yourselves, lads,' he announced unnecessarily. The princess's regally blasé reaction to these developments later suggested to Evans that the monarch's younger sister might herself not be entirely averse to a bit of the other, 'especially with our John'.

Six days later the Beatles played the Hippodrome, Brighton, the first in a series of summer concert parties at traditional seaside resorts like the one lovingly satirised in *French Dressing*. Even the chirpy Paul McCartney later admitted he was beginning to feel the strain, particularly now the actual shows had plunged into orgiastic chaos, dinned out by young fans who howled their way through most numbers. They also shrieked, squealed, wailed and cooed, and there were long periods when they did little else. The band's public appearances now increasingly took place in a gale of shoes and handbags sailing over the footlights, love notes, often pinned to freshly shed knickers, as well as the occasional well-aimed bottle or chair leg. Sociologists would later characterise the whole phenomenon as both a product and a defining symbol of the 'youthquake' undermining traditional society, but at the time the emphasis was simply on informal and immediate fun, rather than any metaphysical concerns about the tedium of mainstream existence. At the art deco Hippodrome, frantic young girls bounced up and down in their seats like popcorn: 2,850 customers, 167 stretcher cases.

But perhaps the most significant moment in world cinema that year came at the 36th annual Academy Awards ceremony in Los Angeles, held in the early evening hours of Monday 13 April, when Anne Bancroft read out the names of the five contenders for the Best Actor award: Albert Finney (*Tom Jones*), Richard Harris (*This Sporting Life*), Rex Harrison (*Cleopatra*), Paul Newman (*Hud*) and Sidney Poitier (*Lilies of the Field*). There was no endearing back-and-forth joshing as there is nowadays, just an actress approaching middle age dressed in a shimmering floor-length ballgown who briskly opened the envelope and read out the winning name: Poitier, who became the first black actor to be so honoured. There was a good deal of applause in the hall as he bounded up in his tails and white tie, but also a number of indignant letters in the next day's press complaining that Bancroft had seen fit to kiss him on the cheek when presenting him with his award. The *New York Times* judged the gesture 'inspiring', if 'regrettably provocative', mild stuff compared with Poitier's anony-mous critics who offered to tar and feather him, if not bash his fucking skull in, for the offence of having been publicly embraced by a white woman. Another paper called the 37-year-old Bahamian American actor, who just a year or so earlier had been scraping by in films like *Virgin Island*, 'the most powerful agent for positive change' on earth.

Elsewhere in Los Angeles, Stanley Kubrick shook hands with Arthur C. Clarke over dinner that week to consummate their deal to write a script then called *How the Solar System was Won*. As noted, the director was fascinated by the possibility of life on other planets, and had had to be talked out of including a lengthy alien invasion subplot to *Dr Strangelove*. 'Stanley was in some danger of believing in flying saucers,' Clarke recalled. 'I felt I had arrived just in time to save him from this gruesome fate.' It would take the perfectionist Kubrick a further four years to bring what became *2001: A Space Odyssey* to fulfillment. In the meantime, the director sold his California man-sion and moved into a home in Barnet Lane in Borehamwood, north of London, if nothing else surely making him one of the few people ever to emigrate from Beverly Hills to suburban Watford. His funds still came from the United States, and he raised almost all his capital there. Kubrick's basic routine was to sleep through the British day, waking at about 5 p.m. in order to do business via telex or phone with the moguls in Hollywood. Most of the established talent to whom he sent the outline of *How the Solar System was Won* wanted nothing to do with a story apparently involving time travel and a tribe of squab-bling apes, so he settled instead on journeymen like Keir Dullea and Gary Lockwood, who were glad of the work, and even the pre-*Rising Damp* Liverpudlian stage actor Leonard Rossiter, somewhat improb-ably transformed into a Russian scientist.

Meanwhile, there was a continuing sharp exchange of correspond-ence between the Lord Chamberlain's office and the principals of Joe

Orton's scabrous comedy *Entertaining Mr Sloane*, which made its West End debut in June 1964 after a provincial try-out. Cuts had been made as a result, but the nation's officially designated moral guardian was still not entirely happy at some of the play's dialogue, or even a number of its stage directions. On 12 June, the Lord Chamberlain sent a closely typed seven-page letter on the subject to the producer Michael Codron, listing some of his reservations on the subject:

' ... and shit on their doorsteps.'
  ' ... old prat!'
  ' ... and give yer arse a chance.'
The direction ("Sloane lifts his hand and touches the point where he judges her nipple to be"). Sloane is *not* to touch the lady's breast.
'You wanted to see if my titties were all my own.'
You are particularly warned that any movements implying or simulating copulation are not allowed, and furthermore that such actions have been described in judgements obiter dictum given in the High Court of Justice as "obscene".
  ' ... I just don't give a monkey's fart.'
  ' ... Bugger.'
  ' ... Grinding to her climax.'

And that was just for the first of the play's three acts, before it delved into matters such as extramarital pregnancy, sadism, bisexuality, murder and an incestuous brother–sister subplot to try the Lord Chamberlain's patience. *Mr Sloane* was some way from contemporary family-friendly fare like *Hello, Dolly* or *Half a Sixpence*, although in retrospect it may have owed something to Harold Pinter's *The Caretaker*, first staged in 1960 and similarly dealing with a calculating intruder arriving to insert himself between two warring siblings in a drama with some of the characteristics of a chess game in which one player thinks he has a winning move only to find he's been outplayed.

Pinter himself was then living in a bow-fronted Regency house on the seafront at Worthing, Sussex, a slightly incongruous spot from which to produce a subversive short story-turned-play, another emblematic Sixties product he called *Tea Party*. Perhaps the most striking feature of this new project wasn't so much its artistic vision, but the fact that it was directly commissioned by the BBC, thus signifying one of those seismic moments – if not the moment – when the Corporation loosened the ties of its editorial corset far enough to embrace a work that was basically the account of a collapse into paranoid delusion of a sanitary engineer, whose ultimate breakdown occurs against a porcelain backdrop festooned with wash basins, lavatory bowls and bidets. This was not your grandmother's idea of acceptable viewing entertainment, especially when subsidised by the TV licence holder. Pinter once told me that *Tea Party* might well be taken as a coruscating satire on Western capitalism, or just as likely – he liked to bowl the occasional well-flighted googly to the critics – 'it could be a technical manual about recent advances in plumbing'. Either way, the *Communist Daily Worker* gave the broadcast a critical rave, and the BBC switchboard lit up like the proverbial Christmas tree. 'I was quite chuffed by it all,' Pinter admitted thirty-five years later.

It seems not too far of a stretch to move from Pinter to the satirist Peter Cook, who at the age of 26 had already starred in a successful transatlantic stage revue, opened and closed nightclubs in London and New York, and provided much of the start-up money for *Private Eye*. In 1964, Cook was busy developing his alter ego, the monotonal E.L. Wisty, for the Saturday-night ITV programme *On the Braden Beat*. In Cook's hands, Wisty had at one time harboured ambitions to become a judge, though sadly his lack of Latin had caused him to fail 'the rigorous judging exams'. This setback had led the character to an alternative career as a coal miner, since on the miner's exam, 'they only ask you one question, "Who are you?", and I got 75 percent on that'. The popular consensus on Cook, who died in 1995, aged 57, was of a dazzling youthful talent – like Ted Dexter (with whom he was at school), almost spoilt by fortune – who later bloated in his secluded north London home like Elvis at Graceland. It's a caricature, if one with a grain of truth. Cook's sometime colleague and admirer Alan Bennett was moved to comment on his friend's 'final years, when some of his talent for exuberant invention deserted him'. If you wanted to fix the time and place when Cook's comic demons were at their most impish, it would almost certainly be the London of 1964.

***

Whether or not you happen to have been a child of the 1960s, most of us sooner or later come to terms with our essential mediocrity, one's youthful dreams of cup final glory or Hollywood superstardom traded in for a well-adjusted life of small victories and inevitable compromises. But not in every case. In early June 1964, a thin, unconventionally featured 20-year-old from the rainy Kentish suburbs should by rights have been completing a three-year degree at the London School of Economics (LSE) before disappearing into a respectable civil service or teaching job, just as he'd long said he planned to do. But unlike most of us, the young man in question – Mick Jagger – didn't settle for a life of modest material comfort, followed by retirement, death, and a few respectful but not overlong obituaries in the local press. Jagger had the necessary ambition and talent for projection, obviously, but he also had that much rarer gift: perfect timing.

The LSE graduation ceremony that year fell on Friday 5 June, and in the normal course of affairs Jagger would have been collecting his diploma at the school's Old Building on London's Houghton Street, then perhaps enjoying a slap-up meal among the red velour banquettes of one of the capital's new Angus Steakhouses with his proud parents Joe and Eva and younger brother Chris, before catching the return train to their small but impeccably neat home in Wilmington, just outside Dartford. But in fact Jagger didn't do that. Instead, he was on stage that evening with the rest of the Rolling Stones, entertaining a riotous crowd 5,000 miles away in San Bernardino, California, marking the occasion of the band's first ever US performance. It was a promising start, if not entirely representative of the Stones' reception in America as a whole. After San Bernardino, the group played four generally less well-received shows in Texas, where they appeared to a backdrop of straw bales and horse manure at the San Antonio state fair. The band's local warm-up act was a tank of trained seals, and immediately afterwards came a performing monkey, who, unlike them, was called back for an encore. After Keith Richards got into a shoving match with an irate customer backstage, he and his colleague Brian Jones went downtown and, for $35 (then around £13) apiece, bought themselves Browning automatics. Richards would never again be without a gun when touring America.

The Stones had similarly mixed fortunes when it came to their first major nationwide television appearance, on the old *Hollywood Palace* show hosted by 47-year-old Dean Martin. Martin and the Stones loathed one another on sight. The generational clash started the moment the band arrived, and continued through their breakneck performance of 'I Just Wanna Make Love to You', during which Jagger repeatedly defied the prevailing showbusiness wisdom that the lower half of a singer's body was meant purely for standing on. Lurching towards the old-fashioned stand mike, Dino then quipped that the glowering young musicians weren't so much long-haired as merely possessed of 'low foreheads and high eyebrows', before introducing a trampolinist as 'the father of the band – he's been trying to kill himself ever since'.

The overall revolution in the state of pop music – at least of the primal sort purveyed by the Stones – was clearly a work-in-progress, further advanced in some regional markets than others. A few days later, a quite different compère, the achingly hip disc jockey Murray Kaufman, bounded on stage to introduce the visiting Englishmen to a raucous audience at New York's Carnegie Hall. Amid Beatlesque screams throughout, the Stones blasted out an eleven-song set, threw down their instruments and ran. Forty-eight hours later, a jet-lagged band honoured a commitment to play the Magdalen summer ball at Oxford for a more select audience of young men in tails and their pukka girlfriends for a fee of £11, or £160 today. But strange as this was, perhaps the single most jarring image of 1964, and the first that most of Middle Britain had seen of the Stones, wasn't the group entertaining a tentful of champagne-swilling undergraduates, but their appearance on that week's edition of *Juke Box Jury*, the popular BBC panel show in which celebrities were asked to judge recent records, forecasting which would be a 'hit' or a 'miss', complete with appropriate studio sound effects. Long-standing convention required that there be a generous minimum 'hit' quota to each broadcast, and even the Beatles had played along on their appearance on the show some months earlier by giving five of the proffered nine selections a cheery thumbs-up.

When their own turn came, on 27 June, the Stones – languidly smoking, and, in their two guitarists' case, vigorously scratching themselves throughout the transmission – voted every song a resounding miss. The *Daily Mail*'s verdict spoke for many: 'The Rolling Stones offended parents everywhere by their behaviour on our television screens.' I once asked Keith Richards if the band's deportment that night had been a calculated pose on their part, or just a case of doing what came naturally. 'Probably a bit of both,' he replied, reminding me of the rule that says the more something is morally censured, the more popular it becomes. He may have been on to something, because since first going on air in 1959, *Juke Box Jury* had typically attracted a weekly audience of between 9 to 10 million viewers. On the night the Stones appeared as guests, no fewer than 18.7 million Britons tuned in, easily the most in its eight-year history, and not far short of the total enjoyed by a major state event like the 1960 wedding of Princess Margaret.

Even at this heady moment, there was still nothing inevitable about the fact that pop (or, as it was still rendered in the press, 'beat') music might prove to be the dominant artistic force of the next sixty years. It's true there was a growing momentum not only for the Beatles and the Stones, but for several other like-minded British groups such as the Hollies, Herman's Hermits, the Dave Clark Five, the Animals and the Kinks, even if the last of these never travelled as far as their undoubted talent would seem to suggest, who in the space of a few short months went from curiosities to stars. This was especially true in America, where whole arenas filled up with youthful crowds shouting for more, which was precisely what the bands were designed to give them. The 'British Invasion' pioneers embraced extravagance: flying pageboy haircuts and sometimes simple but increasingly fantastical lyrics, flashy instrumental solos and even flashier stage costumes which forsook the traditional matching suits for a stylistic mishmash that presented them as a combination of debauched medieval troubadour and futuristic space cadet.

But the musicians themselves still lived surprisingly frugally. The Hollies' singer Allan Clarke remembers the Rolling Stones at their first meeting in June 1964 as 'five corpse-pale guys tumbling out of the back of a smoke-filled van', whereupon they 'stretched, belched a bit and wandered off for a warm-up session at the local pub.' In those innocent days before discovering the charms of consciousness-expanding drugs, the Stones as a rule confined themselves to downing pints of beer and popping the occasional amphetamine to get through as many as fifteen shows a week. Their poverty format wasn't just a pose: in the final week of June, the band performed eleven sold-out concerts, played on three national TV shows and generally continued to provoke decent society. That Sunday night, their co-manager Eric Easton presented each of the musicians with a cheque for £6 5s (£90 today), along with the disappointing news that a scheduled performance in Cleethorpes had been cancelled because of a local bylaw prohibiting entertainment on the Sabbath. For the Stones, life in Britain in 1964 still involved disapproving council watch committees as much as it did adoring young groupies throwing their smalls at them.

That Fleet Street's moral panic about the plague of pop music exceeded the more modest ambitions of the actual carriers of the virus was shown by the headlines that greeted the latest Mods and Rockers skirmishes to break out at intervals on the coast between Brighton and Hastings. Newspapers deplored the clashes as being of 'disastrous proportions' and labelled the participants as 'vermin' and 'louts'. A perhaps overcaffeinated editor at the *Birmingham Post* wrote a leading article that might not have shamed the pages of *Pravda* in the 1930s when denouncing the rival adolescent groups as 'internal enemies' of the UK, who unless checked would 'bring about the disintegration of the nation's character'. The magazine *Police Review* unsurprisingly took a similarly robust line, arguing that the young people's lack of respect for law and order could cause violence to 'surge and flame like a forest fire'. Truly, it must have seemed to the average British householder sitting over his or her morning paper in June 1964 that the entire country had become a sort of proto-*Mad Max* wasteland peopled by feral gangs partial to leather-heavy wardrobes and violent explosions, with names such as Nightrider, Toecutter and Ironbar.

At least that was the media version of the national agenda in the middle days of 1964. In the more arid, if no less obsessive, tones of the Douglas-Home Cabinet, as minuted by its secretary Sir Burke Trend:

4 June 1964. Downing Street.

The Chancellor of the Exchequer: We must do something, both for our international obligations and for the sake of the housewife, on the matter of relaxing apple and pear quotas.

The Prime Minister: But there remains the matter of timing. Why act before the election at all?

The Secretary of State for Industry: Because quotas have been unchanged for ten years, while our own production has risen by 57 percent and overseas production has also increased. We have a favourable trade balance with Italy, and ought to help on such foodstuffs. Nothing is to be gained by delay when all our commercial policy is at stake ... The new policy for horticulture which involves substantial exchequer assistance has not comprised any limitation on the reduction of quotas, as opposed to tariffs.

The Minister of Agriculture: Many European countries are more protective of apples and pears than we are. Long-term policy must be settled by discussion with them. In the interim, my proposals represent the maximum the National Farmers Union would accept. A figure of 800 tons can be argued both ways: it is trivial in relation to completely liberalised imports, but of great help to us presentationally to keep our quota stable.

The Minister for Health: We must beware of what may appear another sop to the Common Market.

The Chancellor: But we must be similarly vigilant on prices.

The Minister of Agriculture: We should say for now that quotas remain unchanged, but thereafter will be under review ... Apples and pears are incontestably sensitive items, and the proposals we suggest represent the maximum degree of flexibility the industry can be expected to accept.

The Secretary for Industry: There will be no wider agreement under the K Round until 1967. And prospects for international agreement on apples and pears would seem remote in any event. We should concede some relaxation on the grounds of our own interests. It would be wholly inconsistent with our trade policy to refrain from making a not insubstantial advance, or to bind ourselves not to make further advances during the lifetime of the next parliament.

The Prime Minister [in conclusion]: We should not relax such quotas before the election. We may merely say that some change regarding apples and pears may arise after 1 January 1965, but not do so until the campaign.

The Foreign Secretary: We must help the Italians where we can.

The Prime Minister: Apples and pears, indeed. But we must wait until after the election.

***

Later that afternoon, the House of Commons debated such matters as the Scottish marriage laws, legal aid, cremation regulations, concessionary bus and train fares for old people and, climactically, apples and pears. There was no obvious sign among the House's deliberations that the nation was in imminent peril of moral collapse, although one Lt Col Sir Thomas Moore, Scottish Unionist MP for Ayr Burghs, not a constituency previously known as a hotbed of juvenile unrest, asked the prime minister what plans he had for 'dealing with the disgraceful hooligans which [*sic*] recently disturbed the peace of our seaside towns', while the Conservatives' John Eden, of Bournemouth, wondered whether the home secretary might not care to introduce legislation to 'restore the use of corporal punishment as a means of dealing with persons convicted of wanton destruction of property and causing injury to others', an initiative even the minister in question, Henry Brooke, a law and order zealot and the butt of some harsh satirical comment from the likes of *Private Eye* and the Saturday-night show *That Was The Week That Was*, resisted.

Superficially a font of almost preternatural calm, Douglas-Home himself was now increasingly exercised about the likely outcome of the next election. Though not publicly announced until 16 September, the event had clearly come to represent a ticking bomb in the minds of both the PM and others. In fact, some news outlets seemed to spend 1964 doing little else but prophesying or anticipating the date Britain would go to the polls. Douglas-Home may have given the impression of having just wandered in off the pages of some bucolic P.G. Wodehouse novel with a brace of freshly shot grouse slung over his arm, but he was also a thirty-three-year veteran of Westminster infighting who was fully capable of calculating the latest electoral odds. As he was painfully aware, the Conservative share of the vote had dropped, in some cases precipitously, in all twenty-one of the by-elections held from March 1963 to June 1964, while Labour's had risen proportionately. County council and municipal borough elections held in May 1964 gave further evidence of a swing to Labour. The Tories reported a net loss of 108 local government seats in England and Wales, compared with a net gain of 152 for their opponents. In the newly formed Greater London Council, Labour now enjoyed the sort of monopoly associated with the National People's Congress in China. The result of a Gallup Poll published on 17 June showed Labour at 49.5 per cent and the Conservatives at 42 per cent, which if accurate would have meant a Labour majority of seventy seats in the Commons. Perhaps it's no wonder Douglas-Home referred to the election quite as often as he did in Cabinet meetings and elsewhere. More privately, he and one or two colleagues thought that there might be a hung parliament and a resulting constitutional crisis, in which a 'disinterested' outsider might step forward to fill the void. The one-time fascist leader Oswald Mosley, then living in France but still periodically returning to stand on a forced-repatriation-of-immigrants platform in by-elections, with invariably disastrous results, and the hero of El Alamein, 76-year-old Field Marshal Montgomery, were both mentioned. Like a number of European leaders of the time, Douglas-Home thought it prudent to meet with senior police and military chiefs to reassure himself of their support in the event of mass public disorder.

Meanwhile, there was that troubling matter of the fruit quotas. The existing rules limited the import of apples to 68,750 tons in the first half of each year, and 15,200 tons in the second, while for pears there was a single annual maximum of 28,000 tons. As we've seen, the Cabinet was now moved to be more flexible in the matter, particularly when it came to accommodating the Italian export drive. Christopher Soames, the minister of agriculture (and quite coincidentally Winston Churchill's son-in-law) had told the PM that he would first concentrate on the pears, possibly with a view to raising the permitted number to as high as 40,000 tons per annum. There were three more lengthy exchanges in Cabinet and at a private meeting in Downing Street between 8 and 29 June. But perhaps something was lost in translation with the centrist Rome government of Antonio Segni, because in a subsequent phone call, Soames awkwardly informed Douglas-Home that the agreed pear quota had changed. Instead of being raised to 40,000 tons, the figure was now somewhat bigger. 'It will actually be half a million tons.' 'Pears!' Douglas-Home scrawled in apparent exasperation across the draft agenda for the Cabinet of 2 July 1964. The PM was just then facing a significantly worsening balance of payments deficit, pressure at the polls, and an imminent London conference of seventeen Commonwealth states, with a constitutional crisis brewing in Southern Rhodesia over its 'whites only' apartheid policies and the nation's youth still busy pelting each other with rocks at every opportunity, and he was worried about pomaceous fruit imports. As ever, there was the side of politics that involved well-intentioned and sometimes even quite intelligent people who were quietly doing their jobs to the best of their abilities, and then there was the triviality and rhetorical wasteland that characterised so much of the public discourse, where people talked about the future of Western civilisation but actually spent their days agonising about matters like Quinces and Red Bartletts.

GREAT SOCIETY

One rainy Wednesday morning in February 1964, 55-year-old President Lyndon Johnson summoned his principal speechwriter Richard Goodwin and a special adviser named Bill Moyers to join him in the White House basement swimming pool.
'We entered the area,' Goodwin recalled:

> to see the massive presidential flesh, a sun bleached atoll breaching the placid sea, passing gently, sidestroke, the deep-cleft buttocks moving slowly past our unstartled gaze. Moby Dick, I thought ... 'It's like going swimming with a polar bear', Moyers whispered. Without turning his head, Johnson called across the pool: 'C'mon in, boys. It'll do you good'.

Stripping off, the two middle-aged counsellors jumped in nude to join their similarly clad commander-in-chief, who promptly 'began to talk as if he were addressing some larger, imaginary audience of the mind'. Calling out over his rising and falling shoulder, Johnson announced his intention to 'outdo Kennedy' and create 'my own program, different in tone, fighting and tough'. As the two aides splashed away to keep up, their chief would occasionally pause in mid-flow in order to stand upright at the shallow end, reach out with a wooden stick to hook onto a nearby bucket full of ice cubes, drag this to the edge of the pool, tip some of the contents over his head, and then shake vigorously with the shock. Goodwin felt Johnson's 'immense vitality' as, in between these ablutions, he detailed a list of specific proposals: the total elimination of rural poverty, nationwide hunger relief, urban regeneration, wholesale racial equality, subsidised health insurance for the elderly and vulnerable, and the full realisation of the American Dream – all that would move the nation, and surely, he believed, mankind itself to some 'distant but attainable vision [of] universal harmony'.

What Goodwin and Moyers were witnessing as they floundered around in the buff in the White House pool was nothing less than the first draft of the legacy which Johnson, now just ten weeks into his unplanned presidency, meant to leave the world. This was different to the usual practice of post-war democratic government, an actual vision of events rather than the seemingly permanent apparatus of crisis management that characterised most administrations. After towelling off, Goodwin consulted with Eric Goldman, a Princeton history professor now serving the president as the informal head of a 'quiet brain trust', or house intellectual.

Goldman thought that the president should articulate his view of mankind's destiny in public, and that, in terms of a popular slogan, the goal of 'post-affluent' America was probably best caught in the title of Walter Lippmann's 1937 book *The Good Society*. Goodwin liked the idea but decided to kick it up to 'the Great Society'. Johnson would first use the phrase in an address on 22 May to the graduating class of the University of Michigan at Ann Arbor. According to Goodwin, the speech was to be 'a statement of national purpose, almost prophetic in dimension, that would bind citizens in a "great experiment" ... The idea was to make people sit up and say their president was really thinking about the future problems of the world.' To Eric Goldman, it 'bespoke what Johnson thought about America, and put in clear and sometimes ringing tones what he felt he wanted for our country'.

The address itself again showed that strange if somehow compelling mixture of high national purpose and Hollywood-style bathos that continues to distinguish most American political discourse today. 'For a century,' Johnson informed the Michigan students:

> We have labored to settle and to subdue a continent. For half a century we have called upon unbounded invention and untiring industry to create an order of plenty for all of our people. The challenge of the next half century is whether we have the wisdom to use that wealth to enrich and elevate our national life, and to advance the quality of our human civilization ... For in your time we will have the opportunity to move not only toward the rich society and the powerful society, but upward to the Great Society ... one where man is more concerned with the quality of his goals than the quantity of his goods.

To reach this desirable place, Johnson continued, Americans should commit to three things: first, they needed to rebuild their major cities, demolishing slums, erecting gleaming and affordable new housing projects, with convenient shops and efficient transportation for all; then, pledge themselves to 'America the beautiful' by increased protection of the nation's air, water, mountains, forests and other natural resources; and last, overhaul the country's public education, building literally hundreds of new school systems across the land that would 'encourage excellence' and 'offer an escape from poverty'.

In addition to these three priorities, Johnson noted towards the end of his speech, there might conceivably be 'other emerging challenges' in the course of America's high-minded new crusade, but the 80,000-strong crowd sitting in the university's sun-dappled football stadium was in no mood to quibble, giving the president a long standing ovation as he reached the climax of his remarks.

Encouraged, Johnson's voice rose as he continued, 'For better or worse, your generation has been appointed by history to lead America toward a new age.' Another roar of approval erupted. 'So, will you join in the battle to give every citizen the full equality which God enjoins, and the law requires, whatever his belief or race, or the color of his skin?' Johnson asked, his weather-lined face sweeping inquisitively from side to side. 'Will you join the battle to give every citizen an escape from the crushing weight of poverty? Will you join the battle to make it possible for all nations to live in enduring peace, as neighbors and not as foes? Will you join the battle to build the Great Society?' the president shouted climactically, by now pumping his fists aloft like a prizefighter. The crowd's roar this time was truly deafening; he had clearly struck the most responsive possible chord.

On the plane back to Washington, Johnson pronounced himself well pleased. Rarely one for a public drink, he allowed himself an exception here and requested a stiff Scotch, which he wanted served in a plastic cup, before admitting he didn't much care for the term 'Great Society'. It was too hokey. 'Sure he was an idealist, but it was really just a bumper sticker for the press,' Bill Moyers said later.

Somehow predictably, alongside Johnson's lofty ambitions and confidence in American exceptionalism, there was the more prosaic reality of what Harold Macmillan had characterised as 'events', while coming to describe his own premiership as 'one damn thing after another, [the problems] colliding and overlapping and refusing to form an orderly line for one's attention.' Perhaps the leader of the free world never did interest himself in the likes of pear crops or many of the other routine preoccupations of his counterpart in Downing Street, but there were still plenty of other unwelcome constraints on his time. Foremost among them was the steady American escalation in Vietnam.

To be fair, this was not entirely Johnson's fault. His predecessor in office had both expanded the number of US military advisers in the area from 685 to 17,000 and acquiesced in the coup that led to the removal and murder of South Vietnam's president Ngo Dinh Diem, on the basis that his successor would be more likely to defeat the communist incursion from the north, a grave miscalculation on Washington's part. Johnson inherited this situation, then made it much worse. Bill Moyers would remember the president telling him in the early days of his administration: 'Those bastards think with Kennedy dead we've lost heart. They think we're yellow and don't mean what we say.'

'Who?' Moyers asked.

'The Chinese,' Johnson replied. 'The fellows in the Kremlin. All those bastards. They'll be taking the measure of us. They'll be wondering just how far they can go ... I'm not gonna let Vietnam go the way of China,' the president continued. 'I told [the diplomats] to go back and tell those generals in Saigon that Lyndon Johnson means to stand by our word, but, by God, I want something for my money. I want 'em to get off their butts and get out in those jungles and whip hell out of some commies. And then I want 'em to leave me alone, because I got some bigger things to do right here at home.'

In short, Vietnam should by rights have become just another issue that Johnson believed would ultimately yield to his irresistible political will. All he needed to do to prevail in the matter was put the fear of God in his generals on the ground and educate the folks back home about the reasons for their army's presence in an inhospitable land 9,000 miles away. An April 1964 Gallup Poll showed him the scale of the challenge. Sixty-three per cent of American adults 'evinced little enthusiasm, or even paid attention' to the problems of a colonial quarrel in South East Asia, while in another poll 78 per cent of young people between the ages of 16 and 21 had heard nothing about the conflict, figures that would both change significantly over the next twelve months. As a result, Johnson believed it would 'really be cheaper in US blood and treasure to CONTAIN the Reds in the Vietnam area. The KEY POINT is this course of action: communication with the public so they understand what we are doing and WHY' (emphasis in the original).

On 22 June, Johnson signed National Security Order No. 308, declaring 'domestic understanding and support essential to the success of increased United States operations in South Asia', not a subject he had cared to include in his rousing 'Great Society' address of just a month earlier.

It has to be said that several of America's domestic affairs also lagged some way behind the great Jeffersonian vision of Johnson's oration at the University of Michigan. The future Nobel-winning novelist Saul Bellow, though something of that rarity in the arts world, a social conservative, was nonetheless deeply troubled by the state of his nation that spring of the Great Society. In the preface to a 1964 book called *They Shall Overcome*, Bellow wrote: 'The lives of southern Negroes are not protected by law.' The truth of this statement, he continued, was accepted by all politicians, and, 'until the civil rights movement becomes effective most Americans will accept it too.' For the present, 'Negroes and those who join with them ... have been persecuted, bullied, terrorized, abused, jailed, maimed and killed', a catalogue of misery 'documented on every page of this book'.

It might seem strange from our perspective to remember that the America of round-the-clock multi-channel colour television, and gaudily lit shops piled with every conceivable consumer luxury, was also a country whose treatment of a sizeable minority of its citizens had evolved little if at all since the Civil War era. In 1964 the nation's social fabric was still sufficiently loose for the owners of the popular Heart of Atlanta Motel, to give just one example, to feel able to refuse admission to dark-skinned patrons, and for the matter to be argued all the way up to the US Supreme Court that December. The judges ultimately ruled against the hotel, although theirs was not necessarily the consensus view of the American public at large. Included within the Court's decision was the case of the Pickrick Restaurant adjoining the segregated hotel, which had similar policies when it came to serving minority customers. The restaurant's owner, Lester Maddox, later ran successfully for Governor of Georgia, where even his Republican opponent Benjamin B. Blackburn felt moved to report 'no accusation of corruption was ever made against him', by no means invariably the case in that particular office. After leaving the governor's mansion in Atlanta, Maddox ended his career as half of a nightclub comedy act alongside his former employee Bobby Lee Fears. Billing themselves as 'The Governor and his Dishwasher' they performed intellectually undemanding minstrel routines around the South, with a black-faced Maddox on harmonica and Fears on banjo.

The events at the Heart of Atlanta motel and its adjacent restaurant were not entirely unrepresentative of what President Johnson described as the 'centuries of oppression and persecution of the Negro citizen' in the United States. Race relations at the local level often fell short of the egalitarian ideal enshrined by the nine robed justices in the nation's highest court. Many provincial hotels and restaurants continued to offer only a muted welcome to their minority patrons throughout 1964. When a number of both black and white guests entered his swimming pool one hot afternoon that June, the owner of the Monson Motor Lodge in St Augustine, Florida, took the precaution of pouring liberal amounts of muriatic acid over the heads of the bathers in order to 'flush the scum out of the water', the cause of a future lawsuit unfavourable to the management's interests. The author can confirm that at least one municipal pool as far away as Tacoma, Washington, was drained each Monday night in the summer of 1964 and new water was added on Tuesday. Monday was 'Colored' day.

When successive waves of the British Invasion bands hit New York that summer, they were amazed to find not only deliriously enthusiastic crowds of teenagers awaiting them at the airport, but also a steaming, potholed city inhabited by grim-faced men and women serviced by street-vendors offering such delicacies as trotter and offal pie or vivid green 'vomit fruit', and fire-and-brimstone street preachers announcing the imminent end of the world. The murder rate in the United States as a whole rose by 50 per cent in the years from 1962 to 1966, and the number of armed robberies doubled. It seemed to some people that the Great Society might be falling apart even before it got properly started. As Keith Richards once said, 'America was a gas with all the air-conditioning and colour TV, but as soon as you stepped out of your cocoon and hit the street it was another world.' The land of the free was then 'a bit basic', Paul McCartney confirmed, adding that the Beatles had refused to go on stage at the 35,000-seat Gator Bowl in Jacksonville, Florida until the show's promoter had assured them in writing that their audience would not be segregated. About 40 miles down the state turnpike, the town of St Augustine remained a scene of near nightly confrontations between blacks, whites and police throughout the summer of 1964, so much so that early in June FBI agents reported back to their director J. Edgar Hoover that the local sheriff, L.D. 'Bubba' Davis, had seen fit to deputise members of the Ku Klux Klan to help maintain public order, an initiative even Hoover thought 'ironical'.

Britain had had its own Heart of Atlanta moment as far back as July 1943, when the 41-year-old West Indian cricketer Learie Constantine, a future high commissioner and the first black man to sit in the House of Lords, arrived with his wife and teenaged daughter for a scheduled four-night stay at the Imperial Hotel in London's Russell Square. The manageress had taken one look at her intending guests and told them that they would be welcome for one night only. Should they attempt to prolong their stay, she added, their luggage 'w[ould] be put out on the street and the door locked'. In Constantine's subsequent lawsuit, the High Court ruled that 'although the plaintiff is a man of colour, no ground exists on which the defendants were entitled to refuse to receive and lodge him on the premises.' While the law limited the award of damages to 5 guineas, the case was widely seen as a turning point in the long campaign for British racial equality, and the eventual passage of the Race Relations Act of 1965. The home secretary of the day heralded the legislation as imposing a 'complete ban on discrimination based on colour, race or ethnic origin', and representing a 'new spirit of total fairness to every British citizen's treatment' as a result. Over the next sixty years, the minister's faith in the 'total fairness' enshrined in the 1965 Act might have seemed excessively hopeful, if not naïve, even if the law meant that seaside landladies could no longer openly display signs announcing 'No Blacks, Irish or Dogs' in their windows.

It says something about the peculiar circumstances of 1964, and the transitional state of what then passed for acceptable public behaviour, that the bawdy American comic Lenny Bruce should first be invited to appear at Peter Cook's club in London, a private, members-only establishment, and thus beyond the Lord Chamberlain's purview, only to then be banned from the UK 'in the public interest'. Even this sanction was mild compared with Bruce's treatment that year at the hands of American officials. There was, for instance, the memorable night at the Café Au Go Go in New York's Greenwich Village, where among other skits he performed a piece ruminating on two recent and widely revered First Ladies. Bruce first declared that 'Eleanor Roosevelt had the best tits of any broad in the White House'. Going on to display news photographs of Jacqueline Kennedy frantically crawling over the back of the convertible in Dallas after her husband had just been shot, the captions for which suggested she was trying to get help, the comedian labelled them 'bullshit'. In his opinion, Mrs Kennedy had merely been 'hauling ass out of there'. Other segments of the night's programme were not as elevated as this. Charged with obscenity, Bruce was found guilty at trial that December and sentenced to four months' imprisonment. Some of the recordings of his shows are more obviously funny than others, but the essence of the act was plainly to skewer as many as possible of his fellow countrymen's hypocrisies on race, sex and religion, with an almost audible smirk in his voice as he did so. Lenny Bruce died on his bathroom floor in 1966, at the age of 40, a syringe in his arm – a scene the authorities encouraged reporters and photographers to record at their leisure for the next several hours. The music producer Phil Spector later expressed the opinion that 'Lenny really died from an overdose of police'.

Such uncongenial treatment of society's outsiders, whether racial campaigners like Martin Luther King or subversive clowns like Lenny Bruce, was perhaps distinctive to the United States. But its generally dismissive tenor would have been familiar across the Atlantic. In school, in church, on the backbenches of Parliament, and in the dowager tones of both the broadsheet and tabloid media, many Europeans were still rooted to the habits and conventions of an earlier era. Much the same thing could be said of South Africa, where the protracted Rivonia Trial of Nelson Mandela and ten other defendants accused of 'recruiting persons for training in the preparation and use of explosives' and 'acting in such ways to further the objectives of communism' finally reached its climax on 12 June 1964: a guilty verdict in ten of the eleven cases, and the subsequent detention of a man who went to prison at the age of 45 and emerged again at 71 to become his country's first democratically elected president.

Mandela's eventual death in December 2013 was the occasion of a collective sense of bereavement perhaps not seen since the Kennedy assassination fifty years earlier. It might seem barely credible that he could ever have been judicially condemned to death in 1964, but such an outcome had been widely expected at the time. A fellow judge would later claim that he persuaded the presiding magistrate, Quartus De

Wet, to change his mind over a cup of tea in the latter's chambers only minutes before he returned to court for sentencing. De Wet, it seems, had been keen on hanging. The reading of Mandela's own subsequent statement from the dock took four hours, and he spoke the last paragraph from memory, looking straight at the bench as he did so:

> During my lifetime I have dedicated myself to this struggle of the African people. I have fought against white domination. I have cherished the ideal of a democratic and free society in which all persons live together in harmony and with equal opportunities. It is an ideal which I hope to live for and to achieve. But if needs be, it is an ideal for which I am prepared to die.

Whether you look on this as a ringing declaration of the God-given rights of all men on a par with Kennedy's June 1963 assertion '*Ich bin ein Berliner*', or Martin Luther King's 'I have a dream' speech of later that summer, or, conversely, as little more than an extended greeting card plea for universal harmony, it remains the potent testament of a flawed but inspiring individual then under imminent threat of losing his life. Mandela was not in fact a natural orator, and some of his personal affairs, among them his handling of both women and money, arguably reflect better on him than others. But in the end his particular gift was as a conciliator, and in the charged racial atmosphere of 1964 that was surely enough.

Then of course there was the great collective prison known in 1964 as the 'Eastern Bloc', comprised of the USSR and its client states in central Europe, South East Asia and a few impoverished outposts of central Africa and Latin America. As a rule, domestic policy in such places was not known for its pervasive tolerance of human rights or of dissent to the central regime. Nikita Khrushchev was still clinging to power that spring, albeit in an atmosphere of such paranoia that he bugged not only the offices of his Kremlin rivals but his own quarters, on the basis that 'I don't even trust myself.' Early on the morning of 15 April, his colleagues from the Moscow politburo dutifully arrived at their leader's suburban dacha to celebrate his 70th birthday. Khrushchev's burly, 57-year-old deputy Leonid Brezhnev cleared his throat and read a fulsome prepared statement: 'Dear Nikita Sergeyevich! We, your close comrades in arms, members and candidate members of the Presidium, and Secretaries of the Central

Committee, extend special salutations and fervently congratulate you, our closest and inseparable personal friend, on your birthday.'

At that, brushing tears from his eyes, the beetle-browed Brezhnev hugged Khrushchev and presented him with a framed copy of the just-read speech, while two men in grey overalls wheeled in a vast mock-teak combined black-and-white television and radiogram set, bearing a large metal plate with the inscription: 'From your ever-loyal comrades at work in the Central Committee and the People's Council of Ministers.' These formalities over, there was prolonged applause, and, despite the earliness of the hour, many toasts were drunk proclaiming all parties' undying loyalty and allegiance to the boss.

Just six months later, the same Leonid Brezhnev stood up at a closed-door session in the Kremlin and informed Khrushchev that his policies had for years 'contradicted Lenin's teaching' and 'fucked up' both industry and agriculture. What was more, he was guilty of treating his colleagues 'like shit', Brezhnev continued. Khrushchev had fallen into the habit of 'making decisions over lunch', had 'ignored others' opinions', and even seemed not to care much about propagating the communist ideal.

When Khrushchev finally rose to his feet to defend himself, Brezhnev cut him dead, shouting, 'You have no friends here!' Lest the point had been missed, he added, 'You're through! A corpse! This is the end!' After some more in this vein, Brezhnev remarked that Nikita Sergeyevich had fallen so low as to refer to his fellow politburo members as mere 'dogs peeing on curbstones', and that, all things considered, it would be best if he now 'voluntarily retired from office'. Khrushchev did so, and Brezhnev himself duly assumed the reins of state until his death eighteen years later.

While Brezhnev seems to have felt his predecessor in office had grown unacceptably soft in his attitude to the West, Khrushchev's rhetoric had not always been notable for its folksy and constructive embrace of the policy of peaceful coexistence with his country's ideological foes. There was the moment in November 1956, for instance, when he informed a room full of Western diplomats: 'Whether you like it or not, history is on our side. We will bury you.' Eight years later, the Soviet hardman greeted attendees of the 1964 British Agricultural Exhibition in Moscow by noting that their prime minister had done 'nothing but, so to speak, offer us his ass' – a startling image to be associated with the courtly Sir Alec Douglas-Home – 'and we will oblige him by kicking it as hard as we can'. Khrushchev then displayed one of those baffling mood swings that constituted the basic throughline of his character when he approached Dr John Knowles, a Colchester-based exhibitor at the fair, and warmly complimented him on the size and apparent potency of two male cockerels which, after a thorough inspection, he declared to be 'superior in every way' to their Soviet counterparts. Late that night, a large man in a dark suit and trilby presented himself at Knowles's hotel room and announced that the supreme leader would look on it as a personal favour if Knowles could supply him with a male and two female birds which he would like to keep for breeding purposes at his dacha. Knowles sensibly complied with the request, and later received a signed photograph of a beaming Khrushchev holding the three birds under his arm in return.

Khrushchev's subsequent departure was one of the more abrupt falls from the heights of totalitarian power without the added presence of a firing squad. It was a crude and undignified exit for the leader of one of the world's two acknowledged superpowers, whose volcanic outbursts of temper had at one time led tens of thousands of ordinary Americans to dig deep fallout shelters in their gardens and even the serenely placid Douglas-Home to privately admit to doubts about 'the merit of spending one's days worrying about the price of milk, [while] the larger question of whether or not mankind will survive for another generation remains unresolved'.

But at least Khrushchev was allowed a peaceful, if painfully obscure, retirement, eking out his slow-motion existence surrounded by his children and grandchildren. This was not an option available to the estimated 160 individuals killed over the years while attempting to breach what Khrushchev and his sock-puppet first secretary of East Germany's Socialist Unity Party, Walter Ulbricht, fondly knew as 'the anti-fascist protection device' – or Berlin Wall, as others preferred to call it – at the front line of the Cold War, quite apart from the millions of those forcibly separated from family and friends, or any contact with the Free World, as a result.

Although denied at the time, it's now known that six individuals died at or near the Wall during the summer of 1964, five of them young men between the ages of 18 and 29. Crass as it is to use the word 'only' in relation to civilian casualties, it might at least be applied to the proportion of female victims of the Ulbricht regime's shoot-to-kill policy. Of the eight women and girls known to have lost their lives at the Wall from 1961–89, perhaps the most wrenching case was that of the bespectacled 37-year-old Berlin housewife Hildegard Trabant, who was killed on 18 August 1964. She had been attempting to flee through a disused S-Bahn tunnel when she was spotted by a border guard named Kurt Renner and ordered to turn around. Trabant did so, taking several steps back towards him, at which point the 20-year-old Renner shot her in the head. It was later thought that she might have been fleeing primarily to escape her abusive police officer husband rather than to reach the freedom of the West per se. Thirty-four years after being officially commended for his 'exemplary behaviour', Renner was arrested and tried for Hildegard Trabant's murder, found guilty, pleaded that he had merely been following orders, and got off with probation.

THE OTHER BRITAIN

Somehow it seems only a logical if ghastly extension from the horrors committed in the name of the East German state at the Berlin Wall to the events taking place in west London at intervals throughout 1964, dubbed, in that mixture of scandal and prurience that typified the Fleet Street culture of the day, the Hammersmith Nude Murders – or, at the more populist end of the market, the strange case of 'Jack the Stripper'.

Early on Sunday 2 February, a man was walking his dog by the side of the Thames about halfway between Chiswick and Brentford when he saw what he first took to be a shop mannequin washed up on the embankment. On closer inspection, the shape turned out to be a nude woman, her face battered and her underwear stuffed in her mouth, whom police later identified as a 30-year-old prostitute originally from Heddon-on-the-Wall in Northumberland named Hannah Tailford. She had been strangled or choked, apparently during or shortly after sex. Two months later, the body of a 25-year-old Nottinghamshire woman called Irene Lockwood, also, as the jargon of the day had it, on the game, was discovered nearby. She had been viciously assaulted and drowned, and was pregnant at the time of her death. Just a fortnight later, 22-year-old Helen Barthelemy, from Ormiston in Scotland, was found dead in an alleyway in Brentford. She, too, had been savagely beaten, genitally mutilated and whipped about the abdomen and buttocks, before being strangled. At this stage, *The Times* felt moved to inform its readers that 'the police believe the nude woman found this week near the Thames foreshore was murdered,' a conclusion perhaps already reached by the roughly 15 million readers of the less diffident *News of the World*, with its barely concealed glee at this opportunity to dwell on the asphyxiated women and their intimate body parts on the pretence of a concern for public safety.

The next victim, 30-year-old, Scottish-born Mary Fleming, was similarly found dead in a Chiswick doorway. Her nude body had been splashed with paint. Then 21-year-old Frances Brown, another Scot, was discovered strangled and dumped in a car park in west Kensington; and finally Bridget O'Hara, 27, from Dublin, found lifeless behind a storage shed on a trading estate in nearby east Acton. The murders ceased after 11 January 1965, and have never been conclusively solved. One theory is that the women were in some way linked to a pornographic blue-movie ring, and were disposed of before they could cause embarrassment to the club's upper-class clientele. A police review in 2021 concluded that the most likely suspect had been a west London security guard named Mungo Ireland, who later committed suicide by carbon monoxide poisoning, leaving behind a note for his wife that read: 'I can't stick it any longer.' And finished: 'To save you and the law looking for me I'll be in the garage.'

Quite apart from the central tragedy of the innocent victims who lost their lives, the Hammersmith Nude case was memorable for the sheer variety of peculiarly British media obsessions it touched on. The box denoting a particularly lurid or violent crime clearly got a tick. The salacious box got ticked as well, because of the fact that the victims were all young women, and all professional sex workers. And also to be considered was pure lechery: the papers got to talk a good deal about otherwise taboo subjects like vaginas under a spurious cloak of public-interest reporting, and as a result by around June 1964 millions of middle-class Britons were settling down each Sunday morning to immerse themselves in a journalistic demimonde with a marked tendency to concentrate not so much on the poor women's lives or on their bereaved families, but on the clinical state of their sex organs.

★★★

At around 8 p.m. on Tuesday 16 June 1964, a sandy-haired 12-year-old with an engagingly wide grin like that of the Milky Bar Kid in the popular TV commercial, dressed in jeans and a zip-up jacket, left his family's terraced home in Longsight, Greater Manchester, to join his younger brother Alan and his three other siblings at his grandmother's house two streets away. Alan later described his brother as a 'carefree sort [who] had little time for anything but laughter and nature, [someone] who loved animals and summer flowers'. The boy was thought to be a bit solitary, but he compensated for this by creating a self-contained world, collecting butterflies, moths, beetles and ladybugs. Steady and methodical at school, he was well-behaved if academically modestly gifted, a sweet-natured child with no enemies. Although old enough to make his own way to the house where he was to spend the night, the boy was short-sighted and had broken his wire-frame glasses the day before, so his 30-year-old mother Winnie made sure he got safely across the street and on his way to his destination before waving him goodbye. Heavily pregnant with her sixth child, Winnie then turned away to walk to the bingo session she attended each Tuesday and Saturday night. She never saw her son again.

The boy's name was Keith Bennett. After parting from his mother on the far side of Stockport Road, he turned the corner to Dallas Street to be confronted by a friendly young couple in their twenties who asked if he would mind helping them load some boxes into their white van parked nearby. It's not definitely known if he then voluntarily got into the couple's vehicle or if they in some way persuaded him to do so. After that they drove for about half-an-hour up an increasingly remote stretch of the A635 before stopping at a lay-by near to where a brook cut through the purple-green summer grass of Saddleworth Moor. Dusk was falling. At that point the man remarked that he had previously lost a glove on the moor and wondered if their new friend might help him look for it. The two duly walked off into the darkening hills, leaving the woman behind in the van. It somehow only adds to the poignancy of the tale to see how amiable the unsophisticated young child seems to have remained throughout it all.

There was no phone in either Mrs Bennett's modest home, nor in her mother's, and as a result it would be another twenty-four hours before the family finally appreciated that Keith was missing. The police came and took a few cursory notes, assuming that the boy had simply run away for a while. 'It happens,' one of the two attending officers remarked. Eventually they arrested Keith's stepfather, James Johnson. In those days, suspicion always fell on a missing person's family members. Johnson was later released without charge, and Keith's disappearance remained unsolved until 1987, when it was determined that he had been a victim of one of the most notorious couples ever to have haunted the public imagination. Their names were Ian Brady and Myra Hindley, and they had already killed at least twice before they opportunistically accosted young Keith Bennett after he cheerily waved goodbye to his mother on his way down the street that warm midsummer evening. Brady had simply walked with Keith out onto the moor, then strangled him with a piece of string and buried him there. His body remains undiscovered to this day.

Brady, a name now synonymous with evil, was born in 1938 in the proverbially depressed Gorbals area of Glasgow, where his unmarried waitress mother promptly put a card in a shop window offering her baby for sale. Taken in by an eccentric older couple with several other adopted children on the premises, he showed early signs of being self-obsessed and psychotically violent. During a routine game of cops and robbers, his fellow classmates remembered that Brady had once tied up another boy and set fire to him. A relationship with a teenage girlfriend later ended abruptly when he threatened her with a flick-knife unless she consented to pose erotically for him and 'let him do things to my bum'. Brady was a hoarder of pornography, sexually precocious, who was said to go for every girl he met. His 'courtship' method was direct: he grabbed and started undoing buttons. Although spurned as often as not, the sheer volume of his efforts brought him some success. Essentially uneducated, but with a half-baked interest in the works of Dostoyevsky, Nietzsche and Hitler, it seems fair to say that he was that not-unknown creature, the literate psychopath.

In 1962, Brady met Hindley, a young typist, while working as a clerk at a Manchester chemical plant. She was later to describe him as her 'god'. The two soon began an intense relationship based on a mutual dislike of the rest of society and their taste for Brady's bizarre and often perverse fantasy world in which Hindley sometimes found herself posed naked but for a white hood placed over her head. The Labour politician and social reformer Frank Pakenham, Lord Longford, later made something of a public career of his efforts to rehabilitate certain hard-core criminals. As a rule, he was not one for the snap psychological judgement on any of the subjects of his charity, but he made an exception in Brady's case. The killer of Keith Bennett was 'brilliant but bonkers', Longford later confided, a verdict with which it's hard to take serious issue.

Hindley, born in Manchester in 1942, and raised in the blue-collar area of Gorton, seemed to be one of those young women, not uncommon in the industrial north of England at the time, destined for a life of cultural and material poverty that could leave them looking haggard and washed-up before their 30th birthday. Her father was an abusive alcoholic, and she spent most of her childhood with her grandmother. At 16, Hindley was an unambitious, unremarkable, though not unattractive school-leaver, already in the dead-end clerical job where she met Brady. To her, he was irresistible, a dangerous and smooth-talking rebel who made an alluring change to the surfeit of 'pillocks' who comprised the bulk of her social circle. Hindley later said that Brady was the only man she had ever met with clean fingernails. She quickly fell under his spell, and was dragged into his demi-monde of paranoia, sadism and pornography. Her essential role, in the case both of Keith Bennett and others, was to lure the children who became Brady's prey, and then to passively look on as he murdered them and disposed of their bodies. They mimicked to the point of caricature the basic pattern of earlier killer couples, from the James Dean-wannabe Charles Starkweather and his barely teenaged sidekick Caril Ann Fugate, who between them murdered eleven people in a maniacal tour of rural Nebraska in the late 1950s, to the much lionised Bonnie Parker and Clyde Barrow, who gunned down nine police officers and four civilians in a robbery spree in the central United States during the depths of the Great Depression – although, at least it could be said of the latter that, in contrast to most serial killers, the clandestine and furtive types who lead seemingly normal lives, they were the sort of brazen outlaws who somehow always capture the public imagination. We seem to relish all the details we can get about the monsters who do the terrible things we would generally prefer not to do ourselves, and also the satisfaction of reading about their punishment after feasting on the gory details of their crimes.

There was clearly no romantic appeal for any but the most twisted imagination to the depraved acts we now know as the Moors Murders, although there was no shortage of press or public interest in them at the time, from the harrowing events on the moors themselves to the still-iconic mugshot of Hindley, taken in 1965, with her peroxide hair swept up and back, and a surly, almost defiant look in her eyes, surely one of the definitive images of evil incarnate of the twentieth century.

On Friday 12 July 1963, telling Hindley he wanted to commit the 'perfect murder', Brady instructed her to drive a van around south-east Manchester while he followed on a motorbike; when he spotted a likely target he would flash his headlight. After only a few minutes, he noticed a pretty 16-year-old schoolgirl named Pauline Reade, who was walking down Froxmer Street in Gorton, dressed in a pink twist-skirt and white stiletto shoes, on her way to a dance at the local Railway Social Club. In a ghastly preview of the Keith Bennett murder, she was enticed into the van and driven up to Saddleworth Moor, where, on the pretence of looking for a lost glove, Brady walked her out of sight of Hindley and up onto the hills, where he cut her throat with sufficient force to all but sever her spinal cord, burying the necklace she was wearing that night in the wound. When Hindley later incuriously enquired whether he had also raped the child, Brady replied, 'Of course I did.'

At about six in the evening of Saturday 23 November that year, the day following President Kennedy's death in Dallas, a popular and mischievous 12-year-old named John Kilbride, dressed in grey flannels and a short jacket with distinctive, football-shaped buttons, was out earning pocket money by sweeping up, as he did most Saturdays, at the Ashton-under-Lyne market in Manchester. While on a brief break, sitting on a bench and eating some biscuits, he was approached by Hindley, who asked him to help her load some boxes into her car. The child smilingly agreed, and she offered him a lift home; Brady was driving. On the way, they once again used the ruse of wanting to find a lost glove to take the darkened road up to Saddleworth Moor. Once there, John Kilbride was assaulted, strangled and buried in a shallow grave by the side of the road, later identified by a picture of Hindley calmly posing there.

If the Moors Murders, to which we'll return later, seem to set a scene of pervasive violence in British working-class society, whose denizens habitually killed, stole, lied and cheated as they slithered around in a sea of immorality, the story also reveals some of the joyless detail of life as it existed for the average resident of a large industrial area in 1964: streets of undifferentiated red-brick houses packed together as tight as dominoes, where indoor plumbing was far from universal, family members took a bath with bowls and pitchers in front of the kitchen stove, being 'on the phone' was a distinct novelty, and a heavy winter fog often descended, bringing a return to wartime blackout conditions and leaving spectacular rime deposits on cars and houses. Social revolution might be in the air in the form of the Beatles and the Stones, but looking out over many British streets on the darker days of 1964 was to be immersed in a scene of Dickensian antiquity. If the householder in question happened to own a television set, he or she might have noticed that some of the more go-ahead programmes had recently begun to air stories about anti-nuclear protesters and angry students, or the plight of prostitutes and the otherwise sexually or socially marginalised, without recourse to a Dalek-like voiceover to disguise the individuals' identities. Such broadcasts were 'all but abolishing shame', in one author's phrase, but for the most part unthinking conformity and respect for one's elders remained the default position for Britons in every walk of life. Tragically, it was this same deference to the 'grown-ups' of society that led a series of young children to trustingly climb in a car to be driven off by a soft-spoken couple who seemed so normal.

The Beatles land in New York in February 1964 for the 'Big Bang' moment of pop music. The cap just visible behind Paul McCartney's head belongs to the record producer Phil Spector. It was a symbolic position for Spector, whose own career would also be obscured by those of the new arrivals. (Library of Congress)

Ronan O'Rahilly, the young Irish nightclub owner who launched Radio Caroline.

The police intervene in one of the clashes between rival gangs of Mods and Rockers that enlivened Margate and other English seaside towns in the chilly spring of 1964. (Trinity Mirror/Mirrorpix/Alamy Stock Photo)

The early Rolling Stones; you would have got long odds in 1964 that they would still be in business sixty years later. (Archive PL/Alamy Stock Photo)

Princess Margaret gets around.

Alec Douglas-Home, Britain's accidental prime minister for a year, who against the odds nearly won a general election. (Wikimedia Commons/Allan Warren)

George Brown visits President Kennedy in the White House, at least proving they once met. (Robert Knudsen/White House Photographs/John F. Kennedy Presidential Library and Museum, Boston)

Bruce Reynolds (right) and other future Great Train Robbers celebrate a successful job with their wives. (Wikimedia Commons/Karen Hogan)

Peter Sellers and Britt Ekland. He had a series of heart attacks, she was fired from a film and between them they lost their dog during the excitement of their whirlwind romance. (Allstar Picture Library Ltd/Alamy Stock Photo)

Elizabeth Taylor and Richard Burton: Hollywood royalty, if in his case at consort level.

Stanley Kubrick, who apart from being a revolutionary filmmaker remains one of the few people ever to emigrate from Beverly Hills to suburban Watford.

Cassius Clay, at age 22, defied pre-fight predictions to become world heavyweight boxing champion in February 1964. Two days later, Clay let it be known that he would answer only to the name Muhammad Ali. (Library of Congress)

Clockwise from above: Terence Conran in his element. (Independent/Alamy Stock Photo); Mary Quant; Britain's briefly famous vocal trio The Paper Dolls, seen wearing Quant's most celebrated design. The miniskirt offered women a chance to feel bold and enfranchised, and provided a tantalising hint of underwear for men.

England's enterprising cricket captain Ted Dexter (right) strides to the wicket with his Sussex County teammate Jim Parks. (PA Images/Alamy Stock Photo)

The swashbuckling Dexter figure of the jet-propelled racing world Donald Campbell, who broke both land- and water-speed records in 1964. (GP Library Limited/Alamy Stock Photo)

Ken Russell, who directed his first feature film, a soggy seaside comedy called *French Dressing*, in 1964. He's seen here on the set of another film with Michael Caine.

Peter Cook, who developed his monotonal alter ego E.L. Wisty in 1964. Rebuffed in his ambition to become a judge after his lack of Latin had caused him to fail 'the rigorous judging exams', Wisty opted for a career as a coal miner instead.

The American comic Lenny Bruce, later said to have died of 'an overdose of police'. (Archive PL/Alamy Stock Photo)

Simultaneously terrifying and absurd, Nikita Khrushchev began his term as Soviet leader in 1953 expounding his vision of a new communist world order, and ended it eleven years later obsessing about the construction of Moscow lavatory seats. (Library of Congress)

Perhaps Khrushchev's most enduring legacy was the so-called Anti-Fascist Protection Device, or Berlin Wall, as others came to know it. (Library of Congress)

Winston Churchill, who bowed out of the House of Commons in July 1964 at the age of 89, seen here with the American financier Bernard Baruch. (Library of Congress)

Robert Boothby, a fitfully brilliant Tory MP who combined formidable oratorical skills with the morals of an alley cat. (Wikimedia Commons/ Allan Warren)

Sean Connery during the filming of *Goldfinger*. (ETH-Bibliothek Zürich, Bildarchiv/Fotograf: Comet Photo AG (Zürich)/Com_ C13-035-006/CC BY-SA 4.0)

Roman Polanski with his young actress wife Sharon Tate, who later became a victim of the psychotic Manson cult.

The eye-catching 'monokini', worn here by the model Peggy Moffitt, which attracted widespread public interest but never quite found a mass market in the British climate. (© William Claxton, via WENN Rights Ltd/Alamy Stock Photo)

Clint Eastwood in *A Fistful of Dollars*, the first in his celebrated spaghetti-western trilogy.

Tyneside schoolchildren waiting excitedly for Harold Wilson on the election campaign trail. Wilson's Pied Piper effect on the young was unprecedented in British politics, although America had seen it all before with John F. Kennedy. (Tyne & Wear Archives & Museums)

The pipe-smoking Wilson (he preferred a cigar in private), who duly took Labour back into power in 1964 after thirteen years of opposition, seen with President Lyndon Johnson. Johnson won the US election that year in a landslide, even if it all went wrong for him from there.

Sam Cooke, the wildly popular American singer whose December 1964 death was ruled justifiable homicide, despite evidence to the contrary.

Stanley Matthews, whose thirty-three-year-long football career ended only after he was knighted at the age of 49 on New Year's Day 1965.

III

SUMMER

MADMAN MUNTZ

I t's not unusual for a large, industrialised nation to be socially and economically polarised between the haves and have-nots, but in the case of Britain in 1964 it almost begins to look like a form of schizophrenia. Statistics can only ever tell half the story, if that, but it's worth noting that the economists Peter Townsend and Brian Abel-Smith concluded at the time that some 14 per cent (around 7.5 million) of Britons lived in a 'state of scarcity', a figure that had doubled since 1955. Of course, the term was relative compared with the real horrors of Victorian slum life, and was defined by Townsend and Abel-Smith as those with an income less than '140 per cent of the National Assistance scale, plus rent.' In material terms, it meant that about one in seven British citizens was unable to afford commodities such as a family car or central heating, let alone take a foreign holiday, although at the extreme end the report noted that there were 'scores of documented cases of families who sleep with the lights blazing to keep the rats away ... children dossing down on wet floors and mothers cooking over an open fire'. Whatever your definition of the word 'poor', this was a lifestyle some way removed from the government's cheery promise of the 'comfortable environment, with all modern conveniences' of Milton Keynes or one of the other new towns laid out on a Ministry of Housing planning board, with their neatly cultivated gardens and parks, and rows of excitingly pastel-hued weatherboarded homes for those who commuted into London for work but preferred to believe that they lived in the countryside at the evenings and weekends.

A striking feature of the British economy as a whole in 1964 was the equivocal reputation of the nation's manufacturing sector. The individual circumstances varied, but in the early Sixties Britain's factories were for the most part staffed by men (and some women) who were siphoned into literally hundreds of long-established craft unions. As the social historian Tony Judt says:

> British Leyland's car plants [then] counted 246 different unions with whom management had separately to negotiate every detail of work rates and wages. The determination to avoid a return to the horrors of the 1930s, when men and machines decayed in idleness, trumped all consideration of growth, productivity or efficiency. Strikes – a symptom of labour militancy and incompetent management alike – were endemic to post-war industrial life.

When later invited to compare the figures of days lost to strike action in Britain to those in her former mortal enemy, West Germany, Ray Gunter, the minister of labour, was forced to admit:

> Data for stoppages of work due to industrial disputes known to be official or partly official are available only on a calendar year basis. There were 2,243,000 such days lost through stoppages in 1964 [while] the number of days lost through sickness notified to the Ministry of Pensions and National Insurance was 287,000,000. I do not have information about voluntary absenteeism. The comparable number of days lost through all stoppages in West Germany that year was 1,846,025 [or roughly 150 times fewer].

Gunter was gracious enough to admit that Britain's industrial performance in 1964 gave 'no cause for complacency'. Much this same conclusion had been reached by the Conservative Cabinet in its economic review in July 1964, which had referred both to a mood of 'near-anarchy' on the shop floor and to a 'total abdication of responsibility' on the part of management. 'It is one thing for dustmen to take their unofficial action,' the Cabinet noted. 'But this same tendency has now taken root in many other sectors of the labour force which have no history of militancy, including nurses, firemen, teachers and even those in the Civil Service. The question [arises] as to where all this might lead.'

Reviewing the UK's perennial balance of payments crisis, with the current trade deficit hovering around £500–800 million, with gold and currency reserves of just £787 million and external liabilities of £3,861 million, a Treasury report of July 1964 coyly referred to a 'cumulative disequilibrium' for which 'currency readjustment might be an appropriate or even a desirable part of any remedial package,' an initiative duly taken by the Labour government in 1967. Meanwhile, the pound was still overvalued, which made it hard for Britons to sell enough abroad to compensate for sterling's chronic deficit against the dollar. Rebuffed again by General de Gaulle in its bid to join the European Community, Britain still compensated for this trade vulnerability by its privileged access to protected markets in the Empire and Commonwealth.

Representatives of this latter group met from 8 to 15 July 1964 in London's Marlborough House, where as it happened much of the talk was not about the vicissitudes of trade but the rogue apartheid regime in Southern Rhodesia. In the great rolling phrases, so compelling in their beauty and simplicity, of even the conference's shorthand notes, 'The ... unwillingness of the Government at Salisbury to make basic concessions in its existing enfranchisement provisions has been met in turn by HMG's disinclination, under the conditions which now exist, to relinquish sovereignty.'

Ian Smith, the former RAF fighter pilot recently installed as prime minister of Rhodesia, presented a formal statement of his own to be read out at Marlborough House: 'There continues to be an emphasis upon the fundamental rights of individuals, and these rights, whether written or unwritten, form through the Commonwealth the standards against which the relationship between the individual and the state is judged.'

Smith's four-point domestic agenda, published that summer, cut more to the chase. It read: 'No forced integration. No lowering of standards. No abdication of responsible government. No appeasement of the Afro-Asian bloc.'

Perhaps some of the social extremes of British life in 1964 can be glimpsed in the richly tinted figure of Reginald Manningham-Buller, Privy Councillor and QC, first Viscount Dilhorne – which, in a voice so fruity it could barely be understood by outsiders, he pronounced Dill-urn. An estimable public servant in his way, Dilhorne, as we'll informally call him, serves as a striking example of the nation's rich inheritance of often charming but intellectually negligible high public officials. Born in 1905 and schooled, with a certain inevitability, at Eton and Oxford, where he took a third-class degree in law, he was called to the bar in 1927, served in the lower reaches of the wartime Churchill coalition, and then became successively the UK's Solicitor General, Attorney General and, from July 1962, Lord Chancellor, in which role he wrote the first report on the Profumo affair, insisting that there had been no security leaks involved, that ministers had acted properly at all times and that most of the blame in the matter was on the 'depraved' osteopath Stephen Ward, who had since killed himself. Steeped in the robust Edwardian values of his youth, Dilhorne believed in the right-eousness, honour and integrity, and above all in the authority, of the law, which he exercised freely, in both written and oral form. He had a certain amount of moral and personal charm, it was said. But he lacked the gift of evoking admiration for it: on the contrary, he displayed an unfailing capacity for making enemies. The journalist Bernard Levin somehow caught a public mood when he rechristened him 'Bullying-Manner' and, when elevated to the peerage, 'Lord Stillborn'. Anyone familiar with Anthony Powell's twelve-book sequence *A Dance to the Music of Time* need look no further than the comic ogre of that work, Kenneth Widmerpool, though without his latter-day socialist conver-sion, to get some of the flavour. There was the Britain of the Beatles and the Stones and of Mary Quant and Terry Conran, in short, and there was the one still submerged in all the pageantry of an ancient Persian court as represented by a grandee like Dilhorne. In some ways, the Sixties took their time to fully get swinging.

There was a palpable sunset mood to events in the House of Commons on the afternoon of 27 July 1964, when, with some diffi-culty, the 89-year-old Winston Churchill rose to his feet to address the chamber for the last time. His remarks seemed to be in the form of a response to a statement by Rab Butler, the foreign secretary, who was about to leave for Moscow. According to the author Eric Gill, who witnessed the occasion:

There, sunk in the seat below the gangway traditionally reserved for the Father of the House, was the figure of Sir Winston ... He was, as ever, immaculately dressed in a black parliamentary suit with the long white cuffs of his shirt protruding from the sleeves of his jacket, the familiar dark spotted bow tie and a gold watch chain hung like a garland across the front of his waistcoat, and a white handkerchief cascading from his breast pocket. It was everyone's vision of Churchill. When the moment came I could hear an audible murmur from Sir Winston, though I could not detect exactly what he was saying, if indeed he was saying anything at all. [After] that he glanced at his Order Paper and evidently decided it was time to leave.

Watching Churchill move slowly off with a colleague on either arm, Gill had a picture of the old *Queen Mary*, with two tug-boats servicing the rumpled but still majestic figure in their midst. 'Then Sir Winston turned to face the Speaker, bowed to the chair and at last took his leave of the House he had served for so long.'

First elected to parliament in 1900, during the reign of Queen Victoria, Churchill had survived long enough to see a time of lost certainties and ignominious debates about needing to apply to the central banks of the world's wealthiest nations to help support the value of sterling. Hansard makes no mention of the final remarks of a man once so eloquent, now reduced to a few inaudible grunts, on 27 July, although it does record a handsome tribute the prime minister paid his retiring colleague in the next day's session:

I move this motion, conveying our unbounded admiration and gratitude ... in the knowledge that all who have ever served here with the Rt. Hon. Gentleman will feel that they share at once in the sadness and the grandeur of this essentially parliamentary occasion. Sadness because the Rt. Hon. Gentleman's long membership of the House is coming to an end, and grandeur because of the honour and the lustre which the parliamentary career of the Rt. Hon. Gentleman has brought to it.

Even the relentlessly progressive Harold Wilson, so reflexive in his distaste for the air of social entitlement and musty decay he associated with the previous thirteen years of Tory rule, could add only:

The terms in which the Prime Minister has moved this motion are acceptable to the whole House and will be welcomed by all of us ... We are speaking today not as representatives of parties, but as Members of a House united by a common bond of admiration and affection for the most distinguished and best-loved of our fellow Members.

Churchill himself then retired to his London home at Hyde Park Gate, where he died on 24 January 1965. His state funeral lasted for four days. The great orator's last words were apparently spoken to his son-in-law Christopher Soames, who had himself just left ministerial office: 'I'm so bored with it all.' Churchill was widely eulogised as the outstanding leader of the century (only later was it in vogue to dwell on his mistakes), although, perhaps characteristically standing aside from the near-universal consensus, the great contrarian Evelyn Waugh wrote privately:

> For the past week my drive has been worn into pot-holes by telegraph boys bearing extravagant offers from newspapers to describe Sir Winston's obsequies. I have of course refused. He is not a man for whom I ever had esteem. Always in the wrong, always surrounded by crooks, a most unsuccessful father – simply a 'Radio Personality' who outlived his prime. 'Rallied the nation' indeed! I was a serving soldier in 1940. How we despised his orations.

Less public than the Churchill encomia, the government and its security forces were also engaged in July 1964 in the final instalment of the long-running saga of the KGB's 'Ring of Five' that had seen the flight to Moscow of, first, Guy Burgess and Donald Maclean, then of Kim Philby, followed by the private confession on 23 April 1964 of Anthony Blunt, who was nonetheless permitted to stay on as Surveyor of the Queen's Pictures, a director of the Courtauld Institute and honorary fellow of Trinity College, Cambridge, among other sinecures.

This latest twist to the story involved the 50-year-old former civil servant John Cairncross. A testament both to the misconceived idealism among Britain's intelligentsia in the 1930s, and to the comic futility of MI5's hunt for embedded communist moles, he was the academically precocious son of a Glaswegian ironmonger and his schoolteacher wife. From these inauspicious but radical beginnings, he had gone on to read modern languages at the Sorbonne and Cambridge, and was approached by the KGB shortly after joining the foreign office, from which he transferred to the wartime intercept station at Bletchley Park.

Cairncross seems to have been motivated primarily by his belief that by passing on Western atomic secrets he was simply helping a sorely pressed wartime ally – Stalin – who had been unfairly deprived of this information by a right-wing establishment clique. This was a not-uncommon view at a certain level of British academic and professional life in the years around 1941–45. Some of Cairncross's spycraft was of the sophisticated John le Carré school; at other times he was known to take the more direct route and smuggle decrypts out of Bletchley Park by the expedient of stuffing them down his trousers. He was well paid for his services. Cairncross eventually moved to Cleveland, Ohio, to take up a university teaching post, but an MI5 deputation finally came calling for him early in 1964. In an exquisitely phrased top-secret Cabinet memo of 20 February:

It is not clear whether Cairncross could, in fact, be returned to this country. His offences are not extraditable; and the United States government might therefore be reluctant to deport him to the United Kingdom, even if they had the power to do so, which is itself uncertain. Nevertheless, they might find some means of returning him to us, just as we had found it possible to decide to return [the Soviet spy Robert] Soblen to the United States.

Even if Cairncross were returned to this country, we should not necessarily be able to secure his conviction. The confession which he has apparently made in the United States has been volunteered in return for certain inducements, and it would not, therefore, be admissible as evidence. Moreover, it is doubtful whether we could properly initiate, or a court be likely to endorse, action in respect of espionage which must have ceased at least twelve years ago – the more so since it could be represented as having been directed to the benefit of a country which, for a large part of the period in question, was an ally of both the United Kingdom and the United States.

'For these reasons,' the paper concluded, 'we should not at this stage entirely close our minds to the possibility that the most expedient outcome of the affair might be for Cairncross himself to decide to leave the United States for some third country without ever returning to Britain.'

In short, it was to be, and indeed it was, hushed up. The Cabinet continued to revisit some of the fine detail of the Cairncross affair during the spring and early summer of 1964, before concluding:

Should this individual in fact be returned to the United Kingdom, it would remain to be seen whether his interrogation on his arrival would produce any evidence on the basis of which he could be brought to trial; and if we cannot get anything out of him, the matter might not end with his conviction but, on the contrary, prove of some little discomfiture to HMG.

In the end, Cairncross was not brought back to the UK in handcuffs to face trial for espionage. In 1967, he voluntarily moved on from the American Midwest to Rome, where he worked for the UN Food and Agriculture Organisation as a translator. Twelve years later, he was publicly exposed by the *Sunday Times* journalist Barrie Penrose. Even then, no official action was taken in the matter. Apart from anything else, as the foreign secretary had told his Cabinet colleagues in 1964, there was the 'potential awkwardness' of the fact that Cairncross's older brother Alec was currently serving as head of the Government Economic Service. 'We would thus be seen as employing someone whose close relative was a self-confessed Communist spy,' the Cabinet secretary noted drily. In the event, Cairncross served a one-year prison sentence in Rome on unrelated currency charges, moved to France on his release, and just had time to write his memoirs before he suffered a fatal stroke while visiting England in October 1995, at the age of 82.

★★★

Whole books, some of them quite readable, have been written on the ghastly appropriation of Beatlesque pop music by some of that band's only fitfully talented spawn in the 1970s and beyond, so perhaps it's again best to be brief and say that in 1964 the primary idea was still to entertain the paying audience rather than to present a politicised or 'countercultural' message for frequently mercenary ends. As we've seen, the Beatles themselves led the field in terms not only of sales but also of the decadent lunacy that often attended their concerts. All four band members were now regularly presented backstage with children in wheelchairs, whose hysterical parents shouted, 'Go on, kiss him! Make him whole again!' Outside hotels, a brisk trade was done in the group's used bed linen, as well as in hairs allegedly pulled from the combs of the lovable Scousers who just a year or two earlier had all been broke and living with their mums and dads. Not for nothing did John Lennon go on to observe that the Beatles had become 'bigger than Jesus'. He and Paul McCartney were now reportedly each making an eye-watering weekly £300 (£4,400 today) from their songwriting duties, and even Ringo was thinking in more ambitious terms than putting enough away to open his own hair salon.

In a canny bit of packaging, the Rolling Stones, in reality two impeccably well-spoken grammar school boys and their three generally docile colleagues, were busy further developing an image as the Beatles' mutant cousins. Like the Fab Four, their band was now fast becoming a brand that was far more commercially valuable than the slightly unprepossessing individuals who sheltered beneath it. One obvious sign that summer of the direction things were going was the front-page story in the music weekly *Melody Maker*. After reading some of the things the press had had to say about them on their first tour of America, the group's young hustler-manager Andrew Oldham was able to suggest the classic headline: 'Would You Let Your Sister Go With A Rolling Stone?' ('I wouldn't myself,' he noted.) The question echoed the sentiments not only of the mainstream press, but of a growing number of worried parents on both sides of the Atlantic. The Beatles, the theory went, may have wanted to hold your hand, but the Stones' aim was elsewhere. It was to be an enduring and, in Mick Jagger's case, timeless image, although Oldham's caricature of the band as priapic shaggers may have been a touch ahead of reality. FBI records of the first American tour characterise all five Stones as 'liberals' (*sic*) who had apparently 'announced their intention to financially support Dr Martin Luther King', but, so far as could be ascertained – and the bureau took the precaution of bugging their hotel rooms – 'have not consorted with any women of loose morals'.

Sitting around their modest two-room flat in north London's Mapesbury Road one night early that summer, Keith Richards began playing a child's plastic keyboard and doodled a tune, which he gave to Mick Jagger. Several hours later, Jagger had managed to come up with a chorus and the title 'Shang A Doo Lang'. The two young pop Turks sold this first fruit of their collaboration to the singer and future *Carry On* actress Adrienne Posta at her 16th birthday party. Also present that night were Paul McCartney, McCartney's friend John Dunbar and Dunbar's 'chick', a slim, tooth-white girl who looked like something out of a Scott Fitzgerald novel: Marianne Faithfull.

Appraising Faithfull's cascading blonde hair, seraphic smile and ample figure, Andrew Oldham had a sudden vision of 'an angel with big tits', and signed her on the spot. A blushing Mick Jagger then ambled up and introduced himself by pouring his glass of wine down Faithfull's dress. Keith Richards followed in turn, asked his new work associate a perfunctory question about her singing voice, and took a cab back to Mapesbury Road to write the melody of 'As Tears Go By', which, with a discreet guitar backing from the young Jimmy Page, went Top Ten later that summer. The song particularly impressed the Stones's Brian Jones, who would come to note ruefully that 'it actually took Keith three minutes to write a three-minute tune', and to rapidly curtail his own compositional ambitions as a result. The essential formula that sustained both the entry-level Beatles and Stones was to give classic American rhythm and blues a commercial facelift, without necessarily losing all the wrinkles. The song was also a career high for Marianne Faithfull, who spent much of the rest of the Sixties as a celebrity without portfolio.

It's necessary to add only that it was the Stones, and emphatically not the Beatles, whose vaguely subversive manner became the template for the scores of bands, some more technically sound than others, to emerge in their wake over the course of the next sixty years. The basic model amounted to about equal parts scorn for pomposity and convention, along with an old-fashioned ability to 'put over' a song. The Stones went about this no fewer than 186 times in 1964, each concert typically beginning with collective frowns from the stage, a largely perfunctory inspection of the instruments, and then a grunted introduction of the first number. A fast-paced package of percussive American electric blues and whirling, anti-virtuosic dance moves followed, all the more compelling amid the Stones's initial show of indifference. The band's jiggly front trio and studiously bored back line quickly became a pop archetype, and a role model for those packing their local Gaumonts and Odeons that summer to digest Jagger's Tiller-Girl hoofing, a lusty beat and Brian Jones progressing backwards and forwards in a series of malignant hops, mouthing lewd endearments to the female members of the audience as he did so. The rock concert as we know it continues to take its basic business plan from this blueprint; the Stones themselves remain the extreme exponent of the British attitude that whatever others hold seriously must be intrinsically slightly ridiculous.

Whatever Victor Lownes had to say on the subject, it's a matter of debate whether it truly was bliss to be alive that year, but you could make a case for saying that to be young and to possess any sort of an ear for a good pop tune was something akin to heaven. The British singles chart of 1 July 1964 lists the first three songs in descending order as: The Beatles ('A Hard Day's Night'), the Stones ('It's All Over Now') and Dusty Springfield ('I Just Don't Know What to do with Myself'), with the likes of Elvis, the Animals, P.J. Proby, Roy Orbison, the Beach Boys, the Dave Clark Five, Billy Fury, the Shadows and the Hollies coming up behind. To adapt the phrasing of the popular ad tagline of the day, if there was ever a serious rival to this particular line-up of best-selling hits, one would like to hear of it.

There may be a certain grim humour to the fact that the small but potent blast of youthful energy seen in the UK music chart of July 1964 stood in such contrast to the prosaic routine of most adolescents as they went about their daily lives. There were many individual exceptions to the rule, but on the whole most young men and women were more concerned with the realities of making ends meet than with acting as the shock troops in the social revolution. 'Playing the game' remained the byword. The unwritten social code, specifically as it concerned young people, might be roughly summarised as this: females were the guardians of morality; they were made of finer stuff than the males and expected to act accordingly. A young woman might step out with a friend or two of the opposite sex, but the basic endgame in life was to find a romantic match that would lead to the altar, or at least, increasingly, the local registry office, and then to live happily ever after. Young men enjoyed more leeway, and were expected to succumb to the blandishments of sex from time to time, but it was still a long way from there to the pervasive culture of 'everyone's at it', or the feeling on certain tabloid papers that it was high time to dispense with the former air of fusty servility and replace it with that unique blend of moral indignation, gossip and bare breasts that would remain the popular template for the next half-century. The illusions of Empire and some of the insular confidence of the ruling elite may have been wounded at Suez, and finally killed off with Profumo, but after sailing serenely in one direction for so long the ship of state was only now slowly coming about. In short, not everyone was 'at it' in 1964, and it sometimes struck those of a certain age that Britain increasingly resembled a family with the wrong members in charge.

It must seem to some of those same people that they have spent their whole lives on the brink of a yawning financial abyss. There's perhaps no need to quote at any length the politicians' successive bromides on the subject, except to briefly note the comments of the wartime Cabinet minister Albert Alexander, lately raised to the peerage as Earl Alexander of Hillsborough, when he rose to address the matter of 'our island's prospects' in the House of Lords that summer of 1964, which at least have the merit of clarity.

'It is true there are some signs of economic progress,' Alexander allowed:

> The output which has been coming recently from steel and the manufacture of cars and in engineering in general has been a slight relief, and I hope it may go forward. But, looking at the matter all the way round, there is no real room for confidence ... Our plight today is largely due to the decline in the advance we made in the first few years after the war, when other countries were in the throes of reconstruction as to their general equities, trade and output. During that period, our exports rose and we were very nearly the top nation in the world in percentage of trade. Now we have very nearly fallen down to the bottom of the ladder ... Our island is at present simply not competitive, and if we persist [in] a policy of go-as-you-please, think-how-you-like, with no good overall plan, letting things take their course, then the nation will be very much worse off for it in the times ahead.

To turn from the more abstract overview of affairs to the way in which flesh-and-blood Britons actually lived:

In the spring 1964 budget, the chancellor, Reginald Maudling, as usual raised the price of a pint of beer and a packet of cigarettes, which by July stood at about 2s 2d (£1.80 today) and 5s (£3.90) respectively, the latter roughly the same as for a gallon of petrol. Maudling's Labour shadow and soon-to-be successor 'Sunny' Jim Callaghan remarked in the Commons on 20 July:

> The government has now increased the price of energy through the returns which the electricity boards are required to make upon their capital assets. Road haulage rates are to go up by 5 percent. The price of smokeless fuel is to be increased by £1 a ton in the autumn.

This weekend beef prices have risen so much that it is cheaper to buy a turkey. The minister of agriculture has cast himself in the role of a 20th-century Marie Antoinette. If the present trend continues, 1964 will be the worst year for rising prices since the Korean War of 1950–51, but without the same cause.

Most of those thrilling to the sounds of the Beatles and the other pop luminaries in that summer's charts would have done so with a device such as a Philips Valve Record Player or an RCA Victor Victrola, at the top end of the range crafted in aluminium or steel, but more often merely a plastic box roughly the size of a small suitcase with a leatherette trim and retailing at around £15 (£220 today) – not cheap, in other words. There were, it's true, some modest cost-cutting innovations in the field that year, many of them the product of the fevered brain of Earl 'Madman' Muntz, a 50-year-old fast-talking Chicago entrepreneur who in 1964 marketed both the world's first functional widescreen TV and the 'Muntz Stereo-Pak', the latter better known successively as the four-track and later eight-track cartridge. From Los Angeles to Luton, the ability to listen to whatever you wanted to while out driving, rather than to endless hours of canned Mantovani light orchestra music and sonorous BBC news bulletins, came about largely because of a manic, folically challenged American huckster typically dressed in red PVC and a Napoleonic hat who would scream in his own broadcast commercials: 'I want to give 'em away, but Mrs M. won't let me!' (It somehow fails to come as a surprise to learn that Muntz was at one time also the world's biggest used-car dealer.)

Muntz's essential sales philosophy was expressed by 'K.I.S.S.' – 'Keep it simple, stupid'; to that end he was known to carry a pair of shears in his pocket with which he'd begin snipping away at the wiring in the back of a standard radiogram with no immediate loss of function – 'most of it's just junk,' he would inform his audience. He even invented the acronym 'TV', because the skywriters he'd hired to promote his latest range of sets couldn't get the full word out in time before the smoke trail from their planes evaporated. Our modern household lives owe a good deal to this motor-mouthed Midwestern high-school dropout with a distinct resemblance in both looks and speech to the comedian Phil Silvers, of Sergeant Bilko fame, crossed with a classic over-the-top, mad-scientist act that would have been looked on with caution by Boris Karloff.

THE COLOUR PROBLEM

One of the few issues about which the British left and right broadly agreed in 1964 was the desirability of planning. In the post-war years, a line of thought emerged both at home and overseas that took as its root a deep and enduring faith in the ability of governments to solve large-scale problems by mobilising and directing people and resources to collectively beneficial ends. One obvious target of the planners' attentions lay in the provision of the nation's healthcare services, which allowed successive administrations to intervene in the day-to-day lives of their citizens in the belief that this would usher in a better, safer and ultimately happier environment, or, if you prefer, a sanitary dictatorship devoted to the cult of health. Of course, there had been previous attempts to regulate and improve matters such as the nation's diet or the state of its physical fitness. But it was only in the mid 1960s that it became an article of faith, enshrined in state policy, that nature invariably awards the crown of longevity to those who follow the latest, and therefore, the best, lifestyle advice. Alas, nature, as any self-respecting doctor will attest, is neither just nor unjust; it is impervious.

The United States likes to take credit for this landmark development in the unwritten social contract between the state and its citizens, in the form of the 1964 report by that nation's surgeon-general, the strikingly named Dr Luther Leonidas Terry Jr, on the negative health effects of tobacco use. But in fact the Americans, as they often do, were merely giving definition to an already existing truth. Two years earlier, the British Royal College of Physicians (RCP) had taken advantage of Ash Wednesday to use what was then a novel technique – the press conference – to announce that tobacco-related lung cancer was now killing sixty-three Britons each day, a mortality rate that was the highest in the developed world. This last statistic was perhaps sobering enough. But what distinguished the RCP report from the reams of other drily academic pronouncements on the subject was the call for the government to 'do something' to actively discourage smoking. In this context, it's worth noting that in the six years 1957–62 inclusive, England's seventy-nine local authorities spent the sum of £3,624 on educational material relating to smoking, an annual total of around £7 12s, or some £145 in today's terms, per authority. Over the same period, the tobacco industry invested £39 million (£740 million today) in promoting its products.

The RCP report did lead in short order to a ban on cigarette advertising on television, and all that ensued, although there's some evidence to suggest that the successive official constraints proved counter-productive, at least among younger consumers. When men like the reedy-voiced Anthony Barber, the health minister, began to say in 1964, 'You must do this – it's for your own good,' the instinct among much of his audience was to do the opposite. 'If the government says it, it's probably cobblers,' was the sort of thing the interviewer for the BBC's *Tonight* programme heard when he ventured out onto the streets following the release of the British statement endorsing the US surgeon-general's report. The cold fact remained that more than two-thirds of all adult British males, and nearly half of all females, regularly smoked cigarettes in 1964, and that 'practically everyone' in the upper tier of society, from Princess Margaret down, enjoyed a drag. Sixty years later, the overall smoking figures are significantly lower, but paradoxically it's the most vulnerable members of the community who suffer most. Today 48 per cent of British men in the poorest social class die before they reach the age of 70, compared with 22 percent of those in the richest social group. Half of that difference is accounted for by smoking. In the Princess ward of Knowsley, Merseyside, said to be the most deprived area of England, 53 per cent of the population smoke, compared with a national average of 24 per cent. By contrast, in the nation's most affluent ward, Keyworth North in the East Midlands, only 11 per cent of the population light up. It seems fair to conclude that these were not the long-term consequences the various social engineers had in mind when they began to vocally assert themselves in British life around 1964.

★ ★ ★

There was no shortage of tobacco users, both in the public stands and the players' dressing rooms, when England began their third cricket Test with Australia at the Headingley ground in Leeds in July 1964. The place was the 'scene of a vast and often raucously loud congestion', in E.W. Swanton's phrase, with spouts of white smoke rising from the houses at the Kirkstall Lane End, grey but at least initially dry skies, and a pitch that in Swanton's opinion had 'perhaps not quite the lasting properties that all concerned had reason to expect'. The visitors had the better of the argument on the first day after Ted Dexter had won the toss for the third consecutive time and chosen to bat. England managed just 268, probably about 50 under par, and Australia replied with 389. Fred Trueman greeted the tourists' fourth man in, Peter Burge, with a swift one to the jaw, but the batsman, chewing throughout as vigorously as for a TV commercial, had the last laugh, scoring 160 in just over five hours at the crease.

Little went right for England the second time around. Parfitt had his knuckle broken off his first ball; Dexter himself, atypically subdued, added just 17 in eighty minutes, and Barrington, too, chose to rely on defence, remaining scoreless for close to an hour. British self-effacement could hardly go much further than this. Australia were left needing only 109 for victory and knocked off the runs for the loss of three wickets with more than a day to spare. It was a match of individual distinction, rather than one of communal brilliance. Perhaps in the end victory went not so much to the better side as to the one that played better.

Three weeks later, the teams regrouped to play out a stale draw at Old Trafford, where Australia's captain Bobby Simpson scored 311 in a shade under thirteen hours, and Barrington replied with an equally languid knock of 256, his first Test century in England after hitting nine abroad. Plenty of runs, then, even if the essential bat–ball contest which helps sustain interest on these occasions never really materialised. The result meant that the visitors retained the Ashes. Over the five days a total of 108,000 spectators paid £36,340, or about 6s 6d (£5 now) apiece at the turnstiles, among them both the prime minister (briefly a first-class cricketer in his youth) and the leader of the opposition Harold Wilson. Wilson despised cricket, but was not a man over-burdened by ideological baggage, and quite pragmatic enough a politician to stand a few drinks in the public beer tent when the opportunity arose.

Elsewhere in sport, a crew from Vilnius defied the odds to beat the University of London in the final of the Grand Challenge Cup at Henley; 50-year-old Scobie Breasley romped home on Santa Claus in front of a 200,000-strong crowd at the Derby; and, as we've seen, the American Tony Lema won the Open Championship at St Andrews, his only such success before he and his pregnant wife died in a plane crash near Chicago. Lema earned £1,500 (£22,000 today), and is remembered for his calm, methodical approach to his game, 'assessing each shot as if by reference to some built-in electronic computer, gauging angles and distances'. On the whole, professional sportsmen were less consumed with science than they are now. 'You just more or less walked up to the ball and banged it,' Jack Nicklaus once informed me. Nicklaus lost by five strokes to Lema at St Andrews.

There may be no atmosphere quite like that of England in its annual midsummer display of the world's most pastoral sports played to the highest competitive level. It's truly a timeless occasion. But the early to mid-sixties as a whole appear as a transitional era, in which conventions of social deference and traditional attitudes still held sway, but where a new spirit of egalitarianism was beginning to trump politics, religion and even class as the arbiter of collective behaviour. A 1955 government report called 'The Colour Problem' had estimated that two-thirds of Britain's white population held a 'low opinion of black people or disapproved of them'. Nearly a decade later, legislation like the Commonwealth Immigrants Act had gone at least some of the way to removing institutional prejudice based on race. But there was still ample scope for individual acts of discrimination, whether in the form of a muttered remark on the street or in the extortionate price for accommodation often reserved for minorities. An American college business lecturer named Paul Heppe would long remember taking an overcrowded train that summer of 1964 from the 'pristine, wide-open avenues' around London's Euston station to visit family friends living in Wolverhampton.

'It was a big shock for someone who thought of England only in terms of Big Ben and the changing of the guard at Buckingham Palace,' Heppe recalled:

> The train rolled through a scene that looked like the aftermath of a nuclear war. As you went further north there were rows of crooked-looking houses, or shacks, lining the side of the track, faces at the windows that seemed to have a ghastly winter pallor even at the height of summer, and a sort of greasy pall of smoke that lay everywhere and clung to your clothes for days afterwards.

Heppe, who happened to be gay, was as struck by the area's prevailing social mores as by its air of physical decay. 'You heard words like "spade" and "coon" uttered without reproach pretty much everywhere, and I won't even mention the charming local epithets for anyone suspected of being gay. They weren't enlightened.'

★ ★ ★

On 12 July 1964, the 2 million or so readers of the tabloid *Sunday Mirror* were treated to a front-page scoop that seemed to offer the perfect cocktail of low doings in high places involving the political establishment, sex and violence. 'Peer And A Gangster: Yard Probe' ran the arresting headline in the *News of the World*'s principal competitor as the defender of the nation's sabbath rectitude, above a story as lurid as any of the paper's staple diet of implausibly well-upholstered actresses, errant choirmasters and unusual domestic practices on suburban housing estates.

'A top level Scotland Yard investigation into the alleged homosexual relationship between a prominent peer and a leading thug in the London underworld has been ordered by Metropolitan Police commissioner Sir Joseph Simpson,' the story read:

> The peer concerned is a household name, and Yard detectives are looking into allegations that he had a 'relationship' with a man who has criminal convictions and is alleged to be involved in a West End protection racket.
>
> I can reveal that the investigation embraces:
>
> 1. Inquiries into Mayfair parties attended by the peer and the East End thug.
>
> 2. The private week-end activities of the peer and a number of prominent public men during visits to Brighton.
>
> 3. The relationships that exist between the East End gangster, the peer and a number of clergymen.
>
> 4. Allegations of blackmail against people who know of these relationships.

It soon emerged that the peer in question was 64-year-old Robert Boothby, a bumptious and fitfully brilliant Old Etonian former Tory MP and junior minister who combined formidable oratorical skills with the personal morals of a bisexual alley cat. The 'thug' was 30-year-old Ronald Kray, who with his twin brother Reggie bestrode London's gangland from the late 1950s up to the time of their eventual arrest in May 1968, carving a reputation – sometimes literally – that they used both to make money and inspire fear. In 1955, they had taken over the Regal billiard hall in the East End, where Ronnie attacked members of a Maltese gang with a cutlass after they unwisely tried to extract protection money from him and his brother. The twins branded another business rival with a white-hot poker, and in due course Ron strode into the Blind Beggar pub in Whitechapel and calmly shot dead a local gangster called George Cornell in front of shocked witnesses. Cornell's offence had been to call Kray a 'fat poof'. 'I'm homosexual, but I'm not a poof,' Ron had indignantly corrected him.

On reading the original *Sunday Mirror* story, Boothby lost little time in engaging the services of the superbly corpulent lawyer Arnold Goodman, widely known as 'Two Dinners', who put pressure on the paper not only to retract its story but to pay his client a staggering £40,000 (or £600,000 today), tax-free, by way of apology. The *Mirror's* chief mistake was to have implied that there was a homosexual relationship between the peer and the gangster, whereas Kray was instead acting as a procurer of rough trade for Boothby, who had a public reputation as a ladies' man – carrying on a three-decade-long affair with Dorothy Macmillan, for six of those years the prime minister's wife – but who was in fact vigorously and recklessly bisexual. In time this gave the *Mirror* splash of July 1964 its final if then unusable twist, that of the establishment cover-up. It was to be a further forty-nine years before files released by the UK National Archives disclosed how closely the Boothby–Kray axis had been followed by both the security services and the home secretary, concerned that the whole affair might erupt into a renewed Profumo scandal.

The documents describe how one morning in 1964 both Krays had arrived at Boothby's home in London's Eaton Square, after several cheques were stolen from him at a restaurant owned by the twins, whose reputation for dispensing summary justice was already well established.

An MI5 memo reads:

> Their alleged reason for the call was to apologise to Lord Boothby for any inconvenience caused to him over his cheques. They explained that one of their chaps had been responsible, but that he was now no longer with them and highly unlikely to do that sort of thing again.

The report concluded: 'Boothby is a kinky fellow and likes to meet odd people, and Ronnie obviously wants to know those of a good social standing, he having the odd background he has; and, of course, both are queers.'

Although Boothby always insisted that his £40,000 windfall from the *Mirror* had gone straight to charity, a large chunk of it in fact made its way to the Krays, who used it to bribe police officers when subsequently under investigation for threatening a rival Soho club owner. The old rogue remained shameless in his denial of his sexual involvement with the twins. In an interview at the time, Boothby said: 'My familiarity with them has been brief and quite proper. My lifelong experience is that the best way to treat the press is with perfect frankness and tell the truth. This is what I have done.'

FOG OF WAR

While Robert Boothby was busy collecting both his payout from the *Sunday Mirror* and a certain amount of abusive private correspondence, much of it anonymous ('Everyone knows of the slimy, stinking life you lead,' read one choice example. 'You are a perfect disgrace to Britain, and the sooner you clear off the better, along with that pansy friend of yours'), across the Atlantic President Johnson's mind was concentrated on the matter of his fellow Americans' relationships with each other. This found expression in the Civil Rights Act, ratified by a 73–27 vote of the US Senate and signed into law that July. Johnson, a Texan who had accommodated himself to segregation for most of his career, has been widely praised for his courage in personally steering legislation that was far from universally popular, and which among other things sought to redress a state of affairs in which only 12,000 of the 3 million black students in the American south attended integrated schools, and black infant mortality was twice as great as white in the nation as a whole. But perhaps the president's unwavering devotion to the cause of equality was motivated by more than just high-minded altruism. He noted in private as the struggle to ensure the Act's passage through Congress began:

> I'm gonna try and teach these nigras that don't know anything how to work for themselves instead of just breedin'. I'm gonna try to teach these Mexicans who can't talk English to learn it so they can work for themselves, [and] get off our taxpayers' backs.

These remarks stood at some remove from the president's soaring ora-torical flourish at the time of the bill's enactment into law, when he took the opportunity to inform the American public:

All men are entitled to the blessings of liberty. Yet millions are being deprived of those blessings because of the color of their skin. This cannot endure ... Our constitution, the foundation of our republic, forbids it. The principles of our own freedom forbid it. Morality for-bids it. And the law I will sign tonight forbids it.

The 1964 Civil Rights Act still has a mythical quality in the minds of many Americans: the transformative moment when the recently televised scenes of shoeless children campaigning against school segregation, being bitten by Alsatians and knocked off their feet by water fired with sufficient power to rip bark off a tree, finally caused enough ordinary citizens to call time on a prevailing status quo essen-tially unchanged since the end of the Civil War a century earlier. But the most reliable opinion polls of the time tell a more nuanced tale. As quoted by the widely respected historian Robert Dallek in his biography of Johnson, the number of those actively opposed to the president's civil rights efforts hovered at or just above 30 per cent, while less than 15 per cent of respondents favoured more aggressive affirmative action of the sort the White House had in mind. To guard against some of the political fallout of the 1964 legislation – which at least notionally barred racial, religious and sex discrimination by employers and labour unions – Johnson enlisted the help of his slain predecessor's 38-year-old brother and serving US attorney-general, Robert Kennedy. 'I'll do just what you think is best on this. We'll follow what you say ... I'll do whatever you want me to do in order to get it done,' he told him.

In short order, Johnson also sent word to Senate Democratic leaders to seek Kennedy's approval on everything relating to the contentious new bill. Why would he do that? a journalist later asked. 'He didn't think we'd get it through,' the then-former attorney-general replied. 'Johnson didn't want to bear the sole responsibility if it flopped.' Kennedy believed that 'for political reasons it made a lot of sense for LBJ'. The president couldn't lose, in fact: if the bill failed, 'it was [Kennedy's] fault, but if it succeeded he would still get credit'.

Meanwhile, Johnson ordered the FBI to wiretap Kennedy's home and office, and personally arranged the running order of the 1964 Democratic convention in Atlantic City to ensure that 'the brat', as he referred to the nation's top law-enforcement official, didn't speak until after Johnson's hand-picked candidate Hubert Humphrey was safely installed as his running mate. Declassified FBI documents reveal that the president was concerned that his young Cabinet colleague and potential rival was a 'burning zealot' who might 'use the Kennedy name' to 'whip up the negro problem in America' to his, Johnson's, detriment. Such was the reality of what the president told the American people was 'our country's historic destiny to stir the souls of men in far corners of distant continents who, like us, hunger for the freedom of all God's children'.

★ ★ ★

As a child of 7 I was lucky enough to spend part of the summer of 1964 not in our naval-issue home in suburban South Merton but at my uncle's house in Anaheim, near Los Angeles, where I was told he'd 'done well for himself' in real estate. It's perhaps difficult to convey the shock of suddenly finding yourself on the other side of the Atlantic in those days, almost as if you'd stepped through the looking-glass from a monochrome world into the voluptuously tropical dream-scape of southern California. There were backyard swimming pools, multi-channel colour TV shows introduced by a garishly hued cartoon peacock, and loaded, doorstop-sized cheeseburgers, to name just three commodities notably short on the ground in the average British household of 1964. Everything seemed to be open all night, and even to my untrained eye it was obvious that public displays of flesh and representations of unconstrained sexual abandon both on screen and in the city streets had advanced well beyond the point of socially acceptable behaviour back home in Surrey.

But perhaps nothing spoke more to the essential promise and reality of American life than the moment when one of my new 7- or 8-year-old local friends introduced himself to my middle-aged uncle at the latter's front door by extending his hand and cheerily announcing, 'Hi, John.' There was something peculiarly and on the whole attractively liberated in the boy's instinctive assumption – and my uncle's immediate acceptance of it – of the general equality of conditions that prevailed in America.

There was another side to the picture, too. The place had a sort of aggressive contemporaneity, neon-lit, consumer-driven and above all youthful, but even among the neatly manicured front lawns of upscale Anaheim, home of the original Disneyland, there were signs of the social unrest and inner-city disturbances that were to become a near-annual summer event throughout the US for the next sixty years. In particular, it seemed local acquiescence to the new Civil Rights Act was only piecemeal, because early in my stay in California I saw on the news that several customers had been evicted from a nearby diner where my family and I sometimes ate by other patrons wielding baseball bats. When I went to the neighbourhood toy store with my newly acquired best friend Duane, who had emigrated with his family from Mexico some years earlier, I noticed how he always paused for a moment in the shop's doorway in order to make eye contact with the man behind the counter. About thirty years later, the adult Duane told me that this was a habit then common to many of those with black or brown skin, and was intended as a way of saying, 'Don't worry, I'm not trying to steal anything.'

Throughout the summer, there were frequent reports of racially charged unrest in the Los Angeles papers. One night there were vivid images on my uncle's oval-shaped Zenith TV, with its accompanying 'space command' remote control, of men and women hurling flaming Molotov cocktails through plate-glass windows, and uniformed men on horses firing tear gas back at them, which for a moment I took to be one of those gritty new prime-time series like *The Asphalt Jungle* or *87th Precinct* I so enjoyed. It somehow had the look of a cracking police drama to it. But after a minute, I realised that what I was watching wasn't a fictional show. It was a news report about a full-scale race riot taking place 3,000 miles away in New York. In due course, we were told that the problem had begun when the superintendent of an apartment block on the east side of Manhattan had taken exception to the presence of several black youths sitting on his building's front steps and proceeded to turn a hose on them while shouting 'Dirty n******, I'll wash you clean.' One of the young men remonstrated with their assailant, voices were raised, and an off-duty policeman who had witnessed the scene from across the street drew his service revolver and fatally shot a 15-year-old black boy named James Powell, allegedly after the latter had waved a knife at him. Six days and nights of unbridled carnage ensued. Seven hundred and twenty individuals were injured, one rioter died after being shot in the head – it was never established by whom – 465 men and women were arrested and property damage was estimated at $1.8 million, or about $32 million today. Two weeks later, the original officer involved was cleared of any wrongdoing by a grand jury, and all charges against him were dropped. The New York police commissioner, a man called Michael Murphy with thick grey hair like steel wool and a face that seemed to have been built in a foundry, explained: 'There were no violations of the rules, and all procedures were followed.'

Shortly after his January 1962 decision to escalate American involvement in Vietnam, President Kennedy gave two speeches in which he apparently foresaw that the growing conflict in the region might come to polarise American politics. In the first, he criticised liberals 'who cannot bear the burden of a long twilight struggle'. They were impatient for 'some quick and easy and final and cheap solution to the communist threat – now'. Kennedy saw the right's criticism of his Vietnam policy as equally deluded. Their depiction of limited American intervention as mere 'appeasement' amounted to 'a campaign of suspicion and fear' much like the Red-baiting tactics popular in the 1950s, but which were now part of the 'grand illusion', as Kennedy privately summarised it to his brother, that the US could 'win compliance and influence people by bombing the shit out of them'. Two and a half years later, I witnessed a small and mutually distressing example of this growing divide on the subject of America's role in Vietnam when, one night in Anaheim, my uncle loudly requested that his visiting younger brother leave the family dinner table and not return as a result of his 'pinko' views on the matter, a scene that surely reflected in miniature the widespread turmoil surrounding the issue as a whole that all but tore the US apart in years ahead. I was shocked by the force with which the door of the house slammed behind him.

Matters then took a fateful turn when, on the Friday night of 31 July 1964, as part of a highly classified programme of covert ops against North Vietnam known as Plan 34-A, Johnson ordered the USS *Maddox*, a Second World War-era destroyer, to steam along a predesignated course just outside the Gulf of Tonkin, about 150 miles east of Hanoi, to gather intelligence on the enemy's shore defences and other military facilities. With a certain inevitability, the North Vietnamese in turn sent torpedo boats to harass the warship appearing off their coast and to usher it back into international waters. The *Maddox*, supported by planes from a nearby US aircraft carrier, took poorly to this development, with the result that one Vietnamese boat was sunk and another was damaged, with the loss of four lives, as the American party left the area.

Two days later, the *Maddox* and her sister ship USS *Turner Joy* resumed their patrol, coming to within 10 miles of the Vietnam coast. Just before midnight on 3 August, the *Turner Joy* duty radio operator reported that the US convoy was apparently being shadowed by hostile gunboats, and that based on their speed and course 'action by them [seemed] imminent.' For the next several hours, both US ships fired rather randomly into the night, and repeatedly dropped depth charges, to deter their supposed pursuers. With daylight, however, the Americans could see no sign that they had actually come under attack. Instead, the *Maddox* and *Turner Joy* found themselves sailing alone on a calm blue sea with only a few passing dolphins for company. Assessing the situation, the captain of the *Maddox* felt compelled to signal back to the Pentagon that 'Review of action makes many apparent contacts and torpedoes appear doubtful. Freak weather effects on radar and overeager sonarmen may have accounted for many reports.'

Robert McNamara, the brisk, 48-year-old US secretary of defence, whose wire-rim glasses, centre-parted oily brown hair and self-confident manner all gave Johnson the impression of 'a human calculating machine', later admitted that even he had had his doubts about whether the crews of the *Maddox* and *Turner Joy* had ever been firing at anything but a few flying fish. Pressed further on the point in the 2003 documentary *Fog of War*, McNamara reflected on the testimony he had given on the issue to the US Senate nearly forty years earlier, which led in turn to arguably the greatest American foreign policy debacle of the twentieth century: 'I learned early on never to answer the question that is asked of you,' he said. 'Answer the question that you wish had been asked of you. And quite frankly, I follow that rule. It's a very good one.'

Johnson himself showed that clarity of mind for which his supporters most admired him when McNamara roused him with a phone call in the pre-dawn hours of 5 August to report that two American ships had come under unprovoked attack by Vietnamese gun boats. It's not given to many of us to be called upon to wake out of a deep sleep, and then to issue immediate orders with the potential to start a full-scale nuclear exchange. According to the record, the pyjama-clad Johnson listened to the voice at the other end for a moment and then said: 'Oh? Now, I'll tell you what I want. I not only want those patrol boats that attacked the *Maddox* destroyed. I want everything in that harbor destroyed. I want the whole goddamn works destroyed. I want to give them a real dose.'

The result was that later that day Johnson sought and quickly obtained congressional support not only for immediate retaliatory strikes, but also a formal declaration backing increased US action in South East Asia as a whole. That evening, he told the American public in a televised speech about the 'brazen attack' in the Gulf: 'Aggression by terror against the peaceful villagers of South Vietnam has now been joined by open aggression on the high seas against the United States of America.'

The Tonkin Resolution, approved by an 88–2 vote of the US Senate, and one of 414-0 in the House of Representatives, duly gave 'approval and support for all measures deemed necessary by the Commander-in-Chief to repel and counter future attacks on the armed forces of the United States.' Johnson was delighted by this mandate, not least because it helped sustain the belief that he was just as tough on America's foreign adversaries as his hawkish Republican challenger in that autumn's presidential election, Barry Goldwater. US air strikes began almost immediately on selected targets in North Vietnam, the opening salvo of America's decade-long overseas nightmare. Of course few people recognised it as such at the time, least of all those in a position of any influence over events in the White House. The Tonkin resolution was 'like grandma's nightshirt – it covers everything', Johnson noted happily, with that gift for metaphor he displayed throughout his long career.

The president was also far too shrewd an operator not to grasp the electoral advantages afforded by Vietnam. Throughout the late summer and early autumn, he would consistently deny that he was doing anything but order a commensurate strike against Hanoi, the mandatory minimum, as it were, called for by the enemy's outrageous behaviour at Tonkin. Goldwater, by comparison, was a 'reckless warmonger' and 'shit-stirrer' not to be trusted anywhere near the nation's nuclear button. After his overwhelming victory in November, Johnson promptly authorised the escalation he had promised not to undertake, if even then remaining wary about letting the American public in on the full facts of their country's involvement. 'I consider it a matter of the highest importance,' he informed McNamara in early December, 'that the substance of this position should not become known unless I specifically direct it.' The president's idea seems to have been that he could bomb the troublesome North Vietnamese into silence before most people back home got to know enough about it to protest – if so, a presidential miscalculation to rival Kennedy's before it in approving a ramshackle attempted land invasion of Cuba, or Richard Nixon's collusion in a botched cover-up of the 'third-rate burglary job' at Washington's Watergate building that followed.

★★★

If the furious, invisible activity seething under the apparently tranquil surface of the Tonkin resolution was largely hidden from the American public, it was a complete mystery to the British. Even in the course of a lengthy Cabinet paper that summer entitled *An Anglo-American Balance Sheet*, Vietnam merited only two rather grudging sentences: 'The Americans need our support for their policies in south-east Asia, and [of] course we will generally give it. This may lead to some decline in our reputation for impartiality and thus of our general influence in the area, not least with the Americans themselves.'

Rather than trouble themselves with the nuances of a foreign policy intrigue in a little-known country on the other side of the world, most Britons were then more concerned with the fickle late-summer weather. Rain prevented a ball being bowled on the last scheduled day of the final Test match against Australia at the Oval, and bad light had interfered at regular intervals beforehand. Fred Trueman took his world record 300th Test wicket, and his young county colleague Geoff Boycott scored his first international century, a typically studious affair of nearly six hours, but things petered out from there into the fourth drawn match of the five-Test series.

It was also raining 200 miles away to the north-west, where Liverpool and West Ham drew 2-2 to share the FA Charity Shield, played in front of 38,000 fans, most of them standing on the terraces, at Anfield. There was no extra time, no penalty shoot-out and no replay. A week later, Sunderland's 15-year-old goalkeeper Derek Foster became the English first division's youngest ever player, a record he held until 2022. BBC 2's *Match of the Day* made its own debut later that evening, airing black-and-white highlights of the day's Liverpool–

Arsenal tie to a viewing audience of 20,000, less than half the total of those actually present at the ground. The new weekly programme was not universally welcomed in the football world. *The Times* asked why any self-respecting journalist like Kenneth Wolstenholme would wish to be involved with this 'tedium of recycled sport'. Later in the year several clubs attempted to block a renewed deal with the BBC from fear of a drop in gate attendances as a result. Today around 4 million people tune in each week to what's become a British institution older than most of the population, with a theme tune that's as recognisable to some as the national anthem, originally recorded by a classical composer named Barry Stoller ('not a football guy') in a north London basement studio, which he did for 'scale' union fees.

In the arts it was the summer of William Golding's *The Spire*, Roald Dahl's *Charlie and the Chocolate Factory* and Ian Fleming's *You Only Live Twice*. As noted, Fleming himself died in August 1964, having at least lived long enough to see two of his James Bond novels successfully launched as films, but narrowly missing the release of the surely definitive *Goldfinger*, with its central cast of Bond, the eponymous rogue bullion dealer, and a blonde-framed vision named Pussy Galore. The last went on to compete at the box office with *A Shot in the Dark*, *Mary Poppins* and *My Fair Lady*, and, perhaps moving a rung down the artistic evolutionary ladder, the likes of *Father Came Too!* and *Carry On Cleo*, while *The Mousetrap* celebrated the twelfth consecutive year of its apparently unstoppable run in the West End – with the possible exception of *Goldfinger*, 'all stuff you could safely take your gran to', as Terence Conran once said.

No one's gran was likely to have been present at the 3,000-seat Empress Ballroom in Blackpool when the Rolling Stones appeared there on a jungle-hot Friday night at the end of July 1964. It was the start of a three-day Scots bank holiday, and the barrel-vaulted old theatre was packed to capacity with day-tripping Glaswegians ('many of them,' Bill Wyman fastidiously notes, 'drunk'). First on the card was the 24-year-old Tom Jones, belting out his debut single 'Chills and Fever'. More than fifty years later, a fan named Matthew Kite could remember that it was so hot in the room that the fireman on duty backstage, with total immersion in his role, had taken to throwing buckets of water over both the performers and the first rows of the audience. Metaphorically fanning the flames, Jones then writhed and poked his crotch at the crowd throughout his peak decibel twenty-minute set, thus launching a long-running tradition: amid the screams, the first pairs of hurriedly shed lingerie came sailing over the footlights to land on the stage.

Next, the Rolling Stones. Excited by the obvious potential for chaos, Brian Jones (no relation, although he might as well have been) immediately began taunting the male members of the audience while mouthing amorous suggestions to their women. The Stones in turn came under a barrage not of bras and knickers, but of insults and shaken fists. Characteristically, Mick Jagger kept his distance while Keith Richards moved over to the centre of the action, the better to give the ringleader some verbal in between songs. Minutes later, the choppy intro to the band's recent single 'Not Fade Away' was cut short by the guitarist taking a gob of spittle to the face.

Even for those who had long experience of Keith's occasional flashes of temper, the tirade which thundered through the hall for the next several moments came as a shock.

'You Scotch *cunt*,' Richards shouted. At that he took one step forward, looked down, drew back his spindly right leg, and plunged a steel-toed boot into his critic's face.

In the ensuing riot, some £3,000-worth of musical equipment was immediately demolished, the theatre's municipal red-and-gold curtains were torn to shreds, a well-aimed bottle of beer brought down an antique chandelier, and one indignant customer climbed a safety rope at the side of the stage and swung there, apelike, from the rigging. A few minutes later, a further group of disgruntled ticket-holders succeeded in pushing a Steinway grand piano over the edge of the stage to the concrete floor below, thus ending its service for the night. Brian Jones later claimed that he had been hit over the head with a heavy BBC-issue microphone stand by a mob chanting 'Scotland, Scotland!', and then 'fucking nearly decapitated' by a cymbal flying through the air. 'Sensing trouble', as Jones later remarked with some restraint, he and his colleagues rapidly brought their tenure to an end. The five band members were spirited out of the building over a roof and placed in a police van, which eventually deposited them by the side of a road some 20 miles away on the B5208, leaving a reported £10,000-worth of damage, seventy-four arrests and fifty-eight injuries in their wake. It took Blackpool City council a further forty-four years to relax their ban on the Stones or any other such 'beat' group performing in their town.

Impressive as this was, in some ways it was eclipsed by what followed two weeks later at the Stones's concert at the Kurhaus theatre in The Hague, which if nothing else proved that adolescent frenzy in 1964 wasn't confined merely to the British Isles. Overexcited fans removed the band's microphone leads as early as the first number, leaving Mick Jagger and Charlie Watts to perform as a duet with drums, tambourine and maracas. Power was then partly restored, but even this arrangement came to an abrupt end in the face of a full-scale stage invasion. Keith Richards would later remember turning to look back at his colleague Ian Stewart, who was filling in on piano that night, and seeing only 'a pool of blood and a broken stool – he'd been hit over the head and taken to hospital'. Some years later, Richards would admit that at that point the thought had occurred to him that this might not be the occasion of one of those classic Sixties outpourings of peace and love. 'I fucked off at top speed,' he noted.

The subsequent damage to the hall itself was extensive, with Bill Wyman tutting that 'chairs were hanging from light fixtures [and] tapestries were torn from the walls,' as Jagger, Richards and Jones once again hurriedly left the premises, Charlie Watts adopted a distinctive crouching posture at his drum kit, and Bill himself stood stoically playing the bass, his face deadpan. But this was to prove only a prelude to a night of widespread civic looting and vandalism. 'Flames lighted the heavens,' the weekly *Haagsche Courant* wrote of the scene. 'One heard shots arising from the [theatre area], and riot police advanced on the crowd ... The wave of fanatical concertgoers soon spread to the town, where 6–7,000 chanting teenagers went on the rampage, many of them adorned with banners and flags, although some paraded around naked.'

★★★

The folk memory of life in many of the more deprived inner-city areas of Britain, perpetuated by the likes of the Kray brothers in 1964, was of a soiled, sad place full of feral gangs and entrepreneurs like the Krays themselves who operated in the contentious grey zone between security and extortion. The reported crime data tell a slightly different story. There were a total of 296 homicides, 200 cases of attempted murder and 2,672 of 'serious' or 'life-endangering' offences against the person during the year, compared with 710, 441 and roughly 24,000 respectively in 2022. In other words, statistically you were about nine times less likely to be violently assaulted than you are today. But there was still a wealth of bizarre and often graphically bloody offences for the 79,252 policemen on duty in England and Wales (one for every 807 citizens, compared with one to 462 today) to investigate. Among other things, the uniquely squalid affairs of the Moors Murderers Ian Brady and Myra Hindley took what later proved to be a significant turn when, on 15 August 1964, Hindley's 18-year-old sister Maureen married her boyfriend David Smith, a drooling, developmentally challenged youth of 16. The bride was seven months pregnant at the time, and none of her family attended the brief registry office ceremony, apparently out of a sense of shame at her condition.

The Hindley siblings, Brady and Smith did, however, go on to enjoy a sort of collective honeymoon by taking a four-day road trip through the Lake District. On the way, the two women sat in the front of their recently acquired minivan, with Myra at the wheel and the two men in the back. Brady took the opportunity to drink a good deal of beer and red wine of notably recent vintage, and to instruct the teenaged groom on the seat next to him in the ways of the world. 'Work,' he announced at one point, 'is something to pass the time of day. Crime is a lot easier, money-wise.' All three of the vehicle's other occupants applauded the sentiment. Smith later remarked that, gifted a social critic as Brady was, it was Myra who was the more dominant half of their strange partnership: '"You want bloody macaroni again?" she would scream, hurling the tin to the floor in disgust when Ian requested his favourite meal', all part of what Smith called a 'heavy' atmosphere which took as its root alcohol, pornography and a sort of pseudo-appreciation of the existentialist school of literature, with a smattering of the Marquis de Sade thrown in. Back home in Manchester, the two couples agreed to stay in close touch.

Meanwhile, in the early hours of 7 April 1964 the police had found a 53-year-old delivery driver named John Alan West lying in a pool of blood on the floor of the small terraced house where he lived alone on Kings Avenue in Seaton, Cumberland. He had first been bludgeoned and then stabbed to death. Within forty-eight hours, two men had been arrested and charged with West's murder. They were 24-year-old Gwynne Evans and 21-year-old Peter Allen. Both individuals were of below average intelligence and both had criminal records. They knew the deceased from work, and had driven to his house in a stolen car in order to extract money from him. Matters had soon become 'heated', a jury later heard, with the results noted. What perhaps most strikes the modern observer isn't so much the relatively mundane detail of the crime itself, but the speed of the subsequent proceedings: arrested in April, Evans and Allen went on trial for murder in the middle of June, and were found guilty and sentenced two days later. Both their appeals were dismissed on 20 July and they were hung in the early hours of 13 August at prisons in Manchester and Liverpool respectively, making it just over four months from the time of their original offence to their deaths. They remain the last two judicial executions to be carried out in the United Kingdom, where an act of parliament sponsored by a Labour MP and wartime conscientious objector named Sydney Silverman led to the abolition of the death penalty in November 1965.

HERE COMES THE SUN

Sir Alec Douglas-Home, the affable if somewhat vapid scion of a landed family who disclaimed no fewer than six peerages to become prime minister, was in some ways a curious choice as chief executive of a nation grappling with a distinct post-war demographic bulge that seemed to have left it full of young people with ever lengthening hair and shortening skirts, in thrall to an insinuating soundtrack of the Beatles and Stones, and where provincial accents now penetrated even the once exclusively Oxbridge domains of the BBC. Douglas-Home himself had turned 61 that summer, but seemed about twenty years older. He had cut his political teeth as the MP for rural Lanark in the 1930s, and was known as a perfectly competent young lawmaker with a love of hunting, shooting and horse racing – always carrying about with him a form book for the turf – if possessing no great gifts of imagination or insight. At the height of the Great Depression, Douglas-Home had once remarked in the Commons that unemployed coal miners and their families might be brought down from Scotland to the London area to work as domestic servants. Personally genial as he was, the PM did not seem to conspicuously personify enterprise or relevance to contemporary values, and by 1964 his language, the way he dressed and even the way he wore his half-moon spectacles – whatever the formidable brain that might lurk behind them – all made him like a creature from a different galaxy.

On 25 September, having announced the fact some days earlier, the premier saw the Queen to formally ask for a dissolution of Parliament, with the election to follow on 15 October. He had waited until the last permitted moment to do so, and, knowingly or not, placed the opposition party under some financial pressure in the process. Having long anticipated an election the previous spring, Labour had poured time and money into a mass publicity campaign that had palpably run out of steam by midsummer. Perhaps the PM was not quite the amateurish political naïf, devoid of the most basic gifts of oratory or calculation, his critics believed. The Labour firebrand Michael Foot, noting Douglas-Home's tendency to be tougher behind the scenes than his detached, slightly dotty public persona suggested, once called him 'a belligerent Bertie Wooster without a Jeeves to restrain him.'

For all that, a note of gentlemanly diffidence distinguished even the PM's private pre-election remarks, as minuted by the Cabinet secretary on 22 September:

> The [Prime Minister] said that in order to avoid any misunderstanding, ministers might perhaps wish to instruct their departments that departmental information services could properly continue to discharge their normal functions during the forthcoming campaign, provided that they took care to limit these activities to factual explanation of current government statements and administrative decisions, and did not in any way become involved in the advocacy of the government's forward policies from a party political point of view. This instruction would need to be interpreted with reasonable common sense.

Displaying the same spirit of remoteness from the sordid mechanics of a modern democratic election campaign, Rab Butler, the foreign secretary, added:

> The international position is relatively quiescent for the time being, and there would seem to be little action we might usefully take to promote our party's cause, apart from keeping in touch with developments through the United States representative in the Geneva [nuclear disarmament] talks and the secretary-general of the North Atlantic Treaty Organisation.

When the campaign itself got under way, Douglas-Home largely preferred to take what could be called the presidential route of standing above the fray. While many grass-roots Conservative party members yearned for a fighter who could give voice to their concerns that the social fabric of the country was apparently being ripped up before their eyes, and the whole place going to the dogs as a result, the PM chose a more passive path – blaming 'permissiveness', urging people to remain calm, stressing his own credentials as a foreign affairs expert at a time when the Soviet Union might still be thought to present 'a not inconsiderable challenge to our way of life', and avoiding heated rhetorical battles. His was the voice of reason.

Labour's feisty leader Harold Wilson, in some ways a strange mixture of progressiveness and pipe-smoking, Gannex-wearing 1950s Northern tradition, less constrained by any notions of aristocratic reserve, lost no opportunity to remind voters that Douglas-Home was not only a belted earl but that he used matchsticks to help him solve financial problems. Nothing could encapsulate more clearly Wilson's central message that he, a former Oxford economics don, was the technocrat, and his opponent a bumbling innumerate, or, extrapolating from that, a case of professional pitted against amateur, the future against the past.

Wilson had first disclosed Labour's core theme of the 1964 election campaign nearly a year earlier, when he addressed his annual party conference at Scarborough:

> Mr Chairman, let me conclude with what I think the whole message is for this conference, because in this conference, in all our plans for the future, we are re-defining and we are re-stating our Socialism in terms of the scientific revolution. But that revolution cannot become a reality unless we are prepared to make far-reaching changes in economic and social attitudes which permeate our whole system of society.
>
> The Britain that is going to be forged in the white heat of this revolution will be no place for restrictive practices or for outdated methods on either side of industry. In the Cabinet room and the board room alike, those charged with the control of our affairs must be ready to think and to speak in the language of our scientific age.

Reflecting in later years on what became known as his 'white heat of technology' speech, Wilson wrote that his principal goal had been to 'replace the cloth cap [with] the white laboratory coat as the symbol of British labour', a transformation all his successors in office have to one degree or another attempted to duplicate. Perhaps the real question being asked of the British electorate in the autumn of 1964 was to choose between a prime minister who could somehow unlock the hitherto suppressed reserves of intellectual and scientific talent frustrated by companies run by public school boys whose authority was based on unearned privilege rather than merit, and one who could be – and was – caricatured as a hopelessly archaic relic out of the Jurassic era, fossilised, obsolete, and, above all, Old Etonian.

Britain's 'hour of once-in-a-century destiny', as Wilson modestly put it, did not, however, yet obsess the public, if it ever did, quite as much as the politicians themselves. The nation's headlines in August and September were that familiar half-world of scandal, crisis and celebrity trivia that remained the approved formula. Motorway pile-ups, air disasters, bank jobs and murders and industrial chaos and the eternal fascination with the House of Windsor, along with periodic Fleet Street 'investigations' into the more unorthodox household practices of the country's elite, all came around as frequently as stops on the Circle Line. On the day after the PM formally moved for the dissolution of parliament, the *Daily Mirror*, virtually the bulletin board of the opposition Labour party, was concerned not so much with the historic opportunity this provided for societal change, as with the front page splash: 'Test Tube Babies Inquiry Set Up'. The next day's paper was similarly exercised with a report on the nation's supply of tranquillisers, while the inside pages saw stories under the arresting headlines: 'Rolls Reward For Finding Parrot', 'Punched At The Private Eyes' Club', '80 Escape As "Pyjama Express" Crashes', 'BOAC To Go Ahead With Mass Sacking', 'Maid Savaged By TV Star's Dog' and the surely inimitable 'Machine-gun Shock In M'Lord's Stolen Suitcase', all of which took precedence over the fine detail of the election.

The society photographer Cecil Beaton was born in 1904 and, with his elaborately foppish frock coats and tendency to himself pose for the camera with a budgerigar poised on his arched finger, was perhaps not entirely representative of the invigorating new Britain of which Harold Wilson had spoken. Nonetheless, his account of a journey that autumn from London to a wedding party in Northumberland captures the materially gilded if incandescently empty spirit of a certain side of British life:

A pre-nuptial gaiety in cold dark King's Cross station with Lucian Freud and Ann Fleming, Paddy Leigh Fermor, etc. Arrival in north before daylight, cold, bleak moor scenery, Cheviot Hills, and our goal a turreted black and white Gothic house with light blazing in every window ... Tony [Lambton], whom I like in spite of his appalling caddishness, said that the bridegroom's mother was appearing at the wedding in a dress she had bought for £20! – that the father had got drunk last night – while the bride had refused to talk to her fiancé on the telephone, shouting that the whole thing was a mistake, hence the father took to the bottle, fell, hurt his eye and had to be guided to bed. [When I] arrived the bride's mother, still in plaster with a broken leg from a go-karting accident, was shouting at people to leave her Clapham Junction bedroom while she dressed the children's hair. Tony himself was yelling to the bride in the bath, 'Why in the world didn't you sign that document as you were told? Now the whole thing is ruined and we'll have to pay death duties.'

Even a P.G. Wodehouse or an Evelyn Waugh might not have been disappointed by the comic potential of a certain strain of British country house life that existed even in the rapidly approaching white light of Harold Wilson's revolution.

Beaton, though not indifferent to the charms of an attractive woman – as well as Garbo, there were affairs with the American dancer Adele Astaire, sister of Fred, and the London socialite Doris Castlerosse – was more personally inclined to his own sex. He had learned to be discreet about it, because, although no longer subject to the death penalty, as had been the case until late Victorian times, 'acts of gross indecency with male persons', even when the parties were consenting adults, remained punishable by a minimum term of two years' hard labour. Beaton wrote in his diary of the gradual 1960s change of attitude on the subject:

Of recent years the tolerance towards this matter has made a nonsense of many of the prejudices from which I myself suffered acutely as a young man. Even I can only vaguely realise that it was only comparatively late in life that I would go into a room full of people without a feeling of guilt.

If Queen Victoria had possessed more understanding than we could expect of her, the world would have been without so much suffering. Fear of blackmail, fear of prison, fear of loss of all worldly hope in their professions could have been avoided by thousands. Politicians would not have suffered the sudden axing of their career from the moment of 'scandal'.

'For myself I am grateful,' Beaton concluded:

Selfishly, I only wish that this marvellous step forward could have been taken at an earlier age. It is not that I would have wished to avail myself of further licence, but to feel that one was not a felon and an outcast would have helped enormously during the difficult young years.

This was all very encouraging, but it would only be fair to add that in 1964 most attitudes to any deviation from prevailing rules of conduct, whether moral or physical, might strike us today as somewhat rigid. Apart from the strictures of the law itself, published references to any gay or lesbian activity still tended to be couched in phrases like 'the abnormality' or 'the condition', while even in his report recommending the partial decriminalising of such acts, the former public school headmaster Sir John Wolfenden preferred to use the odd code name 'Huntley and Palmers' – the biscuit manufacturer – Huntley for homosexuals, Palmers for prostitutes or pimps. Tony Gill on the *Sketch* was told that the words 'unnatural', 'pervert' and 'vice' were acceptable usage for stories involving male inversion, but that any reference to lesbianism should be brought first to the notice of a city editor who 'appeared to quite enjoy hearing any details that might be going about heaving breasts and spanking and the like'. This last individual's personal tastes seem to have been commendably inclusive, because he was later arrested following an incident in the changing room of the menswear department at Harrods and left his position at the paper as a result.

★★★

When the *Daily Mirror* of 28 September 1964 led with the front page splash 'Whose Finger On The Tranquillisers?' the paper was chiefly concerned with the introduction and rapid availability in Britain of the 'miracle pick-me-up', Valium. The drug had first come on the UK market in the summer of 1963. Within eighteen months, Valium use had reached what we would classify today as epidemic proportions. GPs wrote 2 million prescriptions in England alone in the period from March 1964 to February 1965, and the annual figure would reach 4.8 million by the end of the decade. In time Valium became, along with LSD, the physically smallest icon of its generation, if one with vast consequences. Many of those originally introduced to the drug or its derivatives as young men and women would find themselves struggling with their addiction many years later. Valium's triumph inspired every large pharmaceutical company to market an antidepressant of its own: Upjohn was soon competing with Xanax; Wyeth would grow wealthy from Ativan. The typical user of the day was characterised as a stressed housewife who became hooked in her suburban home – much as portrayed by the Rolling Stones in their song 'Mother's Little Helper' – or as a tranquillised zombie, like the women in Jacqueline Susanne's bestselling novel *Valley of the Dolls*, but the truth is that most such drugs are no respecter of age, sex or social class; they destroy lives indiscriminately.

'My wife Joan says Valium turned me into a robot,' a retired Oldham electrical engineer named Keith Andrew would reflect, some fifty-eight years after first being prescribed the drug. 'The tablets calmed me down at first,' Andrew says:

> But within a few months I began to feel nothing at all ... They dulled all my emotions and I withdrew into a shell. I just went to work and fell asleep in a chair when I came home. I then started to have regular panic attacks and insomnia, too, while my weight fell from more than 11 stone to 7 stone 10 lbs. My GP kept writing my repeat prescriptions.

It was not just the lives of stereotypical stuttering, hollow-eyed junkies that were ruined, in other words, but those of millions of otherwise productive men and women at all levels of society: people crippled emotionally by their dependency, whether enabled by a doctor, or more inclined to steal and lie to feed a habit not generally compatible with a stable family life. It's surely one of the strange paradoxes of the 1960s that so many mood-altering substances intended to expand human potential should have proved so damaging and, in all too many cases, fatal.

A brash new kid now entered the jauntier end of the Fleet Street block in the form of *The Sun*, launched, initially in broadsheet form, on 15 September 1964. The paper rose out of the ashes of the old trade union *Daily Herald* and, as we've seen, had ambitions to share in Harold Wilson's vision of a Britain in the grip of a white-hot revolution, positioning itself as the news outlet of choice for the men (and to a lesser extent, women) in their crisp white lab coats whom Wilson saw as the future. The somewhat unlikely cabal behind the paper its owners boasted would be a 'beacon of truth ... geared to the bracing mental attitudes and new interests of the mid-1960s' were the 63-year-old Winchester- and Oxford-educated media baron Cecil King, who would later go on to seriously propose that the country's democratically elected prime minister be removed from office and replaced by a ruling junta led by Lord Mountbatten; and King's editorial director Hugh Cudlipp, 51, known equally for his abrasive charm and commitment to the Labour party until he, too, came to fear that it had travelled too far down the road to extremism and, as Baron Cudlipp, defected to the Social Democrats in the House of Lords.

In keeping with Wilson's ideal, the new paper was designed to symbolically cast off the old cloth cap and brown overalls of the British working man and embrace the exciting, technocratic future that apparently lay just around the corner.

'Look at how life has changed,' *The Sun's* first editorial noted:

> Five million Britons now holiday abroad every year. Half our population is under 35 years of age. Steaks, cars, houses, refrigerators, washing-machines are no longer the prerogative of the upper crust, but the right of all. People believe, and we believe with them, that the division of Britain into social classes is happily out of date.

The Sun, or rather Cecil King, a man whose socialist zeal did not preclude him serving as a part-time director of the Bank of England, nor whose pursuit of the truth extended to believing that the Holocaust had occurred, spent £400,000 (£6.4 million today) on a campaign to promote the new daily, with TV commercials branded with a blazing sun and the slogan 'Time for a paper born of the age we live in', along with a less well-publicised champagne party at London's Café

Royal to toast the new symbol of social equity and classlessness. King also splashed out a reported £30,000 on christening mugs for British babies born in September 1964 to celebrate their good fortune in arriving at the same time as *The Sun*, and as much again on supplying free beer to their parents. The paper initially fulfilled all its backers' hopes for it, selling a daily 3.6 million copies at threepence each. But the collective euphoria seems to have worn off, because the figure had halved by the end of the first week of publication. By the end of 1964, King's once upbeat charts and graphs had to be turned upside down as newsstand sales fell to less than a million. Five years later, *The Sun* was down to around 700,000, which gave an enterprising young Australian media tycoon called Rupert Murdoch the opportunity to buy the paper on knock-down terms and promptly relaunch it as a tabloid, ironically with an 'exclusive interview' with Harold Wilson in the first issue, if discreetly tucked away inside, behind a front page splashed with the headline 'Horse Dope Sensation' and several photographs of skimpily clad (if not yet quite topless) young women. Such was the promise and reality of King and Cudlipp's British media revolution.

★★★

When it came to the autumn 1964 election, *The Sun* made no bones of its support for the populist new age of affluence and technology apparently represented by Labour. 'We are a radical newspaper,' the launch editor Sydney Jacobson informed one of his reporters, who dutifully published the fact. For reasons that are part of the inscrutable workings of Britain's election process, *The Sun* quickly rose to a position of tribal leadership among first Labour and then, under Murdoch, Conservative prime ministerial hopefuls. Seeking the editor of *The Sun*'s blessing would become a ritual of self-abasement that successive candidates aspiring to high office would undergo for the next sixty years. The resulting spectacle in 1964 was partly comic and partly tragic. At one extreme, there were comments such as, 'Now that you see me in the flesh, I hope you'll agree that I'm not really the ogre I'm made to look on the televisor [*sic*],' as Douglas-Home told the paper by way of an 'unprecedented insight' into his character while on the election trail. At the other, there was the same PM's perhaps ill-judged boast that 'What had been a trickle of immigrants from the Commonwealth has now developed into a flood, [and] we saw that if it was not brought under control it would create very serious problems. So we brought in legislation to stop them.' This last remark was deemed to be 'vile', at least to *The Sun*'s pioneering vision of a multicultural Britain.

It was mild stuff compared with the scene on the streets of the Birmingham suburb of Smethwick (Oswald Mosley's old manor), then possibly the most colour-conscious of the nation's 630 parliamentary constituencies, where the Conservative candidate Peter Griffiths may not have uttered, but never disowned, the widely heard campaign slogan, 'If you want a n***** for a neighbour, vote Labour.'

Pressed further on the issue, Griffiths, a 36-year-old local headmaster and borough councillor, remarked only that the phrase was a 'manifestation of the popular feeling. I would not condemn anyone who said it. That is how people see the situation in Smethwick. I would say it is exasperation, not fascism.' If nothing else, Griffiths could at least claim to have been born and bred in the Black Country, as opposed to his Labour opponent, the scholarly and liberal-minded shadow home secretary Patrick Gordon Walker, who had held the seat for the last nineteen years, but happened to live in London's genteel Hampstead Garden Suburb. Walker had opposed the introduction of the immigration quotas cited by Douglas-Home; Griffiths wanted them to be significantly tougher. It all led to one of the most charged election campaigns ever seen in the UK, with busloads of activists arriving daily from Labour's Transport House headquarters in London, to be met by supporters of the Conservative candidate brandishing explicitly phrased placards, some of which might later have run afoul of the terms of the Racial and Religious Hatred Act.

Griffiths may have played to people's anxieties about a housing shortage in Smethwick by blaming the problem on immigrants, but the local Labour party could hardly aspire to the moral high ground on the matter. As configured in 1964, it was far from a model of inclusiveness. Several of the Labour-affiliated working men's clubs specifically excluded black people, while other places of entertainment expressed their disapproval by a codified entry policy akin to the apartheid system in South Africa, sometimes reinforced by more robustly applied tactics that might have won an admiring nod from the Kray brothers. 'Colour bars were common here at that time,' a retired Smethwick social worker named Harbhajan Dardi would recall more than fifty years later. 'Barbers would make the Asian customers wait three, four, five hours while they cut white people's hair. In those days [local] pubs had a no blacks rule. People like me couldn't get served.'

When the final results were counted, Gordon Walker lost on a 7.2 per cent swing to the Conservatives that reduced his vote from 20,670 in the previous election to 14,916. The following week, Griffiths duly took his seat among lively scenes in the House of Commons, where Harold Wilson claimed that the new member should 'serve his term here as a parliamentary leper.' At that, twenty Conservative MPs promptly left the chamber in protest at Wilson's remarks, and Griffiths himself observed, 'If Harold wants a fight, he can have one.' He lost his seat at Smethwick in the next election, wrote a book entitled *A Question of Colour*, and later re-emerged to take Portsmouth North for the Tories, holding the seat until the 1997 Labour landslide. He 'made little impact in those latter years,' the *Telegraph* concluded, 'never quite living down the extraordinary epithet with which Wilson had branded him'. Peter Griffiths died in Portsmouth in November 2013, aged 85.

It's mildly incongruous that in the midst of a local campaign as rancourous and occasionally violent as that of any British general election since 1945, the largest crowds to be seen on the streets of central Birmingham in the second half of September were those not waiting to hear Peter Griffiths or his Labour opponent speak, but queuing to pay their 3s 9d (£3 today) to escape for two hours into a fantasy world whose most potent images were those of a nude young woman killed by being smothered in gold paint, a mute Korean assassin with an unusually lethal bowler hat, an all-female flying circus spraying nerve gas over the US bullion depository at Fort Knox, and a laser beam pointed at that portion of the hero's lower anatomy most required for his continued success as a womaniser, all accompanied by a breezily melodramatic title song belted out by Shirley Bassey with the ubiquitous Jimmy Page once again on guitar. If some evil force were to eliminate all we now know about the twenty-five-plus James Bond films, only *Goldfinger* remaining, it's a fair bet we could reconstruct from it every outline of the basic formula, every essential character and flavour contributing to the franchise we still flock to today. If *Goldfinger* isn't the best of the bunch, it's the one that can stand as a surrogate for all the others. It's also important as a link between the more modest first two Bond outings and the later big-budget extravaganzas; after this one, with an immediate $42 million ($630 million today) at the international box office, the producers could be certain that 007 was good for the long haul.

Goldfinger, like many of Ian Fleming's fictional tales, was not pure invention. It was inspired by the swashbuckling exploits of the Anglo-Canadian spymaster William Stephenson, whose wartime scheme – ultimately frustrated – to relieve the collaborationist Vichy French government of their gold reserves held on the Caribbean island of Martinique had come to Fleming's attention as a young operative with British naval intelligence. The film had other, more contemporary connections. *Goldfinger*'s celebrated title sequence, with its fast-paced if shamelessly sexist introduction of the film's cast by a series of images flickering over a woman's nude body, was the work of a quirkily brilliant London-based New Jersey transplant named Robert Brownjohn. In the summer of 1962, Keith Richards, then a fitfully employed musician and aspiring graphic artist, had taken his portfolio on a dismal tour of the main West End design houses. Most of the impeccably well-groomed executives he met there couldn't wait to get the pill-chewing young punk out of their offices, but the future Rolling Stone long remembered that the 'cat who did the Pussy Galore [*sic*] titles' had at least been civil to his visitor. Several years later, Keith repaid the courtesy by commissioning Brownjohn to design the cover of the Stones's album *Let It Bleed*, which in its way proved as epochal a Sixties pop artefact as *Goldfinger* itself.

A new kind of action hero also made his debut that month with the first in the Clint Eastwood spaghetti-western trilogy *A Fistful of Dollars*. Eastwood, then a 33-year-old, modestly successful TV cowboy, had been sent a screenplay called *The Magnificent Stranger* after half-a-dozen better-known actors had passed on it. About five pages into the script, he recognised elements of the Japanese director Akira Kurosawa's 1961 samurai film *Yojimbo*. Eastwood thought the dialogue to the project in his hand 'atrocious', but the storyline 'intelligently laid out' with a certain vein of seemingly intentional dark humour. The result was that he agreed to make the film for a fee of $12,000 and economy-class air fare to and from the shooting location in the rugged southern Spanish province of Almeria. 'I figured I'd have some money and a vacation,' he remembered.

There were certain practical difficulties to the ensuing eleven-week project: the film's director Sergio Leone spoke only Italian, Eastwood spoke only English, and most of the rest of the cast and crew spoke either German or Spanish. Because the budget limited his access to a full orchestra, the film's composer Ennio Morricone turned in a soundtrack punctuated by the noise of whistles, screams, gunshots, cracking whips and howling wolves, backed by an incongruously lush soaring chorus. The whole mismatched farrago should logically have gone on to take its place among the likes of *Star Wars Holiday Special* or *Two-Headed Shark Attack* and other would-be dramatic films so bad they're enjoyably funny, instead of which it quickly returned $20 million on its $185,000 budget and made Clint Eastwood a global star, his poncho and half-chewed cheroot as expressive in their way of a certain kind of male élan as Sean Connery's ivory dinner jacket and double-cuffed shirts in *Goldfinger*. For his next outing with Leone, the aptly named *For a Few Dollars More*, Eastwood got $100,000 and first-class air fare.

★ ★ ★

Perhaps the single most compulsory viewing on British television that year, at least if you were under about 25, was Rediffusion's early Friday evening *Ready Steady Go! (RSG)*. Opening with the evocative line 'The weekend starts here!', it was presented from a cramped room at Television House in a gloomy side alley in Holborn, central London, by a 20-year-old woman named Cathy McGowan who got the job after being asked by the show's producers, 'What do you think young people in this country care about most?' 'Clothes,' she said. McGowan herself, whose coal-black eyes and slightly clenched smile gave off a whiff of youthful rebelliousness, was an early patron of the newly opened London fashion store Biba, with its gaudily styled, and, to parents, worryingly androgynous line of gypsy smocks, embroidered caftans and ornately beaded slippers. As the social historian Dominic Sandbrook says, 'She wore all the latest trendy shifts and mini-dresses; and she spoke with an earnest, classless barrage of teenage slang, praising whatever was "fab" or "smashing", and damning all that was "square" or "out".' The resulting atmosphere in the *RSG* studio was akin to a slightly chaotic house party run by children while the grown-ups were away. With engaging frequency, the lights on the stage would fail, the presenter would forget her lines, or a heavy camera would plunge into a group of gyrating dancers. Everything was excitingly casual, breathless, and prone to suddenly go wrong. It was appointment viewing.

The *RSG* episode aired on 18 September 1964, while the adults of the world were waiting expectantly for the starting gun of the general election campaign, saw the Animals, the Zombies and the Hollies in fast succession, before taking it down a notch with Dionne Warwick singing a mid-paced Burt Bacharach ballad 'You'll Never Get to Heaven (If You Break My Heart)'. The following Friday brought Gerry and the Pacemakers, Wayne Fontana and Little Eva of 'The Loco-Motion' fame, while the broadcast of 2 October featured artists as diverse as the scowling 52-year-old John Lee Hooker of Tutwiler, Mississippi, his narrowed eyes and upthrust guitar offering a palpable hint of menace to polite English sensibilities, followed by Lulu and Birmingham's Keith Powell and the Vikings performing their own energetic, if only partly convincing, version of the blues. As some ten million weekly viewers came to appreciate, it was *RSG*, rather than the more tightly choreographed *Top of the Pops*, that would insinuate a winning combination of pop and rock, and even defiantly black American music, into English suburban homes. 'It emptied the streets every Friday night,' Paul McCartney once remarked.

The Beatles themselves twice graced the rather unlovely *RSG* building (it soon moved to new premises in Wembley) in 1964, thus presenting the viewing public with the mildly unusual spectacle of a television studio apparently being kicked to matchsticks by its young audience members. In September, the group was back in America, where, sitting around New York's Delmonico Hotel late one night, they first met the tousle-haired, somewhat dazed-looking figure of 23-year-old Bob Dylan – 'a pop-music equivalent of the wartime Allies converging at Yalta', one eminent rock author has written, although, perhaps deviating from the practice of a Winston Churchill or Josef Stalin, Dylan himself came bearing marijuana. McCartney, traditionally the Beatles' point-man on such matters, put his introductory roach in his mouth, lit it and slipped Dylan's own LP *The Times They Are A-Changin'* on the turntable. A toke or two later, and Paul suddenly discovered the meaning of life, which he had the presence of mind to jot down on a scrap of paper. Squinting at his notes in the cold light of dawn, he read, 'There are seven levels,' which was good as far as it went, even if the particulars were missing.

In scenes out of *A Hard Day's Night*, the Beatles made their post-gig getaway the next evening in Atlantic City by means of jumping off a pier into a speedboat, which took them offshore to a waiting hospital ship. Several hours later, back in the Lafayette Hotel, McCartney rather ungallantly recalled the four musicians as 'knee-high in crumpet, [with] girls being delivered like they were room service'. Regrettably, it was also a theme with the Beatles throughout their career that no joyful experience remained untinged by another, rather less happy one for very long. A few nights later, Lennon and McCartney sat down over drinks supplied by their roadie Mal Evans for what was supposed to be a brief songwriting session, and instead began talking about money. It's unlikely that a self-made near-millionaire of John Lennon's stature could be found who knew less about personal finance than he did. At this point, he still had no idea how to balance a cheque book, nor that loans were generally repaid at interest. When, back home, he casually signed for two new cars, a Maxi and a Mini, he thought that 'the firm' would simply foot the bill. Because it was impossible to listen to Lennon for very long without wanting to impart advice, McCartney now said something responsible about how he and his wife Cynthia might wish to draw up a budget. John went 'mental', Mal Evans reported, 'and told Paul to fuck off'.

On 22 September, the *New York Times* wrote, 'The Beatles flew home to England yesterday with the rings of girlish shrieks and more than $1 million in receipts as the echoes of their month-long tour ... It was considered one of the most successful of its kind in profit, attendance and attention.' The paper added that, while the band left New York in relative quiet, 'four thousand screaming youths gave them an uproarious welcome when they landed early in the morning at London airport'.

In the intervals between debating the merits of the Beatles and the other successive waves of British Invasion bands, America was now increasingly in thrall to 'the most important battle in history for our nation's soul' as Lyndon Johnson, taking a leaf from Harold Wilson's book, called the autumn's presidential poll. It would not be the last race to be so described in a country where every election result must be portrayed as triumph or disaster.

In the steady ratcheting-up of rhetoric that occurs in America every fourth autumn, it's long been true that both Republican and Democratic parties must pretend that civilisation itself hangs in the balance; certain doom will follow should their opponents somehow come to power. On 7 September 1964, the Johnson camp unlocked another level of alarmism: a vote for the president's challenger, the 55-year-old Arizona senator Barry Goldwater, was a vote for nuclear annihilation. Such was the key theme of the widely aired 'Daisy' TV commercial, which remains to this day the most famous political ad ever made, and the template for the pervasive end-of-humanity scare-mongering we expect of a modern campaign.

The spot opened with a shot of a little girl in a field of flowers, picking petals off a daisy as she counts falteringly from one to ten. As the girl reaches nine, she pauses, and a booming male voice then cuts in, this time counting backwards from ten. The camera pans in on the girl's right eye, which dissolves to black, followed by the flash of an atomic explosion. As viewers continued to watch the mushroom cloud, Johnson's distinctive Texan voice exclaimed: 'These are the stakes! To make a world in which all of God's children can live, or to go into the dark. We must either love each other, or we must die!' Lest there be any doubt of the practical message of the ad, an announcer's voice then added: 'Vote for President Johnson on November 3! The stakes are too high for you to stay home.'

Other successive Johnson ads pushed home the same theme: Goldwater, like his near-namesake villain in the latest Bond film, was a dangerous nut, while he, Johnson, was the man of reason who loved all people. (This last part may be true: in Joseph Califano's definitive *The Triumph and Tragedy of Lyndon Johnson*, the president spends a distressing amount of time naked, while reporters had long been aware of a special executive retreat reserved for his use in the US Senate, known as the 'nooky room'.) A few days later, a new ad ran showing a second little girl, this one licking an ice-cream cone. A woman's voice cuts in to explain that nuclear isotopes in the atmosphere are harmful to our children. A nice man in the White House had recently concluded a nuclear test-ban treaty to make the radioactive poisons go away, the voice continued, but 'now there is someone who doesn't like this treaty. He voted against it. He wants to go on testing more bombs. His name is Barry Goldwater, and if he's elected, we might start testing all over again.' A few days later, an American magazine named *fact* (so styled) ran a story under the headline 'The Unconscious of a Conservative', in which, among other things, they claimed that the Republican candidate was mentally unsound and a 'certified schizophrenic'. Goldwater sued and won $65,000 ($1 million today) in punitive damages.

Somehow inevitably, the next Democratic attack ad went on to imply that the president's challenger was a racist, with a film clip showing

Ku Klux Klansmen burning a cross and the voiceover: 'I like Barry Goldwater. He needs our help.' Taken as a whole, the core message was that Goldwater and his brand of conservatism represented an existential threat to the republic, and to warn of the imminent demise not just of American democracy, but of man's continued existence, should he be elected.

By the end of September, opinion polls showed President Johnson with a two to one lead over his challenger, and even other Republicans avoided the seemingly radioactive Goldwater. By and large, the press – these were the days before talk radio and the internet – took Johnson at his word, dutifully calling on their readers and listeners to vote for the incumbent, failing which this might be the last free election in history. Some of these same civic-minded journalists might have been surprised to learn what their commander-in-chief privately thought of them. 'Reporters are just puppets,' Johnson noted to a room full of trusted staff members. 'They respond to the pull of the most powerful. And I control the fucking strings.'

Of course, Johnson was right to highlight the perils of nuclear arms – no sane office seeker, after all, stands on a platform of appealing for enhanced means with which to deliberately shorten man's survival. But in the heat of the campaign, perhaps it slipped the president's mind that the concept of the world's two hostile superpowers targeting not only each other's military facilities, but their civilian populations as well, was a wholly owned initiative of the Democratic administration of 1961–63 of which he himself was vice-president. This new strategy became known as 'Mutual Assured Destruction' – or, with a certain grim aptness, MAD – and its underlying logic was that if neither side could be sure of surviving a nuclear exchange, there would not be one. Both Presidents Kennedy and Johnson had spoken alarmingly in this context of a 'missile gap' that supposedly existed between the United States and the Soviet Union. So wretched was the state of America's home-based nuclear hardware, Kennedy had declared, that his country had had no choice but to place its intermediate-range missiles in Britain, Italy and Turkey, all aimed at the Soviet Union.

By the autumn of 1964 there was indeed a significant disparity between the two sides' nuclear capabilities, but the true balance of power was not quite as Kennedy or, latterly, Johnson had described it. Depending on how the terms were defined, the US had from twelve to eighteen times the number of usable warheads the Soviets did.

In fact, there were only six operational long-range missile sites located in the USSR. Because each missile took a full twenty-four hours to fuel, leaving them vulnerable to attack by the American bombers that continually circled over the Norwegian Sea, ready to move on the commander-in-chief's order to their preassigned targets in the USSR, this meant that the total number of effective weapons at Nikita Khrushchev's (or, from 14 October, Leonid Brezhnev's) disposal was just that: six. 'It always sounded good to say in public speeches that we could hit a fly at any distance with our rockets,' Khrushchev later admitted, 'so I exaggerated a little.' It remains a sobering thought that in the second half of 1964 the primary focus of the leaders of the two rival nuclear powers lay not in curbing the arms race but in exploiting it for political advantage.

There was another incident, meanwhile, at the permanent crisis point of the Cold War, with the fifty-second and perhaps most contentious death at the Berlin Wall: that of 21-year-old Egon Schultz, an East German Volkspolizei, or 'Vopo', officer who was killed on the night of 5 October in a shoot-out with a group of tunnellers escaping to the West. It only later transpired that Schultz had died as a result of 'friendly' fire from one of his own comrades. Long treated as a case of a fallen martyr to a 'gang of imperialist bandits' from the West, to quote Walter Ulbricht, the truth emerged only with the release of East German state files in November 1990, at which point both Egon-Schultz Strasse and other such public memorials in the Soviet bloc were quietly returned to their original names.

Then lucky enough to be in the eleventh year of his tenure as first secretary of the Communist Party of the USSR, if with less of his term ahead of him than he might have imagined, Nikita Khrushchev was clearly still consumed by the topic of Berlin, variously referring to it as 'a cancer', 'a thorn', a 'bone in my throat' and 'the testicles of the West, [to be] squeezed for good effect'. The Soviet hardman was not pleased when on 13 September 1964 West German and US military police fought one of their recurrent gun battles with opposing Red Army and Vopo personnel as a popular East German jockey named Michel Meyer managed to clamber over a barbed-wire fence at Checkpoint Charlie with the help of a rope the American guards threw him, while elsewhere in the city that day Martin Luther King announced, 'Here on either side of the Wall are God's children and no man-made barrier can change that.' In fact, on hearing of these developments,

Khrushchev went on a rampage. If the West truly wanted a fight over the divided city, he announced, they would be 'squashed like bugs', their own towns and villages reduced to 'piles of dog shit'. Any future war was bound to be thermonuclear, the red tsar added, with that ability he had to pass rapidly from the scatological and faintly ludicrous to the frankly terrifying. Following any such exchange, the USSR and United States might survive, Khrushchev supposed, but America's European allies would be wiped off the map, reduced to a 'grease spot' the Russians would in time obligingly 'mop up' as a kind of sanitary service to the remainder of surviving humanity.

Just two days later, Khrushchev claimed in a speech in Moscow that Soviet scientists had shown him 'a monstrous new terrible weapon' that was 'a means of the final destruction and extermination of mankind'. Addressing an audience of politicians visiting from Japan, the Soviet leader added chillingly, 'I have never seen anything like it ... It is power without limit.' But just twenty-four hours later, speaking at a reception at India's embassy in Moscow, Khrushchev was sounding more sanguine on the subject. Perhaps humanity would survive after all, he told his hosts, in another of his characteristic reverses, explaining that his earlier remarks had been misquoted. 'I spoke to the Japanese in Russian, and it was taken down in Japanese and then it was spewed out in another language, like something out of the state circus,' he guffawed. Some Kremlin watchers had come to wonder whether the de facto head of the 400 million citizens of the Soviet bloc might not be clinically schizophrenic. That same month, Khrushchev genially accepted an invitation from the West German chancellor Ludwig Erhard to visit him in Bonn later in the year, although for the reasons noted the Soviet supremo was unable to fulfil the engagement.

★ ★ ★

The Labour party manifesto published in September 1964 ran with Harold Wilson's theme of a white-hot revolution and promised a 'New Britain – mobilising the resources of technology under a great national plan; harness[ing] our wealth in brains, our genius for scientific invention and medical discovery'. Modernisation was the byword. When it came to what, exactly, this plan might be, the document was less specific. But it set the tone for a month-long election campaign in which 'progress' was the dominant theme, and where the diminutive, pipe smoking

Labour leader at times seemed to aspire to the late President Kennedy's aura of charismatic youthfulness. One journalist reported of Wilson's Fifth Beatle-like appeal while on a visit to Liverpool:

> Hundreds of children followed him round ... They asked for autographs, they chanted his name and yelled 'Yeah, yeah, yeah' ... Wilson's extraordinary Pied Piper effect on the young is something quite unprecedented in British politics, and a little uncanny. Some people made a point of touching his car, and then gazing at the hand which had received such a wonderful blessing.

There were still those who stood apart from the pervasive Wilson-mania, preferring to dwell on his slightly dowdy suburban British sensibilities and concealed streak of ruthlessness rather than the Kennedy-ish presidential magic. *Private Eye* was perhaps ahead of the field in going on to produce a cover cartoon showing the Labour leader on his knees, his tongue extended, behind President Johnson, but it expressed a view some people then had of the Atlantic alliance. (Wilson at one time seriously discussed the possibility of Britain becoming America's 51st state, fearing that otherwise the country would become just a 'little Switzerland', his press secretary later revealed.) In fact, criticism of Wilson's personalised campaign tactics wasn't restricted to his political opponents. There were also frequent rumblings of discontent from within his own party. 'We are all extremely anxious about the way the election is developing,' Wilson's colleague Tony Benn recorded in the privacy of his diary.

'The leader is principally concerned with his own position and we have lost the initiative,' the shadow education secretary Richard Crossman similarly complained. 'We've all been downgraded because Harold is absolutely determined to be the sole man.'

Wilson's only close, if usually discreetly concealed, companion on the campaign trail was his brilliant if somewhat mercurial political secretary (and, it was rumoured, firm personal friend), 32-year-old Marcia Williams, the future Baroness Falkender. The consensus was that Williams was clever, strong-willed, ambitious and manipulative, and, at least until the ascent of Margaret Thatcher, arguably the most powerful woman in Britain. These were not female qualities universally admired in 1964. When the *Daily Mail* went on to disclose that Williams had two young sons born out of wedlock, the press fell over themselves in their search for evidence of Wilson's paternity. It later emerged that the children's father was actually one of their own: Walter Terry, political editor of the *Mail*.

Despite Wilson's presidential airs, one or two of his subordinate MPs at least managed to provide a certain amount of entertainment on the campaign trail. Notable among them was the owlish-looking George Brown, the 50-year-old deputy leader, whose undoubted intellect and oratorical flair were matched only by his affinity for single malt Scotch. This latter trait had first come to the public's notice on the evening of 22 November 1963, the day of President Kennedy's assassination, when an emotional Brown, interviewed on the ITV programme *This Week*, slurred out that 'Jack was a very great friend of mine ... I remember it's not many weeks ago I was over there with my daughter, talking to Jackie across the garden wall. One is terribly hurt by this loss,' along with several more reminiscences in the same vein about his 'great pal' and 'brother', whom he had in fact met just twice, both times on formal occasions. The viewers watching at home were at least spared the sight of Brown's off-camera interaction with the American actor Eli Wallach, who in a commercial break following this tribute turned to another guest to enquire, 'Is this bastard for real?' Told that he was a politician of the highest rank, the star of *The Magnificent Seven* snapped, 'I don't care who he is. I'll still knock the shit out of him.'

Brown's contributions to the 1964 campaign were sometimes disastrous, often inspired and always lively affairs, constantly teetering between the scintillating one-liner and the toe-curling gaffe. At one point, he climbed onto an upturned box in the street to suggest that the mortgage rate could be cut to just 3 per cent – 'if not even less', he added, waving his arms around wildly before hugging a passing young woman who, while not immediately disengaging herself, seemed not to actively relish the old soak's embrace. It was left for the chancellor, Reginald Maudling, to drily point out that Brown's mathematics were 'deeply suspect' and to suggest that his Labour opponent might benefit from a lengthy rest cure.

The campaign wasn't all about high-minded statesmanship on the government side, however, as seen by the moment when a purple-faced Lord Hailsham, or Quintin Hogg as he called himself in his role as education minister, lashed out at a poster of Harold Wilson with his walking stick. And Maudling himself was a 'devotee of Bacchus', in the careful words of one obituary. While campaigning, the chancellor carried not one but two briefcases adorned by a ministerial coronet. One contained papers, the other was entirely filled with miniature bottles of gin. When he retired to his hotel each night he drank them with a dash of vermouth.

For the principal Conservative message, Harold Macmillan's 1957 remark that 'Most of our people have never had it so good' was still the tune to whistle to. The Tories' most-repeated party political broadcast showed a young woman dreamily leaning on her vacuum cleaner, then harking back to the dark days of the Clement Attlee administration (when she herself would have been a teenager) and comparing them to the affluence of her spruce new home, with its array of washing-machines, wall to wall carpets and electric cooker. There was no way she was ever going back to a life characterised by inedible Woolton Pie, queues at the butcher's shop, or being exhorted to grow carrots because they helped you see in the dark.

Back at Transport House, Harold Wilson asked the visiting George Gallup, the American-born pioneer of political opinion polling, whether attacking the Conservatives as money-grubbing materialists would heighten his appeal to most undecided voters. When Gallup answered no, it confirmed Wilson's belief that it was high time for Labour to move on from the perennial British battleground of the class war, and accommodate itself to the new forces of consumerism. Or, as he privately put it to Richard Crossman at Transport House on 28 September, 'Of course ideals matter, Dick. But without leaders who can present those ideals in a way to keep up with the times, we're all stuffed.'

IV

AUTUMN

'WHERE ARE WE HEADED?'

Some democratic governments drift more or less serenely from one election to another; others seem to spectacularly lose the voters' goodwill along the way and to never quite recover their all-important aura of competence. The tragicomic events at Suez terminally holed Anthony Eden's Tory administration in late 1956, just as the catastrophic shock of sterling's 'Black Wednesday' would effectively spell doom for John Major's prospects thirty-six years later, to take just two of the many available examples in Britain alone. When all semblance of authority is gone, and the public suddenly comes to look on their political rulers as simply not up to it, then it's just no good carrying on. That particular insult to the electorate's intelligence can never be pardoned. Flagrant mistakes can be patched up, individual foibles and even crimes forgiven over time, mere sexual incontinence excused, and every other form of moral lapse – bribery, nepotism, falsification of official documents on which hang matters of war and peace – all these can be overcome. But never the point at which an elected leader is revealed as a prize buffoon. There's simply no coming back from there.

Perhaps unfairly, this last state of affairs was reached by the British prime minister Alec Douglas-Home shortly after lunchtime on Friday 9 October 1964, when he rose to his feet and attempted to address a large crowd assembled at the new Bull Ring shopping complex in central Birmingham. The PM's subsequent speech did not go quite as smoothly as intended. In fact, it was a fiasco. Douglas-Home had spent much of his political career in the more rarefied atmosphere of the House of Lords and, whatever his other gifts, was not ideally suited to the cut and thrust of a modern political street fight. Even as he now rose, then cleared his throat and began to read off a long list of encouraging data about the future direction of the national economy, a voice from the crowd suddenly rang out: 'Leave off, you old wind-bag!' Douglas-Home seemed to falter momentarily, peering out across the audience through his half-moon glasses, but soldiered on regardless, only to be interrupted by other voices raised in unison, chanting 'Tories Out!' and 'We Want Wilson!' To make matters worse, the prime minister's public address system seemed to malfunction, or at least not to be suitably amplified, with the result that his already thin voice was forced to struggle for ascendance with those of the crowd, 'like the sound of a single flute in a Wagner storm scene,' as one witness put it.

This was bad enough, but soon the supremely dignified PM, the man who had helped to negotiate with Hitler, and met on terms of familiarity with presidents and kings the world over, was confronted by a new challenge – a larger-than-life-sized cardboard 'Homosaurus' with the body of a prehistoric reptile and the face of Sir Alec himself, staring back at him from the front row of the crowd. Blinking rapidly as the monster was raised up before him, the PM struggled heroically to continue with his prepared remarks. But somehow the minutiae of the latest GDP forecasts and the prospects for improved overseas trade failed to carry the increasingly restive audience with him. Some years earlier, on a visit to Washington, Douglas-Home had been taken on a tour of the nearby FBI headquarters, where he had watched a training session in which the bureau's new recruits undertook a nightmare walk down a movie-set street in which pop-up waxwork targets suddenly loomed in a doorway or at an upstairs window, sometimes brandishing a weapon, at others merely a bag of groceries or the family pet, forcing the young agent to take a split-second decision about how to react. It must have been thus that Douglas-Home's speech now appeared to him as he gazed out not only on the hideous spectacle of Homosaurus leering back at him, but also on a wide range of banners and signs imprinted with messages of a uniformly hostile nature. Confronted by these and by a swelling chorus of boos, jeers and catcalls, Douglas-Home, his Adam's apple bobbing rapidly up and down his neck, could only manage to say a strangulated 'Thank you' in response to an applause not yet detectable. After a few more moments of agony, the PM then elected to leave the stage prematurely amidst a rain of shouted expletives and flying debris much like the atmosphere of a typical Beatles or Rolling Stones performance of the era but without the solace of the actual concert.

Douglas-Home may have been an anachronistic and, to some, mildly ludicrous figure, but he had also been around the British political landscape quite long enough over the years to be able to recognise an authentic disaster when he saw it. Appraising the frenzy of upside-down faces mouthing insults through his car windscreen as it then hurriedly left the area, the PM turned to his travelling secretary and announced calmly, 'Well, we're quite finished, I'm afraid.' He later admitted that he had appeared 'hunted' in the almost sadistically lengthy TV news footage of the scene, and that for the remaining week of the campaign, 'nothing really mattered – one had appeared simply not to be in control of events, [something] the voting public will not soon forget'.

The Tories' edifice of respectability, or even of minimum competence, then seemed to crumble further with a singularly ill-advised interview the PM's deputy Rab Butler gave that same day to the *Daily Express*. 'We're running neck and neck,' Butler reflected. 'I'll be surprised if there's much in it. But things might start slipping in the last few days ... If so they won't slip towards us.'

Apart from the PM's spectacular implosion at Birmingham, and the partly balancing spectacle of an overwrought George Brown's slurred outbursts on the Labour side, perhaps the main political drama that month outside of Smethwick came on the streets of the Cardiff South East constituency, where England's cricket captain Ted Dexter had decided to take himself out of contention for his side's winter tour of South Africa and stand as the local Conservative parliamentary candidate instead. His opponent was none other than James Callaghan, the shadow foreign secretary, a sitting MP since 1945, and in due course to become not only prime minister but the first person to hold all four great offices of British state. It was a somewhat whimsical decision for even an acknowledged free spirit like the Milan-born Dexter, who winningly remarked of the whole thing in his autobiography, 'At that time I knew more about Italian politics than English, but the sum total of both would not have made up a five-minute speech to the local Young Conservatives.' The *Sketch*'s Tony Gill went down to cover the proceedings for a day or two in Cardiff, and long remembered the 'superbly comic scene of Lord Ted strolling about the docks in his beautifully tailored suit to meet the locals, before pretending to enjoy an evening nosh-up of Glamorgan sausage and pureed seaweed washed down with a pint at the Pig and Trotter'. Gill was also on hand to record the 'semi-regal' progress of a theatrically avuncular Callaghan, 'chortling away to the crowds seemingly without a care in the world, while his beady eye stared out across their heads through the ranks of the press like a searchlight sweeping by'.

For a politician, Callaghan was a man of some detectable charm, even if it came equipped with a sensitive on–off switch, much like the next Labour grandee to be dispatched by Transport House to Cardiff – the long-serving MP and acclaimed historical biographer Roy Jenkins, who eventually succeeded Callaghan as chancellor. In time, Jenkins broke off from denouncing the 'ludicrous popinjay imported from the drawing-rooms of Mayfair', as he called Dexter, to quietly enquire of Tony Gill if he knew where one could get a decent meal with 'a drop of red' to accompany it. The lawyer Arnold Goodman, an acknowledged authority on such matters, and also present in Cardiff for the day, duly led the Labour contingent into a nearby Italian restaurant, filling the narrow doorway as he passed through it, Gill noted, 'like a supertanker in a canal lock'.

When the final vote came to be counted in Cardiff, Callaghan increased his majority from 868 to just under 8,000, and as a result Dexter decided he might after all quite fancy going to South Africa, where he did rather better, scoring 344 runs in seven innings at an average of 57. England won the series with their heavily fancied opponents one Test to nil.

It's often said that politics can make for strange bedfellows, not least in the heat of a typical British election campaign. Such was the case now. There was the richly hued Jenkins, for example, a liberal-minded man of classic distinction and manifold paradoxes, the croquet-playing, claret-tippling son and grandson of miners, in theory sympathetic to, but in practice somewhat aloof from, what he called 'the demos', of whom an admiring lady once confided, 'I could imagine tearing off his beautiful pinstripe suit only to find another beautiful pinstripe suit underneath.' He went on to be a famously reforming home secretary and an unusually austere chancellor who eventually led sixty-eight Labour MPs into the Conservative lobby in protest at his party's anti-European wing.

Rab Butler, too, was formidably highbrow if notoriously bored by detail, not necessarily an asset in his own career as chancellor, nor when it came to matters such as speaking to the press about his party's election prospects. I was once lucky enough to interview him in his anecdotage as master of Trinity College, Cambridge, when he told me that the 1964 election had been decided by the fact that 'enough people were fed up with the government, not because the whole country was suddenly in the grip of socialist mania'. There was a touching and perhaps mildly comic illustration of this last fact to be seen when *The Sun's* proprietor Cecil King had a gold rod specially inserted on the bonnet of his chauffeured Rolls, so that he could drive around London with a red flag flying inscribed 'Vote Labour' during the campaign. In the coming months, the man whose paper believed that the 'division of Britain into social classes is happily out of date' would find himself locked in debate with the government of the day over the issue of whether he should properly be rewarded with a mere life peerage, or his preferred hereditary earldom, for his services. In the end King conceded the point, with the proviso that his socially ambitious wife be made a Dame.

A *Daily Mail* opinion poll published on 1 October, a week before the prime minister's fateful encounter with Homosaurus at Birmingham, showed the Conservatives enjoying a 2.9 per cent lead in the country as a whole. That day also saw the release of the latest balance of payments figures, which revealed a significant if not unexpected monthly shortfall of £73 million in the nation's accounts. Harold Wilson was not slow to again draw attention to the PM's 'matchstick economics' for the remaining fortnight of the campaign: a golden age of socialist prosperity lay just around the corner, *The Sun* promised in its next editorial, 'if only we all keep our nerve'. A few days later, Quintin Hogg, another one of those rare politicians liable to go enjoyably off-message, told a heckler who raised the Profumo scandal, 'If you can tell me there are no adulterers on the front bench of the Labour party, you can talk to me about Profumo,' a barb said to have caused alarm in the household both of Wilson himself and that of his private secretary. By 14 October, the *Mail* was reporting that the two principal parties were neck and neck in most of England and Wales, although Jo Grimond's Liberals 'may cause mischief with their banal views about devolution in Scotland'.

Early the next morning, news came in of Nikita Khrushchev's abrupt fall from grace in Moscow. The once-unchallenged Soviet dictator was forced to abdicate after several hours of successive denunciations at the hands of his former colleagues, at the end of which they unanimously granted his 'request' to be allowed to resign. Khrushchev was at least spared a show trial and summary execution, and allowed to retire, if effectively under house arrest, with a modest pension. The gift of the television-radiogram set presented to him on his 70th birthday was repossessed by two men in dark suits who called at his home a few days later. Khrushchev himself saw the means of his departure as proof of the 'great reforms' he claimed as his enduring legacy to the state he had led since 1953.

'I'm old and tired,' Khrushchev confided to his son Sergei:

> Let them cope by themselves. I've done the main thing. Could anyone have dreamed of telling Stalin that he didn't suit us anymore and suggesting he go? Not even a wet spot would have remained where he had been standing. Now everything is different. The fear is gone, and we can talk as equals. That's my gift. I won't put up a fight.

In turn, Khrushchev's successor Leonid Brezhnev would continue the ongoing cycle of reform and reaction in Russia that remains the basic template today. The Kremlin's stagnating authoritarian system as it was constituted in October 1964 faced a number of pressing challenges both at home and abroad. Coming just nine days before Khrushchev's fall, the mass breakout at the Berlin Wall that led to Egon Schultz's death again hinted that all was not well in the imprisoned state of East Germany. No fewer than fifty-six individuals safely made their way to freedom on that occasion. A few weeks earlier, fourteen escapees, including eleven children, were smuggled across the border in a refrigerated truck, concealed under the carcasses of slaughtered pigs being transported to the West. In November, Brezhnev was to privately remark that the 'anti-fascist protection device' itself had become a 'public humiliation' for Marxism-Leninism, and should be 'critically assessed', a review that in the end took the Soviets and their East German satellite a further quarter of a century to conclude.

There were compelling economic as well as strategic reasons behind Brezhnev's growing disillusionment with the Wall. Exact figures are hard to establish, but it's been estimated that by late 1964 the USSR was sustaining a defence burden that may have been twice as great as that of the United States, with a GDP only about a fifth of its principal rival. Before long, Brezhnev authorised imports of food and technology to the Soviet bloc from Western Europe and the US, putting him in the equivocal position of relying on the willingness of capitalists to extend credit to maintain internal stability.

The edifice of Marxist solidarity was further shaken at a Sino-Soviet summit in Moscow not long before Khrushchev's fall. The meeting had signally failed to bring about the 'fraternal agreement [and] anti-imperialist harmony and concord' previously expected of it. One senior Chinese delegate to the talks openly expressed surprise at the continuing denigration of Stalin by the current Soviet regime. '"Murderer", "criminal", "bandit", "fool", "shit", "motherfucker", "idiot" – all these curses and others, even more vile,' he remarked fastidiously, 'came from the mouth of Comrade N.S. Khrushchev.' How was it that so many communists all round the world had for so long considered 'some sort of shit' to be their leader? Was Khrushchev himself, the delegate enquired, 'completely clean'?

On 16 October 1964, just two days after power changed hands in the Kremlin, the Chinese government successfully activated Project 596 (or 'Miss Qiu', as it was coyly nicknamed), the country's first nuclear test, a 22-kiloton bomb dropped from a platform close to the Lop Nur salt lake in Inner Mongolia. The device itself was relatively modest, in the sense that it could merely obliterate a city the size of Coventry or Miami but not remove the entire United Kingdom or United States from the map. The Peking government did not bother to disguise its glee, nor its primary motivation in becoming the fifth member of the world's nuclear club. 'This is a major achievement of the Chinese people in their pacific struggle to increase their national defence capability and oppose the Western imperialist policy of nuclear blackmail,' Zhou Enlai, then in the sixteenth of his 27-year premiership, remarked, before adding:

> We pointed out long ago that the treaty on the partial halting of nuclear tests signed by the United States, Britain and the Soviet Union in Moscow was a big fraud to fool the nations of the world … it tried to consolidate the monopoly held by the three offensive powers and tie the hands and feet of all peace-loving races.

The reaction in the West was one of justifiable concern at this 'pacific' struggle by the Chinese government. A hitherto classified paper prepared by the US Defence Intelligence Agency for President Johnson on 24 November 1964 concluded gloomily: 'The Soviet lack of [cooperation] has delayed the schedule of Red China's construction of fissionable material production facilities but, despite this, we believe the CHICOMS have every intention, and are in the process, of developing an extensive, broad-based nuclear weapons program.'

A shorthand note that month by the Cabinet secretary in London similarly reported that 'PM was most concerned at news, [which] officials are to examine'.

There is no comparable record of the Soviet reaction, but according to the cosmonaut Alexei Leonov, the incoming first secretary of the Party did not trouble to conceal his alarm at a Kremlin reception later that month: '"This individual [Mao Zedong] may be a communist or he may be a fascist," Leonid Ilyich told me, placing a steadying arm on my shoulder. "Or he may be just another conquest-minded bandit who is today trying to bring us all nearer to oblivion".'

Whenever there's a significant change of course in a democratic government, as opposed to the Soviet model, two distinct lines of thought seem to emerge. The first might be called the wider socio-economic school, and in the case of Britain in October 1964 it found expression in Harold Wilson's words, quoted in the *Daily Mirror*:

Wilson says there is no place in politics for the gentlemanly amateur, now as obsolete as that snob game, Gentlemen versus Players. Those Etonians who still believe in the survival of the smuggest will want no part of the future landscape. But the young, the dynamic, the brainy, the well-intentioned and the just will flourish in it. So promises Mr. Harold Wilson.

Cecil King or his speechwriter made broadly the same point in a great eve-of-election address at Fishmongers' Hall in London:

Our people [have been] spiritually and materially starved for thirteen long years ... They have seen their ideals and their illusions and hopes one by one worn away by events, [and] by the uneasy feeling that for too long our great vessel of state has been heading for the shoals while the captain and crew blithely sip cocktails on the sun deck.

Set against this, there was the more humdrum reality that after more than a decade, and four successive Conservative administrations, a relatively small majority of people thought it might be time not so much for a grand social experiment as for a modest change of course. The events of 15 October weren't a wholesale, or even a unified 'repudiation of every fundamental principle of the archaic Tory-grandee type clinging to the honeypot of office', as George Brown once put it in characteristic style. The change of government wasn't the result of a 'revolution' at all, in fact, but rather of the pervasive sense among a sufficient number of people, strategically located around the country, that this was perhaps the moment for a new hand to apply a gentle touch to the tiller. It's salutary to note again that in British politics prime ministers generally aren't treated as saints or sun gods, except possibly by their own inner courts. Political power is far more unadorned than in the United States. No 'Hail to the Chief' is required. If enough people become sufficiently bored or listless, the head of government is unceremoniously removed, generally survived only by their memoirs, lectures, and the nation's debts.

Early on the morning of Thursday 15 October, the unseasonably fine British weather broke in a shawl of rain. Two days earlier, George Brown had spoken darkly of unnamed 'agents' of the state who were 'going about, try[ing] to suppress people's right to vote'. He offered no specific examples of this plot; perhaps it was just one of those inspired rhetorical devices that seemed to come to Labour's deputy leader from time to time. Relatively few people in Britain were thought to live in active dread of the knock at the door by the political police in the dead of night. Instead of being deliberately targeted by a sinister Tory dragnet, the only real constraint on participation in the democratic process appears to have been apathy. There was a voter turnout of 75.6 per cent on the day, which may seem high from a modern perspective, but was still significantly less than the figure of 83.1 per cent that had returned the Conservatives to power in 1951. Several 'ordinary English men and women' were invited to give their views to the BBC in the immediate run-up to polling day. An unnamed teacher in his forties from Spalding in Lincolnshire informed the interviewer that in his opinion 'the Conservative party seem to have too many "wild men"', among them the former Cabinet ministers Enoch Powell and Iain Macleod, who had both declined to serve under Douglas-Home, the former now remarking in his constituency address, 'It is essential we introduce control over the number of immigrants allowed in if we are to avoid the evils of a "colour question" in this country for ourselves and for our children.' These 'wild men' would 'just not follow the leader', the Spalding schoolmaster complained. 'There was not any party coordination. They are just going in opposite directions.'

To Kate Armstrong, a 51-year-old retired company secretary from Lancaster, the key concern was the national economy, which she summarised in a pithy four-word slogan the main opposition party might have taken for themselves: 'Where are we headed?' Many of those questioned by the BBC spoke of being materially better-off than in 1951, but of nonetheless worrying about the general direction of the nation's finances. 'We're simply spending money we don't have,' a Rushden, Northants, shopkeeper named Nick Hodges informed the interviewer. Cutting through the blare of the political hustings, that was surely the voice of reason. Few voters appeared to believe that this profligacy with the nation's money might be unique to the Conservatives, and the chancellor was criticised from within his own party for his failure to publish the full cost of Labour's manifesto commitments. ('Life is too bloody short,' Maudling later observed. 'Nobody has time to do a lot of sums about the renationalisation of the road-haulage sector, and nobody would read them even if you did.') Another BBC interviewee, an assistant manager of flight operations at Eastleigh airport in Southampton, thought that it was 'all about a feeling that's really quite intangible that the government has simply been allowed to drift along, sometimes rather aimlessly, for long enough'. Fair play suggested it 'might be time for the other chaps to have a go'.

On election night itself, as quoted by the author Richard Davenport-Hines, Paul Raymond's cabaret in the West End of London had a gimmick. 'After voting closed, five naked showgirls appeared on stage, each with a ribbon in their hair. The one with the blue ribbon represented the Conservatives, the pink ribbon Labour, yellow for Liberal, red for Communists and white for independents.' As each result came in, the girl representing the victorious party took a chiffon scarf of the appropriate colour and tied it round her neck or waist. 'None of the girls wanted to be the Communist, not from political scruples but because they did not want to be shivering without a single scarf for the whole night.'

The young woman with the pink scarves won, but it was a close thing. Labour took 317 parliamentary seats to the Conservatives' 304 and the Liberals' nine, for an overall majority of just four. 'Barely a mandate,' George Brown was left to reflect. If the election result was truly the ignition point for Britain's wholesale social transformation in the latter half of the 1960s, it got off to a slow start. Labour managed a swing of around three per cent, although its popular vote rose by only 0.25 per cent, meaning fewer people voted for the party than in its election defeats of 1955 and 1959. The main shift was that from the Conservatives to the Liberals of 5.7 per cent; four of the Liberals' nine seats were won in Scotland, whose independence their manifesto had demanded. The geography of Britain's politics was essentially the same as it is today, with Labour dominating in London, the industrial midlands and South Wales, and the electoral map otherwise showing a spine of Tory blue. Douglas-Home later remarked that his premiership had effectively been doomed from the moment, just twelve weeks in, when Iain Macleod went into print to accuse the Conservatives of operating a closed shop of Old Etonians to appoint Home in the first place. David Ormsby-Gore, a well-connected former Tory minister now serving as Britain's ambassador in Washington, privately wrote to the outgoing PM with the view that 'almost anything could have tipped the electoral balance: if the news about Khrushchev or China's nuclear explosion had come [a] few hours earlier, or just Rab [Butler] keeping his mouth shut for once.' The Douglas-Home government had been in office for 363 days, the shortest tenure since 1922, and one of the briefest in British history, although an eternity compared with certain more recent administrations.

The 1964 election and the new Wilson regime may not have achieved a revolution in British life, but it at least represented a retreat from the last remnants of the country's imperial heritage and a tactical turn towards the Continent. The government would in time submit the nation's latest application to join the Common Market, only promptly to share the fate of the previous attempt and be rebuffed by General de Gaulle. Always slyly ambivalent on Europe, Wilson soon came to recognise that full membership of the club would be firmly barred until the French president left office. Briefing his Cabinet colleagues on a visit to Paris to discuss the matter face to face, the PM was forced to give a sombre review of events: 'De Gaulle indicated that negotiations for our membership of the European community might be prolonged and, in the end, nugatory. The General's mood was one of apocalyptic gloom about the state of the world and the need to reconsider and reconstruct French policies.'

'Would you care to join the revolution, Comrade?' Wilson had asked, perhaps puckishly, of the twenty-six men and one woman (the minister for overseas development, Barbara Castle) whom he invited over the weekend of 16–18 October to form his first Cabinet. On the Friday afternoon of the 16th, the PM himself, at 48 the youngest to date of the twentieth century, drove to the palace to proverbially kiss hands with the monarch, unexpectedly turning up with his wife Mary and their 20-year-old undergraduate son Robin in tow – 'a bit of a culture shock to us,' the Queen's private secretary later confided. Ted Dexter's nemesis Jim Callaghan was given the poisoned chalice of the Treasury, with Gordon Walker, despite losing his seat at Smethwick, as foreign secretary, and George Brown dispatched to head the newly formed department of economic affairs. There is no definitive tally of how many times Brown subsequently threatened to resign (Wilson once wearily calculated that it was 'about fortnightly'), but he finally succeeded in doing so in early 1968. The Cabinet papers show that even then Wilson was in an agony of indecision over losing his way-ward but fitfully brilliant lieutenant, writing no fewer than seventeen drafts of the letter accepting Brown's decision. The PM himself hung on with his slender lead until calling a snap election in March 1966, when Labour increased its majority to 98 seats over all other parties.

No one can say with total conviction, but there's anecdotal evidence to suggest that most Britons in 1964 had relatively little insight into what was going on in neighbouring European countries, while more exotic destinations like Red China or the Soviet Union remained the remote, enigmatic places of the sort ancient map-makers used to label 'here be dragons'. There was of course no rolling twenty-four-hour news of the kind we enjoy today, limited practical satellite television technology, little casual overseas tourism, and no internet. The daily papers carried a certain amount of foreign news, more carefully rationed in some outlets than others, but in general the reasonably inquisitive British adult knew as much about the goings-on elsewhere in the world, beyond the unavoidable headlines about France's latest European veto or the result of the American presidential race, as he or she did about the far side of the moon.

There was, however, one exception to the generally insular rule: sport. Whether in the form of the annual football European Cup (won that year by Inter Milan), or the successive summer tours by overseas cricketers, or the inevitable parade of foreign-born champions at the

British Open golf or Wimbledon, people could reel off the names of the leading international competitors in their fields without displaying the least comparable interest in those same players' host countries. On occasion, a handful of sporting events with only minimal direct British involvement could even command the nation's headlines. When the 1964 Olympic Games opened in Tokyo on 10 October, a photograph of the Japanese runner Yoshinori Sakai touching the ceremonial torch to the stadium cauldron banished even Alec Douglas-Home and Harold Wilson from the front pages. The choice of Sakai was deliberate: he was born in Hiroshima on 6 August 1945, the day the atomic bomb was dropped on the city, and was said to symbolise his nation's rehabilitation during the years since the 'great disagreement', as the official Olympic programme delicately put it. Adding a further layer of poignancy to the scene, one of those watching the opening ceremony from the stand was 63-year-old Emperor Hirohito, Japan's godlike head of state during that same late unpleasantness. In a thin voice the public had first heard announcing their country's surrender in 1945, he now announced that 'freedom of choice and association is ... a universal principle, and it should know no exceptions.'

South Africa was banned from taking part in the Games over its preference for selecting its athletes on the basis of their skin colour, but ninety-three other nations sent teams to Tokyo. They were the first Olympics to be broadcast live to overseas television screens, using America's new solar-panelled Relay 1 satellite floating 20,000 miles over the equator. By the end of the thirteen-day event, the Soviet Union had won ninety-six medals and the USA ninety. The two Germanys put aside their political differences to field a unified team at Tokyo, and duly came third in the medals table. They would never again cooperate in this way. An Ethiopian named Abebe Bikila won the marathon and 20-year-old 'Smokin' Joe' Frazier took gold in heavyweight boxing, while British interest was largely confined to the long-jump pit, where Lynn Davies and Mary Rand respectively brought home the men's and women's title. The future Liberal Democrat leader 'Ming' Campbell competed for his country in the 200 metres, winning his preliminary heat in a creditable time of 21.3 seconds but failing to advance to the finals. Some people were worried that the fallout from the Chinese nuclear test taking place halfway through the games at Lop Nur might adversely affect the athletes' performances, but the entirely pacific Peking government insisted that there was no problem.

China herself boycotted the Games because of the presence of a team from Taiwan. Apparently gifted at boxing and weightlifting, the Taiwanese delegation did not otherwise flourish in Tokyo.

By late 1964, there was increasingly a second unifying theme shared by people around the world for whom the once-stigmatised 'beat' or 'race' music was quickly becoming a universal language. The Beatles continued to dominate this fast-developing growth field, with yet another frenzied fifty-five-show, twenty-five-town British tour that autumn. It was during this exhausting itinerary that the native exuberance of John Lennon's, and, to a lesser extent, Paul McCartney's songwriting came to be tempered by a certain vein of introspection and even despondency, with titles such as 'If I Fell', 'Baby's in Black' and 'I'm a Loser', all of which suggested their recent success had brought them fame and fugitive prosperity, but not necessarily contentment. The group as a whole had clearly reached the stage at which an artist is forced to carefully consider the fine print of their unwritten contract with the public, often the point at which an inherent emotional instability is further inflamed by the effects of bad advice and hard drugs.

By October 1964, the Beatles had clearly become big business. After the film and record receipts of *A Hard Day's Night* were added up, it was found that the four young musicians, still sharing a communal London flat just twelve months earlier, now had a major tax problem – as well as the tour fees and royalties, the core Lennon–McCartney creative firm, Northern Songs, was being floated on the stock exchange – and management advised everyone to buy property. As a result, John Lennon paid £65,000 (£1 million today) for a twenty-four-room mock-Tudor pile next to a golf course in Weybridge, Surrey, with Queen Anne furniture and a baronial fireplace. On a rare morning off later in October, Paul McCartney was chauffeured down for a songwriting session. As they turned into John's lane, McCartney looked up from his *Daily Mail* and asked the driver whether he was keeping busy. 'Busy?' he said. 'I've been working eight days a week.' Paul walked into his partner's all-black study, sat down at the piano, and told him, 'I've got a great title.'

The Beatles may have led the fold, but by late 1964 several others were coming up fast behind them. Doing their own bit for Britain's export drive, the Rolling Stones were back that October for their second visit to the United States. A summer of relentless touring and recording had worked wonders for their overseas box office potential.

Their manager Andrew Oldham's perverse PR campaign didn't hurt, either. 'The Rolling Stones, who haven't bathed in a week, arrived here yesterday,' several New York-area papers duly reported on 23 October, having taken Oldham's publicity handout at face value. In the accompanying photograph, Mick Jagger was seen to be obligingly scratching himself, while Keith Richards examined the inside of his trousers. Two nights later, 65 million Americans tuned in to watch the Stones top the bill on the weekly *Ed Sullivan Show*, while Sullivan himself strode around backstage with a martini, muttering about the indignity of it all. Amid prolonged screams in the studio audience, the band blasted out Chuck Berry's 'Around and Around' and returned for 'Time is On My Side', a tightly choreographed package of loud guitar, Piltdown Man hair and that serviceable but faintly hostile voice that always seemed to make a threat of the lyrics. The switchboard at CBS (the same media company that would later snap up the rights to four Stones albums at $8 million apiece) was immediately jammed with complaints by parents. Next morning, a rattled Sullivan told the press, 'They'll never be on again. Never. Never. We won't book any more rock and roll groups and we'll ban teenagers from the theatre.' Six months later, Sullivan would beg the Stones to return, while acts like the Doors and Jefferson Airplane began to vie with his show's more traditional fare of elderly Broadway stars, sequined trapeze artists and amusingly prehensile monkeys.

An hour or so after that first Sullivan performance, Mick Jagger and Keith Richards left their bungalow-sized suite and went up on the roof of the Astor hotel in Times Square with Tom Jones and assorted Herman's Hermits, who were also touring the States, to gaze out over the lights of the city. 'Hundreds of kids' were down below screaming their names. The young musicians, who hailed from places like Dartford and Pontypridd, and the area around the Davyhulme sewage works, smiled at each other. Most of them had had to have their parents co-sign their recent contracts, because they were still legally underage to do so on their own. Andrew Oldham himself was just nineteen when he persuaded the Stones to let him manage them. At their first meeting, he had asked the band members simply to 'trust me'. Now, after headlining the Sullivan show, they began to do so.

By then Jagger and Richards had already done the one really imperishable thing of their brief autumn tour, which was to be standing on stage at New York's Academy of Music when the new-journalism guru Tom Wolfe walked in, wearing his trademark double-breasted cream suit with a three-pointed silk handkerchief, a Malacca cane in his hand, to snap one of his indelible social X-rays for that week's *Herald-Tribune*:

'The girls have Their Experience,' Wolfe wrote:

> They stand up on their seats. They ululate, even between songs. The looks on their faces! Rapturous agony! There, right up there, under the sulphur lights, that is *them*. God, they're right there! Mick Jagger takes the microphone with his tabescent hands and puts his huge head against it, opens his giblet lips and begins to sing ...

One way or another, a curious thing seemed to have happened in the musical landscape over the course of just a few months in 1964. What had been a novelty – almost a freak-act – in February had penetrated the mainstream by October. Nobody could say with certainty how or why this happened, and even today we're in the realm of conjecture. Perhaps it was the inevitable birth-cry of the baby-boom generation making itself heard, or perhaps the fact that America itself was only now emerging from its collective shock following the murder of its young president, and thus susceptible to the British Invasion's inoffensive thrills, with their seductive combination of escapism and therapy. The musicians themselves had no clue. They felt their way through the whole experience, acting or ad-libbing, expressing first and thinking, if at all, later. Pressed at the time by an elderly reporter in a business suit and a bow tie, even Mick Jagger, among the most articulate of that often decried breed, the pop star, could offer only:

'It's been very enjoyable ... yes, most enjoyable ... a very successful tour.'

'Now, er, that was not true of the first one, was it?'

'Ooh, *no*,' Jagger said, and emphatically shook his head. 'We only came over here on the first one so we could get ourselves known, so to speak.'

'Uh-huhh.'

'And then we came back and things started happening for us.'

'Well, er ... why did they start happening?'

'I really don't know,' Mick admitted, with a shrugging, search-me gesture of those tabescent hands. 'Some sort of chemical reaction ... seems to have happened, somehow.'

The Stones were the major talking point around New York in October 1964, but far from the only one. The World's Fair, held on a 700-acre site at Flushing Meadows in suburban Queens, attracted 52 million paying customers over two five-month seasons, with an intervening midwinter break, as well as a number of civil rights marches and arrests. On the 26th of the month, just as the Stones were lighting up the Ed Sullivan switchboard, the screen version of the stage musical *My Fair Lady*, with its roots in George Bernard Shaw's 1913 play *Pygmalion*, opened directly across Times Square at the Criterion theatre, proving if nothing else that the sound traditional showbusiness values could coexist with those of the brash new rock and roll upstarts. *My Fair Lady* went on to win eight Oscars, and vied with *The Carpetbaggers*, *Mary Poppins* and *Goldfinger* as the year's most successful films at the global box office.

Later that week, there was an audacious and, it transpired, also mildly comic jewellery theft a few city blocks away at the fortress-like Museum of Natural History on Central Park West. The whole barely credible story later attained canonical status, and was made into at least one feature-length film, reviewed in *Variety* with the enigmatic line, 'Words cannot describe the plot that follows.'

On the wet Thursday night of 29 October, 26-year-old Allan Kuhn and his partner-in-crime Jack 'Murf the Surf' Murphy, who was 27, crept into the museum grounds while a combined lookout-getaway driver cruised slowly around the block in a perhaps incautiously chosen pink-and-white Cadillac with chrome hubcaps. The two Miami-based beach boys, already with a lengthy record of petty crime to their credit, were talented, brazen and sure-footed. After scaling a fence into the building's courtyard, they scrambled up a fire escape to secure a rope to a pillar just above the fourth-floor window ledge of the alluringly named J.P. Morgan Hall of Priceless Gems and Minerals. Clinging on to one end of the rope, Murphy managed to swing across to the window and used his foot to prise open the outside latch. They were in.

'We stood there for a while,' Murphy later recalled, 'making sure no guards were coming, and getting our bearings.' Both he and his accomplice passed some of the time that elapsed by smoking a cigarette. There was still no sound of an alarm, and no one approached them. At length, the two men had simply walked down the empty hallway to the conveniently signposted room where the valuables lay.

Thinking it best to proceed in easy stages, they then each smoked another cigarette. There was still no alarm. At that point, they used tape and boxcutters to open the glass display cabinets and get to their prize. Even when they lifted the stones from their cases, the room remained eerily silent. It later emerged that the wire on the alarms had been disconnected, and the sole staff member on duty had been downstairs watching television rather than making his rounds. 'The guard did not act in an entirely appropriate fashion,' the New York police were later forced to admit in their report of the affair.

No one heard or saw the two thieves as they then stepped back into the night, taking with them twenty-four precious stones, including the golf ball-sized Star of India, the Eagle Diamond and the DeLong Star Ruby, with a total value of at least $400,000, or roughly $6.4 million in today's terms. Incredibly, none of it was insured.

It would be another twelve hours before the loss was discovered, at which point the museum director called a slightly chaotic press conference. Such things tended to be more haphazard affairs than they are now. 'We will scour the ends of the earth for the hoodlums and lowlifes who perpetrated this outrage,' he promised.

As international manhunts go, this one was relatively short-lived. Murphy and Kuhn were picked up at a Miami Beach hotel just a day later. The local police already knew of the pair as dubious characters, high-living beach bums who swaggered around in speedboats and Cadillacs with tanned young women in tow and no visible means of support. New York detectives had already arrested the pair's 25-year-old driver Roger Clark, as he and a girlfriend unwisely drew attention to themselves by repeatedly ordering champagne and caviar while playing loud rock music in a hotel room immediately across the street from the scene of the crime, and following what the police report calls 'applied psychology', he directed them to his hastily departed colleagues in Florida. Murphy and Kuhn were in turn arrested and charged, but then quickly released on bail. They went on to enjoy some of the same Robin Hood status of Britain's Great Train Robbers, widely feted as a pair of lovable rogues who had casually pulled off one of the world's great gem heists. At a wisecracking press conference, they announced that they planned to open a nightclub called The Star of India. The waitresses would wear saris.

There was still no direct evidence linking the two young surfer dudes to the crime, nor any sign of the jewels themselves. They might even have gotten away with it, but for the fact that the actress Eva Gabor happened to see their photograph in her local paper and recognised Murphy and Kuhn as the same two individuals who had relieved her of a $25,000 diamond ring earlier in the year at the Racquet Club in Miami. In light of these new developments, a local judge raised the pair's bail to $150,000 apiece, which proved beyond their means. Returned to jail, they were suddenly willing to negotiate, and led the authorities to a left-luggage locker at the local Miami Trailways Bus station. Inside were two ordinary plastic shopping bags containing the Star of India, the Eagle Diamond and seven lesser gems. The remaining stones later turned up wrapped in a waterproof bag hidden in a public phone box.

Murphy, Kuhn and Clark put up a spirited defence in court, claiming among other things to have been the victims of a frame-up perpetrated by the Cuban government. The jury, however, was unpersuaded by this account, and each of the defendants was sentenced to three years. In 1967, the men walked out of jail free and famous, going on to write a somehow peculiarly American second chapter to their lives. Murphy was later convicted of second-degree murder, imprisoned and freed once more, to become a born-again Christian and travelling evangelist, dying in 2020. Kuhn racked up another conviction for conspiring to receive stolen goods, but went on to become a model citizen with a small landscaping business in the American Midwest, before moving to Alaska to pan for gold. He was last heard of managing an organic beet farm in northern California. Clark, the amiable bungler who drove the getaway car, became a bartender and golf pro at an exclusive country club in Vermont, dying in 2007. Court records show that over the years he received several tickets not for speeding but for 'impeding traffic' by driving too slowly, an ironic fate for an individual once employed as the wheelman in a major metropolitan jewel caper.

In more elevated news, on the morning of 14 October 1964, 35-year-old Martin Luther King Jr, sleeping in an Atlanta hospital room, where he had gone after suffering from exhaustion, was awakened by a phone call from Stockholm. The voice at the other end told him that he had been awarded that year's Nobel peace prize, beating out other shortlisted candidates including the Ethiopian emperor Haile Selassie, the Shah of Iran and the long-serving Labour MP and anti-war campaigner Fenner Brockway. It was an unhappy week for Brockway, who also lost his parliamentary seat in the next day's election.

'We live in a day,' King remarked in his Nobel speech, with the usual tendency to soar to the oratorical heights on such occasions:

> when civilisation is shifting its basic outlook. A major turning point has arrived in history where the presuppositions on which society is structured are being rapidly analysed, sharply challenged, and profoundly changed ... The deep rumbling of discontent that we hear today is the thunder of disinherited and lonely masses, people rising up from dungeons of oppression to the bright hills of freedom. In one majestic chorus the masses are singing 'Ain't gonna let nobody turn us around ...'

Back on the US campaign trail, the hullabaloo raised by President Johnson's 'Daisy' ad did not deter Republicans from commissioning their own, energetically sustained doomsday film. Entitled 'Choice', it showed urban riots, a large-breasted woman in a tight swimsuit, the ecstatic audience at a Beatles concert, and one of the new GTO muscle cars speeding down a dirt road with beer cans flying from the windows. Intended as a montage of American moral decay as Barry Goldwater saw it, other observers might have applauded at least some of the images. For his part, Johnson encouraged a view of himself as more of a statesman than a partisan politician. On his arrival at a campaign stop in New Orleans, he told a waiting crowd of about 4,000, both black and white:

> I am going to repeat here what I have said in every state ... Whatever your views are, we have a constitution and we have a Civil Rights Act, and two-thirds of the Democrats in the Senate voted for it, and three-fourths of the Republicans. I signed it and I am going to enforce it, and any man who is worthy of the high office of president will do the same thing.

Johnson was one of life's inveterate flesh-pressers, never happier than when lighting an election-time fire under his party and administration officials that he stoked with a daily flow of phone calls and memos about everything from getting out the agreed central message about American exceptionalism down to the exact number of promotional posters, badges, bumper stickers, balloons and suitably monogrammed golf balls required at each campaign stop along the way. Yet even he admitted to doubts about the wisdom of exposing himself too freely to his fellow citizens in the charged atmosphere of an election held less than a year after President Kennedy's assassination in Dallas. For one thing, he believed that Fidel Castro's Cubans, rather than the 'lone nut' Lee Harvey Oswald, were behind his predecessor's death. 'Jack Kennedy tried to get Castro, but Castro got him first,' Johnson told his aide Joe Califano in October 1964.

Now the president feared that he too might be targeted, possibly by Cuban kamikaze pilots attacking his plane while on a whistle-stop tour of Florida. The Warren Commission had presented its report late that September, insisting that Oswald had been solely responsible for the events at Dallas, and that the nightclub owner Jack Ruby had in turn acted alone in killing Oswald two days later. Like many others, Johnson remained unconvinced by the official explanation. Perhaps it was the natural reaction of a mind forged by thirty years of political intrigue and backroom dealings that led the president to see conspiracies at every turn, or to inform a reporter, 'We were operating a damn Murder, Inc. in the Caribbean,' adding that Kennedy's death had been an act of retribution which the Cubans might well regard as unfinished business. As a result, Bill Moyers said:

There were times when LBJ didn't want to step off the campaign plane in front of a crowd in 1964. It took a lot of guts ... Once we got back to the plane, and I forget what I said to him, but his answer was, 'Well, nobody shot at me.'

Johnson held his nerve long enough to be safely back in the White House to savour the highly gratifying results of the election as they came in on the night of 3 November. He trounced his Republican opponent by roughly 43 million to 27 million popular votes, and by a 486 to 52 margin in the all-important electoral college. Over the years, America's thirty-sixth president would come to enjoy various nicknames, including 'Mr Glow-Worm' for his habit of shutting off unnecessary lights, and the perhaps less affectionate 'Bullshit Johnson' thanks to his lifelong avoidance of being a martyr to false modesty. For at least the last few weeks of 1964, the president would revel in the sobriquet 'Landslide Lyndon', even if his experience from that point on was to offer a particularly poignant example of how fickle a political mandate can be. Less than four years after his historic victory, following a term in office plagued by violence at home and abroad, Johnson was so unpopular that he did not seek re-election.

MEET THE NEW BOSS

Both sides in the old wartime Atlantic alliance were now led by reform-minded, left-leaning figures who had promised voters a dose of bracing economic and social liberalism to blow their nation's 1950s cobwebs away. Each man had insisted that he had a destination in mind, and a map for reaching it. But did anything really change?

The answer in Britain seems to be that it did, if only on a symbolic level. *Private Eye* ran a striking front cover soon after the October election in which Harold Wilson and his wife Mary were seen standing together at their kitchen sink doing the washing-up, in a way that was somehow hard to imagine of Sir Alec and Lady Douglas-Home. The speech bubble above Mrs Wilson's head read: 'I wish you would do this when there aren't any cameras around, Harold.' It was funny, and like all the best satire it contained a grain of truth. Wilson was undoubtedly clever – perhaps a bit *too* clever, some critics carped – and he was modern. But he was also a consummate politician. Wilson's pledge to social reform had to walk a fine line. He had a razor-thin parliamentary majority, as he was fond of reminding people to help explain his enforced accommodation of his Tory opponents. The MP and future foreign secretary Anthony Crosland later complained that the Labour commitment to sprint for economic growth was 'sacrificed at the high altar of protecting the parity of sterling' by failing to immediately devalue the pound. The journalist and campaigner Paul Foot was on ground well beyond this when he argued that Wilson was 'always an unprincipled opportunist and we were naïve for believing otherwise'. To George Brown, it was clear that 'Harold was left with a deteriorating economy that his own rhetoric had elevated to the issue that mattered more than anything else, but which he had no strategy for fixing.'

It would only be fair to say that Britain's new prime minister became known as a trimmer, a politician associated with tactical manoeuvres rather than with implementing any high-minded vision of the sort he had laid out in his 'white heat' speech and elsewhere. Wilson also had one characteristic flaw in common with President Johnson, almost always a constitutional handicap in a public figure: his deep-rooted paranoia, his conviction that he was always being plotted against, that every tactical setback was proof of some grand conspiracy, in Wilson's case if not to actually assassinate him, at least to silence him politically.

There was a telling, if at the time confidential, example of the way in which vision can be tempered by events at one of the first Wilson Cabinet meetings, which convened at 10.30 in the morning of 12 November 1964. 'Overseas Affairs' and 'The Economy' were each touched on in a few brief remarks by the competent minister, after which the PM and his colleagues busied themselves with a discussion on the matter of 'Remuneration of Ministers and Members of Parliament' that took up the next two hours, at which point lunch was sent in. Herbert Bowden, the lord president of the privy council, opened the discussion with a lengthy recital of the various challenges members of both the Commons and Lords faced in 'giving the virtually full-time service which the proper transaction of the business of their Houses now requires', and concluding that a substantial pay raise was thus in order. Continuing the debate, the Cabinet noted that it might be 'embarrassing to adjust Members' salaries shortly before the announcement of fixed arbitration awards for dockers and railway workers, and some months before the new bands in National Insurance benefits take effect.' Nevertheless, it was agreed with a show of hands that 'the government should not evade its solemn responsibility for acting on the recommendations of a committee which had been appointed for the express purpose of resolving the [financial] embarrassment which members of parliament would otherwise encounter', although, on a point of presentation, 'it might be desirable to attempt to make clear to the public the distinction between a member's basic salary of £2,000 and the allowance of £1,250 for expenses'.

After some further exchange on the matter, George Brown, the architect of a new apparatus of economic policymaking specifically designed to encourage prudence with public money, expressed the view that 'If proper allowance is made for the responsibilities of ministers and for the earnings of individuals of comparable stature in other walks of life, the figure of £8,000 for a senior minister is the minimum that can fairly be adopted.' The Cabinet agreed that this was so, but wondered if perhaps it might be the wrong message to send to the public 'in view of the serious fiscal situation in the country as a whole'. On the other hand, 'for ministers to forgo their fair increase [would] in reality be irrelevant to the government's incomes policy' – which it was helpfully noted 'depends not on a standstill in wages and salaries, but on the achievement of higher productivity' – and, moreover, that 'it would be most unwise to overlook the additional expenditure which

Ministers had found it necessary to incur as a result of the acceptance of office, or the losses which they would sustain by forgoing the other sources of income which had previously been open to them'.

In conclusion, Wilson and his Cabinet colleagues agreed it was all a highly delicate matter to be seen to be awarding themselves pay rises of this magnitude, at a time when the average take-home wage of a semi-skilled male industrial worker was around £850 a year, and for his female counterpart £480, but that it was nonetheless the right thing to do, and that 'the Bill which would be required to increase Ministers' salaries and expenses should be introduced, if possible in time to be debated before Christmas'.

And on that note, after a desultory minute or two spent discussing the matter of arms sales to South Africa, the new Labour Cabinet adjourned.

Wilson would later come to speak of the very real attainments of his first few months in office, wrought under the 'quite exigent circumstances' of Britain's recurrent national economic Armageddon. His administration had 'promoted women in politics, pursued full employment and built new houses at the rate of 400,000 a year', he later noted with some pride. In time, there would also be Labour's Race Relations and Equal Pay Acts, and a marked liberalising of the laws on homosexuality, divorce and abortion, as well as the parliamentary vote to ensure the death penalty would long remain off the statute books – indeed, could be supported only by the most 'mean and ill-spirited' of his political opponents, as the PM put it. In some cases, these were deliberate initiatives, in others more a matter of stumbling into opportunities, but between them they represent a defensible record.

Some of Wilson's critics would nonetheless come to see his first administration as having offered little more than a permanent cycle of crisis management initiatives, as he and his colleagues grappled with the nation's inherited balance of payment crisis. Other commentators would point out the obvious truth that the roots of Britain's financial malaise lay in the previous thirteen years of unbroken Conservative rule, which the PM himself likened to the spectacle of a chronic gambler who can't pay his bills, but who to cheer himself up offers to resolve the matter by placing another bet. A third group would later take what could be called the sociological line on the incoming government, claiming that its real legacy was to encourage the belief that the idea of deferred gratification, like that of the death penalty, or of the inadvisability of having children out of wedlock, now belonged to the dustbin of history. Such observers would point to matters like the epidemic of obesity, the soaring amount of private and public debt, the nation's world-beating rate of teenage pregnancy, and the ubiquity of drug and alcohol abuse as all having had their genesis in the era beginning on 16 October 1964 that led to a gradual erosion of the guardrails defining the limits of acceptable behaviour. If nothing else, Wilson's administration might be said to have drawn a line under the era known as 'post-war', where qualities like stoicism and self-effacement more or less prevailed in daily life, where there was still an entity called the British Empire, and where the phrase 'stiff upper lip' could be – and was – applied without satire. Of course, such judgements were possible only with the benefit of long hindsight. Most Britons in late 1964 would have been focused less on metaphysical notions about the moral decay of the nation, and more on the suddenly apocalyptically wet weather, the latest Beatles single, and the first appearance of the long-running soap opera *Crossroads*, which made its debut on ITV that November.

Across the Channel, General de Gaulle, now at the midpoint of his ten-year term as president of France, no longer troubled to conceal his displeasure at the closeness of the Anglo-American alliance as it stood in late 1964. The general was particularly unhappy that Washington had come to an agreement to furnish the UK with the latest Polaris nuclear missile system, but had offered the French only 'similar' terms. There seems to have been some initial difficulty at the Quai d'Orsay in translating the nuances of the word 'similar', as opposed to 'identical'. It eventually transpired that what both Presidents Kennedy and, in time, Johnson had in mind was to supply France with American-built rockets, which would remain under the joint control of US and French commanders on the ground.

This was unacceptable to de Gaulle, and as a result the French would be obliged to design and build, at immense cost, their own unilateral, six-vessel nuclear fleet, or *force de frappe*, which entered service only in 1971. (De Gaulle himself had left office, and indeed died, prior to its eventual commission.) A new Franco-German concordat, signed less than twenty years after the end of the war, confirmed that by 1964 there were two distinct Western defensive blocs: the so-called Atlantic special relationship, and the 'European project' now increasingly aligned with German and French interests. In firmly announcing his latest veto of Britain's application to join the Common Market, de Gaulle remarked:

> Sentiments, as favourable as they might be and as they are, cannot deny the real facts of the problem ... Britain is insular ... the nature and structure and economic context of her people differ profoundly from those of the other states of the continent ... With Britain's inclusion, there would appear a colossal Atlantic community under American dominance which would soon devour the European community.

Sixty years later, this remains the essential fault line that runs through British politics. For all the undoubted change to the social fabric of the country since 1964, that one issue is as stubbornly polarising today as it was in the early weeks of the first Wilson administration; a full revolution has led the country in a circle.

These would not be the only issues to divide the world at large some forty years before Muslim extremists expressed their dissatisfaction with the West by murdering 3,000 people in a day and triggering the global War on Terror. In Moscow, the new Soviet Communist boss Leonid Brezhnev attempted to mend fences with the People's Republic of China by hosting Chinese premier Zhou Enlai to a three-day Proletariat Revolutionary Gala on the anniversary of the 1917 Bolshevik uprising. The Russian initiative could be counted only a partial success. On his return to Peking, Zhou promptly issued a statement accusing his hosts of 'appeasing United States imperialism' and of seeking to coexist with 'the sworn enemy' of worldwide communism, which nation should be 'effaced, not cuddled or kissed.' By way of illustration, the Chinese went on to shoot down the first of several dozen high-altitude American Firebee drones flying over the south-eastern part of their country, apparently sent there to monitor the movement of troops around the North Vietnamese border. It has been remarked of the Peking government at this time that it picked fights abroad, whether with adversaries or allies, at least in part as a way to maintain unity at home.

There was another, and singularly dramatic, example of the world-wide class struggle in the early hours of 24 November, when five American C-130 Hercules transport planes dropped 320 Belgian paratroopers onto the grassy airfield at Stanleyville (today's Kisangani) in order to evacuate Western hostages being held by armed Congolese rebels; about 1,600 civilians were successfully freed, and twenty-four others were killed in the crossfire. In Rhodesia that autumn, 40-year-old Robert Mugabe and several other figures opposed to white minority rule were detained for subversion and incitement, while Iran's 64-year-old Ruhollah Khomeini was in turn exiled by his home government owing to a difference of opinion about the need for a programme of social and religious modernisation. Like Nelson Mandela before them, both men would later emerge to become what they saw as liberators of their oppressed peoples. Mugabe spent much of his time in prison reading for an external degree from the London School of Economics; Khomeini used some of his own enforced solitude to write a book entitled *The Jurist's Guardianship*, which later achieved wide circulation in the Iran he served as supreme leader.

Clearly, the rule of law was not always the dominant characteristic in the affairs of states around the world in late 1964. Leaving aside the American adventure in South East Asia that accelerated to an intensity few voters could have expected when they returned President Johnson to office, civil wars or coups broke out in Saudi Arabia, Bolivia, the Sudan, Yemen, Tunisia, Cyprus and Bhutan. Haiti conducted a series of televised firing-squad executions of rebels opposed to François 'Papa Doc' Duvalier's dictatorship, and Syria fired some missiles at civilian settlements on the other side of its western border with Israel, prompting Israel to retaliate by bombing strategic targets around Damascus. Taken as a whole, this fell some way short of fulfilling the promised 'year of transformative peace and goodwill' in international relations heralded by the United Nations secretary-general U Thant in his annual address to the General Assembly in January 1964.

'LADY, YOU SHOT ME'

It's been argued that the culture war waged remorselessly today displays some of the same logical trap favoured by the witch-dunkers of the seventeenth century. If the woman drowned, she was innocent; if she lived, she was a witch and should be burned. In the same vein, the person who says they are racist is a racist, and so is the person who denies it. The best thing to do in this looking-glass world is to save time and immediately confess to being an irredeemable bigot in the first place.

In 1964, however, 'racism' wasn't just an effortless and damaging charge to cast on anyone you disliked or disagreed with, or who disagreed with you. It was an observable fact of life. Whether in the ubiquity of 'Paki' jokes, or the sort of casual prejudice captured by a neatly dressed Indian man fitted with a hidden BBC radio microphone to record his experience of trying to get a haircut in central Birmingham ('We're closed, mate,' the barber remarked, 'can you just clear off?'), a certain scepticism about the merits of a fully integrated society was the rule, and widespread social inclusivity the exception.

A curious and tragic incident occurring in Los Angeles on 11 December 1964 seemed to crystallise the always charged debate about race relations in the United States. The smooth-voiced, 33-year-old black singer-songwriter Sam Cooke, then riding high on the twist craze, had enjoyed a string of six top-ten hits over the previous five years. As things stood in 1964, it did not necessarily follow that he was a wealthy man – even for its white performers, the record business was a mixture of inefficiency and corruption – but Cooke had one invaluable companion swimming alongside him as he navigated the shark-infested waters of 1960s American showbusiness: a pipe-smoking 32-year-old 'neighbourhood guy' from New Jersey, sometime Hollywood mogul and future business adviser to the Beatles and the Stones named Allen Klein.

Klein was incredible. 'Weird', 'slimy', 'inelegant', 'ineloquent', 'charmless', 'sinister' and 'castratingly rude' in various accounts – and those were just the more charitable views of colleagues who admired his obvious business skills – he may have been the most chillingly repulsive pop music executive of even that golden era for the genre. Squat, beady-eyed and built like a bag of spanners, invariably clad in ill-fitting jeans and a greasy sweater that offered asylum to stray bits of food, he and his wardrobe were so brazen that both defied ridicule. Klein made his name with a titanically aggressive negotiating style which he conducted on his own unvarnished terms, deploying an almost comic machine-gun rattle of street argot, liberally spiced with ripe fuck-you invective. Casting himself as the Robin Hood of Tin Pan Alley, taking on the mighty robber-barons of the record labels, he convincingly assured clients that he was 'someone who knows how to give these guys some of their own shit back', in time coming to enjoy virtual loyalty-card status in both the US and UK court systems as a result. Pursued successively by the tax authorities and stock exchange regulators in several countries, Klein was eventually found guilty by a New York court of filing false accounts. He had put up a stout defence for himself, even so, invoking much of the fine detail of the Anglo-American tax treaty and other arcane legislation. In the end US District Court Judge Vincent Broderick concluded that Klein had 'lied throughout' his trial, and gave him a two-year sentence, all but two months of it suspended.

Klein met Sam Cooke in the early autumn of 1963, and soon discovered that the singer's record label, RCA Victor, had declined to pay him a substantial amount of accrued back royalties. This oversight was swiftly corrected following a brief but memorable visit to RCA corporate headquarters which wasted no time on pleasantries. 'You've been fucking us over!' Klein shouted at the assembled board members of the 1901-founded company, many of them not far behind it in age. It was his standard opening when doing business, and he followed it with a snapped, 'Haven't you?'

Whatever transpired in the course of the next few minutes, it was enough for the long-serving RCA senior management to agree to a significantly improved offer for Sam Cooke's services. The singer would receive an immediate cash advance of $100,000 ($1.7 million today) for each of the next three years, followed by $75,000 ($1.2 million) for each of two option years. This was serious money for a recording artist of the day, let alone one stigmatised as a mere 'race' performer. There was a modest celebration party that night at a downtown New York club, and following that the two principal beneficiaries of the day's events went outside and, seemingly as an afterthought, scribbled their initials on a contract laid out on a car roof in an unlit parking lot. Apparently it was too dark for Cooke to read the fine print, which made everything payable not to himself but to the Nevada-registered Tracey Ltd, a company solely controlled by Allen Klein.

Sam Cooke died just fifteen months later, in circumstances that still regularly exercise rock music's quite extensive conspiracy mills. The singer had gone to a room at the $3-a-night Hacienda motel in south Los Angeles with a young 'mulatto Chinese-American woman other than his wife', as the police report described her, but in reality a 22-year-old aspiring actress and sometime sex worker named Elisa Boyer. The couple had met for the first time earlier that evening in a fashionable downtown nightclub, where the singer had seemed to be in good spirits and 'merrily waved around a wad of $5,000 in cash from a recent set of concert dates'. At around 2 a.m., Cooke and Boyer got in his new red Ferrari 400 and drove for half an hour to the unprepossessing Hacienda, an establishment catering to short-term, if not hourly, guests, where they signed the register as man and wife. The real Mrs Cooke, Barbara Campbell, mother to Sam's two surviving daughters, a young son having died in a pool accident, was elsewhere in town, apparently reconciled to her husband's occasional nocturnal excursions.

The exact details of what happened next remain a matter of some mystery. Boyer claimed that on their arrival at the motel, Cooke had 'dragged' her into the bedroom, abruptly pinned her to the ground and stripped off her clothes down to her slip and bra. 'I thought he was going to rape me,' she told the police. According to her story, Cooke himself then disrobed and entered the bathroom, at which point his companion grabbed her shoes and skirt from a pile on the floor. In her haste, she explained, she also picked up Cooke's clothes, which contained his wallet and cash. At that point, Boyer ran down the street to a nearby phone booth and made a hurried emergency call to the police, telling the dispatcher that she had been kidnapped.

Cooke supposedly flew into a rage when he emerged from the bathroom to discover that both Boyer and his possessions were gone. Wearing just a sports jacket and a single black shoe – his only remaining items of clothing – he jumped back in the Ferrari and screeched around the corner to the front of the hotel, where he loudly confronted the manager on duty, a 55-year-old African American woman named Bertha Franklin, whom Cooke believed was shielding Boyer. The exchange between the motel employee and her lightly attired guest quickly became heated. 'Where's the girl?' Cooke repeatedly demanded. Apparently unperturbed by the sight of a trouserless man shouting at her through the grilled window of her office, Franklin replied that she had no idea as to Mrs Cooke's whereabouts. At that stage, Cooke put his shoulder to the door of the motel's office, breaking it down, and confronted the woman more directly. 'He grabbed both of my arms and started twisting them,' Franklin testified, 'and kept yelling "Where's the girl?" I started kicking. I tried to bite him through the jacket. I was fighting, biting, scratching, everything.' For many years it was American motel orthodoxy for the duty night manager to keep a stout club or stick close at hand for dealing with obstreperous patrons, and Franklin was no exception to the rule. 'I swatted him a couple of times,' she reported, 'but he kept coming.'

At that point, Franklin abandoned the stick and seized the palm-sized .22 pistol she kept under her desk for interacting with especially unruly guests, and squeezed off three close-range shots. Two missed, but the third struck Cooke in the heart. He was dead by the time an ambulance crew arrived five minutes later. According to court testimony, his last audible words were 'Lady, you shot me.'

Four days later, a Los Angeles coroner's jury ruled Cooke's death a 'justifiable homicide' in view of the 'incontrovertible fact [that] Mrs. Franklin had feared for her physical wellbeing'. Less easily explained was the fact that Cooke's body showed signs of severe bruising around the neck and head. 'It looked like he had been used as a punchbag' said no less a judge than Muhammad Ali, who attended the open-casket funeral in Chicago. The singer Etta James similarly wrote, 'Sam's head was practically disconnected from his shoulders. That's how badly he'd been beaten. His hands were broken and crushed ... They tried to hide it with makeup, but I could see massive bruises on his head.' Had Cooke perhaps been assaulted, some wondered, by a party or parties other than the Hacienda's arthritic female night clerk? A few minutes after police arrived at the motel, Elisa Boyer walked up and calmly introduced herself as an acquaintance of the deceased. She had a single $20 bill in her purse; Cooke's own cash-stuffed wallet was never found.

There remained the central question, too, of why a wealthy celebrity might have wished to drive nearly 20 miles to the unalluring Hacienda in the first place, passing several more salubrious places of lodging along the way, unless it had been specifically suggested to him by his companion. Had Elisa Boyer in fact deliberately lured Cooke to the motel in order for her confederates to rob him? Tactfully described in the press as a 'Eurasian vocalist' (and by the investigating police as a 'real baby doll'), Boyer was subsequently arrested on prostitution charges and in 1979 found guilty of second-degree murder following another hotel shooting. It has to be said that the police enquiry into the whole matter of Cooke's death was cursory at best, and that within less than a week the officially accepted story was that this otherwise gentle-spirited popular entertainer had suddenly plunged through the door of a south LA flophouse in the early hours of the morning while apparently in the grip of a priapic frenzy, and there grappled with a blameless elderly lady who had had little option in the matter but to shoot him dead.

It may be that something like this really did happen. But it's also possible that the story of Sam Cooke's violent and lonely death owed something to the partisan nature of the US criminal justice system of the time – would the verdict have been quite as quickly reached had the victim's name been Sinatra or Presley? – or, equally, that Cooke had been set up for a reason concealed somewhere within the thicket of his financial dealings with Allen Klein, who subsequently paid $350,000 for the remaining rights to his late client's estate, a legacy valued at some $100 million today.

★★★

The Trinidad-born journalist and social campaigner Claudia Jones died in her London home that December. She was only 49, and had apparently suffered a heart attack. Jones, sometimes called the god-mother of multicultural Britain, had been deported from the United States in 1955 to begin a long, generally unavailing struggle against what she saw as the deeply ingrained flaws not only of her adopted country's ruling class ('You expect your enemies to be shits,' she once remarked; 'it's when your friends are shits too that's so disturbing'), but also of some on the political left – uneasy, apparently, with the idea of a strongly opinionated immigrant woman in their midst. She went on to found Britain's first major black newspaper, the *West Indian Gazette*, and played a central role in bringing the annual gaiety of the Notting Hill Carnival to the streets of London. In keeping with her request, Claudia Jones was buried in a grave adjacent to that of her hero Karl Marx in Highgate Cemetery.

If the death of Sam Cooke had left the British press largely unmoved, that of Claudia Jones just a few days later was a cause for positive rejoicing at one end of the spectrum down to polite reserve at the other. There were respectful but not overlong notices in most of the broadsheet papers, and few other signs of communal grief or distress at her passing beyond those of Jones's immediate circle. No one travelled in on their own initiative, as for the death of a modern-day pop star or royal princess, clutching their cellophane-wrapped bouquets to lay at the gates of the deceased's home. Most people at that time preferred not to broadcast the fact that they were grieving, and to do otherwise was thought to be evidence of an unseemly hysteria. If truly distraught, the theory went, you suffered in silence. Perhaps it was all psychologically damaging to repress our feelings as we did and just below the surface millions of ordinary Britons were inwardly seething with barely contained resentment or anger at the way they considered themselves to have been treated by life. Or perhaps a certain amount of emotional restraint might be an advantage in such cases. It's hard to say with any certainty. No one seemed unduly perturbed on the cold winter morning on which Claudia Jones was laid to rest in the plot immediately beside the role model she had revered throughout her adult life. The *West Indian Gazette* survived her by only three issues.

Was Jones right when she spoke about the challenges an Anglo-Caribbean woman might have expected to face in the Britain of her day, where some of the least enlightened behaviour came from within the politically liberal camp? Her own experience seems to merit sympathy. Many of Jones's male fellow travellers treated her as an exotic novelty, if that, and before turning on his tape recorder an interviewer from the BBC who introduced himself as a 'Labour man' once complimented her on her 'lovely rump' – probably an imprisonable offence today. On the other hand, one of Jones's biggest surprises following her arrival in Britain was to see white council road-sweepers cleaning up after the first Notting Hill festivals. 'Caucasian hands doing a coloured man's work – whatever next?' she wrote. Another shock was seeing young women walking around in public with 'indecorously' short skirts. What sort of message was that to send about female self-pride? Perhaps it was all what we would now call empowering. Or perhaps Jones's reaction was only the commonly held view of people over a certain age in the early 1960s. Celia Grigg turned 18 in December 1964, and in the week before Christmas took the train up from her family home near Aldershot to interview for a position in the typing pool on Tony Gill's *Daily Sketch*.

'There was no such thing as a Human Resources department,' she remembers:

It was called Personnel, and the man there was about sixty, with a great bumpy red nose and smoking up a storm. I noticed he was inclined to dandruff. After a few minutes he asked me to stand up and do a full turn for him, and I was young and naïve, so I did. Then he said my dress was all right, but that if I was going to work there I'd have to wear stockings and high heels. No one said a word about my typing skills.

She took the job. A now elderly lady who prefers anonymity adds that she'd applied around the same time for a vacancy at the BBC. The nation's broadcaster was 'white, male and hideously sexist,' she recalls. 'The interviewer was a lecherous old sod in his 40s, and after shaking my hand and looking me up and down, the first thing he said was: "That's a nice skirt, love, but it would look better on my bedroom floor".' She, too, accepted the job. 'There was a boozy Christmas lunch that year. I was wearing a reasonably low-cut party frock, nothing special, and the big game they all played was to roll up bits of the paper-chains hung around the room and then try and chuck them down my cleavage.'

Christmas itself was a protracted affair, says Celia Grigg, who spent some of the time moving out of her family home to a shared flat nearer London:

> Basically, everything shut down for a fortnight. The big thing was to at least have enough coins to feed the electricity meter and not freeze to death. There were no late-night shops, or at least not where I lived in the back end of Croydon, although I think the milkman still came round every morning. The fridge broke down, but there was no problem keeping the bottles cold. You just left them out on the window-sill. We were three girls in the flat and there was always a row of great big sensible knickers hanging stiff as a board on the outside drying line. It was the Swinging Sixties, but the country I lived in was still quite naff. Most places closed early, and even when they were open you saw signs outside cafés saying things like 'Teen-aged customers should conduct themselves with courtesy,' and my own personal favourite, 'We proudly serve only imitation cream on the premises.' You heard some great music, but even then people were shocked by the Rolling Stones not bothering to wear suits and ties when they played at the London Palladium. That really upset people, and there were a lot of indignant letters about 'falling standards' in the press. When I think back on 1964, I think of outraged colonels from Tunbridge Wells, early closing, and frosty knickers hanging on the clothes line.

The heat of Harold Wilson's revolution, then, burned more warmly in some parts of British life than others. There were at least tentative signs that the government might reform some of the nation's more sclerotic institutions to be seen in the Cabinet meeting at Downing Street on 15 December. Douglas Houghton, the MP for Sowerby in West Yorkshire and lately Chancellor of the Duchy of Lancaster, told ministers of his plan to appoint a commission with no less a brief than to 'undertake a systematic review of the English law; carry out consolidation and statute law revision; and put forward specific proposals for reform, on the analogy of the Department of Law in other countries of Western Europe'. Houghton's colleague Tom Fraser, a former Scottish coal miner who had gone into politics as an alternative, now became one of the long line of transport ministers to advocate a 'national plan for the co-ordination of the country's road and rail systems', while George Brown climactically revealed that he had 'just today reached agreement with representatives of both sides of industry in a joint Statement of Intent on prices and incomes, [which] should both contribute to the renewal of international confidence in sterling and provide a firm foundation on which to develop the Government's domestic policies for economic expansion'.

Brown's announcement brought a polite round of applause from his colleagues, and had a certain logic, but for one thing. It required British management and labour to display a mutual goodwill that had largely ceased to exist since the 1940s. For now, the Cabinet recorded its satisfaction with the 'highly satisfactory results' of Brown's discussions, which seem to have come by way of a Christmas economic miracle, before moving on to 'certain outstanding matters of concern'. These included a number of 'unresolved wage claims in several sectors of society', among them groups with no previous record of militancy in the area, 'notably the higher judiciary, who consider that they now have a very strong claim to an increase in their remuneration'. Wilson and his ministers sympathised, but noted, in terms that perhaps owed something to the PM's own background as a maths lecturer, 'The precise quantum of the increment should be a matter for further discussion between the parties primarily concerned.' That concluded the Cabinet's last full session of 1964.

'TIS THE SEASON

While Wilson himself remained diligently at his desk that Tuesday evening, one or two of his colleagues took the opportunity to attend a modest Christmas drinks party held in a private function room on the top floor of the nearby St Stephen's Tavern. As we've seen, George Brown, the man charged with bringing a new sense of discipline to the nation's economy, and Wilson's presumptive heir as premier, then enjoyed a somewhat equivocal reputation when it came to the Bacchic rites. There had already been a mildly unfortunate (if perhaps apocryphal) incident when, on hearing the orchestra strike up a number at a formal embassy reception in South America, Brown had made a beeline for an attractively crimson-clad figure and asked for a dance. Unfortunately, he failed to recognise two salient facts: the band was in fact playing the Peruvian national anthem, and the individual he had approached was the Cardinal Archbishop of Lima.

A teenaged University of London student named Diana Pryce was working part-time at the St Stephen's pub over the Christmas holidays, and was called on to go upstairs several times that evening to resupply the parliamentary group with wine from the bar. Each time she opened the door to the function room where the party was in progress she found some new prank awaiting her. 'Once it was a piece of string tied around ankle-high across the door, the next a plastic jug of water on top of it, and a third, I seem to remember, involved a bunch of balloons arranged in a funny display, accompanied by a lot of naughty male laughter and a song they seemed to have just made up which rhymed "Brighton" and "tight 'un".' Although Brown himself had a good singing voice, there is no evidence that he was personally involved in this composition.

When Wilson was asked many years later what he considered his greatest achievements in office as a whole, he spoke not about his government's incomes policy, nor the fact that he had managed to avoid or delay civil wars in Central Africa and Northern Ireland, nor having resisted American pressure to send British troops to Vietnam. He was most proud, instead, of having made the United Kingdom a 'fairer place', and of having found parliamentary time to reform the laws governing much of traditional family life. Wilson expressed particular satisfaction that he had been able to drag the issue of theatrical censorship into the twentieth century, in order to 'stop the state from interfering with anyone's idea of entertainment'. The Lord Chamberlain's Office remained a potent force of the early 1960s British arts landscape, as seen by their continuing list of objections to the script of Joe Orton's new play *Loot* when once again presented to them for their review in December 1964. 'This remains a filthy play,' the report began unambiguously, before going on to itemise some of its lingering concerns: 'Dialogue on p.3 a mixture of smut and blasphemy ... Blasphemy again ... Voyeurism ... Female genitalia described in crudest terms ... Offensive reference to homosexuality ... The play is unpleasant in many of its details, and [I] continue to recommend it should not be licensed,' the report concluded.

'That's the thing about the 1960s,' says Tony Gill:

People have an idea of all these beautiful young kids parading around in flares and miniskirts, and everything being free and easy. And to be honest there was some of that. You never had less than three parties on a Saturday night if you were under about 40 anywhere in London, and I remember once being at some rich girl's house out near Henley and looking at a double row of Range Rovers and Aston Martins parked out front, testifying to the arrival of Harold Pinter and Roman Polanski and a couple of Beatles. It was that kind of crowd. On the other hand, there were non-stop shortages and strikes, everything seemed to be broken or shut, with a lot of blokes walking around in bad suits and women with frumpy dresses and dodgy teeth. Half your life was bells and beads, and the other half was little Hitlers straight out of the army telling you 'You can't park there, mate.'

Things generally seemed good in the old-fashioned world of print journalism. 'There was a wink-and-a-nod quality to life at the *Sketch*,' Gill says. And a contagious optimism. For the paper's lavish Christmas party that year, the directors flew in the 22-year-old Japanese pop sensation Kyu Sakamoto, who sang his infectiously catchy global hit single 'Sukiyaki' – which, being rendered in the Tanka-poetic idiom, few of those present would have known was actually a stinging rebuke of Western post-war imperialism. 'I woke up in a friend's bathtub in Clapham,' Gill adds.

Roman Polanski, the 31-year-old *enfant terrible* of European cinema who had now migrated to the United Kingdom, recalled it as an 'exciting place ... There was a cultural renaissance with British and Europeans, and also many Americans – all the film-makers, screenwriters and actors who had fled from Hollywood.' At least for an ambitious and well-connected creative artist like him, Britain was clearly the place to be. Within a few months of arriving in the spring of 1964, Polanski was on the fast track to social success as a member of the Ad Lib set, a collective of London's most beautiful people. Located in a cramped, smoky room in a building behind Leicester Square, the Ad Lib itself somehow regularly packed in three or four hundred guests, throbbing, sweating, dancing the conga and crashing into the laps of strangers. Then it would typically be on to the nearby home of a Paul McCartney or Victor Lownes, the latter of whom soon offered Polanski both female companionship and his first taste of LSD. The precocious young future director of *Rosemary's Baby* and *Chinatown* didn't need a subpoena. 'The world's best and brightest people were all in London,' he told me.

They came form unexpected origins, like Polanski himself, a young Holocaust survivor. Perhaps that was what led them to see the special qualities of the place. It was a 'mudge better scene than LA', the director remarked in his then much-mimicked accent. 'Fandastic days', he added, and they got even better when at a party he met the co-directors of the Compton Group, a Soho-based concern specialising in soft-core porn films with titles like *Gutter Girls* and *London in the Raw*. So lucrative was this venture, which had recently swung to a zenith with *My Bare Lady*, that Compton's owners, two East End entrepreneurs with the faintly comic-opera names of Michael Klinger and Tony Tenser, were keen to expand. The company's principals listened politely to the young Polish émigré's insistence that he would one day be bigger than Alfred Hitchcock. Having read the original screenplay Polanski first showed them, an absurdist comedy called *If Katelbach Comes*, aggressively rejected by all the major studios, they could see why a script about a young French woman and her middle-aged transvestite husband living alone in a remote seafront castle might not have been considered an immediately commercial property. But, unlike everyone else, they actually agreed to make a film with Polanski – not *Katelbach*, but a horror story they called *Repulsion*, shot in five weeks that winter on a total budget of £35,000 (£520,000 today), which proved to be his ticket to *Rosemary's Baby* and all that followed. 'I was the king of the scene,' Polanski later remembered, for once throwing modesty to the wind.

Perhaps it's enough to say that, on the whole, the British were now becoming noticeably less interested in the nuances of organised religion or party politics, and more so in consuming and being entertained. By December 1964, over 90 per cent of all UK households owned at least one television set, up from a figure of 62 per cent just five years earlier. People would have settled in that 25 December, a Friday, to a line-up of programmes that ranged from a live broadcast of Billy Smart's Circus to a fiesta of Latin American folk dance on BBC 1, to a special festive transmission of *Ready Steady Go!* and a stream of American imports like *QuickDraw McGraw*, *Petticoat Junction* and *The Danny Kaye Spectacular* on ITV, with the Queen's traditional 3 p.m. message to the Commonwealth acting as the fulcrum and national rallying point on both channels. It was snowing that day across much of the UK, so at least some people might have spent part of the long weekend curled up with a mug of Horlicks and a good book like John le Carré's newly published *The Spy Who Came in From The Cold*, or listening to Petula Clark belt out her new single 'Downtown', that anthem to metropolitan glamour and future karaoke standard, on the family Dansette in their sparsely furnished, pre-*Austin Powers* suburban front rooms.

Britain's rail services were effectively comatose until the following Monday morning, enabling, or in some cases compelling, many people to spend a protracted amount of time with their extended families. Between the pressure to replicate greeting-card ideals of seasonal gatherings, and the tendency of even adult children to revert to old roles when visiting home, perhaps it's no surprise the Marriage Guidance Council, forerunner of today's Relate, reported a 35 per cent surge in the volume of calls during the week of 28 December to 4 January. Even when people were free to move around the country again, they did so either on snowbound roads described by the AA as offering the 'worst driving conditions in history' or on a severely depleted national rail network. Dr Richard Beeching, the efficiency expert brought in at more than twice the prime minister's salary, had already caused the closure of 1,058 route miles of track in 1964, and 800 more would follow in 1965. As a result, huge swathes of the UK were suddenly cut off, including a large part of the south-west, where the acres of ghost lines and rows of phantom platforms serve as a visible reminder of the Beeching axe today. More broadly, the cuts arguably marked the end of Britain's romance with the train and the inexorable rise of the car, with 8 million vehicles already then registered in the UK, up from 5 million in 1960.

On 23 December, Labour's transport minister Tom Fraser told the Commons that Beeching himself would be 'returning to his former post as technical director of Imperial Chemical Industries in the middle of next year, [but] I have his assurance that I shall continue to have the full benefit of his counsel during the months ahead'. Most of this, however, was rhetoric: Beeching's contract had not been renewed, and he left government service on poor terms. It was regrettable, the minister added, that 'this individual, an outstanding servant of the state, [had] attracted such undue attention, much more of it drawn to the person who has undertaken the study of our rail network than to the study itself'. Reading of Beeching's departure from the government, Paul McCartney invited him to sort out the Beatles' finances. He wisely declined.

Before returning to the private sector, Dr Beeching would go on to render one final service to the travelling public by unveiling the new brand for Britain's railways – British Rail – and its familiar double-arrow logo. Later appointed chairman of a commission to reorganise the English and Welsh court system, Beeching died in hospital in East Grinstead, Sussex, in 1985, at the age of 71; the town later named a small road after him on the site of one of the railway lines made redundant by his report.

At least one Englishman's experience that Christmas differed significantly from the world of fresh food shortages and transportation woes on offer elsewhere. This was Keith Richards, the hirsute guitarist and principal creative force of the Rolling Stones, whose crowd-management technique earlier that summer at Blackpool had contributed to the city's worst outbreak of civil disorder since racial tensions had flared into 'Chinky'-bashing riots shortly after the conclusion of the Great War. It was only now, two years into the Stones's still seemingly unstoppable career, that Richards first came to realise that he was suddenly one of the biggest pop stars in the world. The revelation occurred not on a concert stage, but while he was out Christmas shopping in his local, normally decorous north London high street, and a shrill Dame Edna-type woman with a vivid pink rinse suddenly went berserk, lashing out at the young musician for 'singing trash'. Several remarks of an unappreciative nature followed. In time, the woman steered the conversation away from Richards's music to that of his personal appearance, satirically advising him that he should perm his hair. 'You should perm your twat,' Keith promptly replied, thus taking the exchange to the next level.

In short order, Richards's critic was swinging at him with her hand-bag, and a curious crowd had gathered to follow the progress of this apparent generational clash taking place on the streets of Hampstead. After that, both parties continued to bellow querulously at one another for some time, until the crowd became a mini riot, and at length someone plunged through the plate-glass window of a shop in all the confusion. At that, the word 'police' was mentioned, and Richards, apparently thinking it best not to expose himself too closely to the forces of the law, took the opportunity to hail a passing black cab, a photograph of the scene catching a blurred smudge of Keith's jet-black eyes bulging in a moment of frozen shock and his convict's striped jersey slipping from his shoulders, an image that appeared to capture in a single snapshot the end of the old, mutually respectful relationship between a performer and his public and the arrival of something altogether more primal.

Under the circumstances, it's worth noting that the date was Friday 18 December 1964, and that Keith Richards himself turned 21 that day.

★ ★ ★

Coups and counter-coups in Saigon in the last part of 1964 further complicated President Johnson's options as he continued to walk the razor's edge between his commitment to shore up anti-communist forces in the region and his reluctance to 'send our boys 9 or 10,000 miles away from home to do what Asian boys ought to be doing for themselves'. Clearly there were no easy choices in the matter. The widely syndicated American newspaper columnist Joe Alsop wrote on 23 December that Johnson was 'consciously prepared to accept defeat in Vietnam', and taunted the president by comparing his 'cowardice' in South East Asia to his predecessor's actions in the Cuban missile crisis: 'If Mr. Johnson ducks the challenge [in Vietnam] we shall learn by bitter experience what it would have been like if Kennedy had ducked the challenge in October 1962.' Johnson was not pleased to be publicly accused of lacking moral fibre in this way. He was especially unhappy because Alsop happened to be a closeted homosexual and he, Johnson, had gone to some trouble to prevent certain compromising photographs taken of the award-winning journalist whilst on a trip to Moscow from becoming public. 'They [the press] hate me because of my Great Society legislation,' the president complained. 'They don't want to help the poor and the negroes ... but the war, oh, they love the war.'

Johnson later applied a perhaps fitting metaphor when coming to reflect on his competing priorities while serving as his nation's chief executive. 'If I left the woman I loved – the Great Society – in order to get involved with that bitch of a war on the other side of the world, then I'd lose everything at home,' he noted. 'But if I left that war and let the commies take over South Vietnam ... there would follow in this country an endless national debate that would shatter my presidency, kill my administration, and fracture our democracy.'

Presidents always tend to talk this way about the imminent collapse of society, but in fairness to Johnson his early progress in Vietnam was steady and deliberate rather than showy and divisive. The full gravity of the situation on the ground seemed to come home to him only when the beloved all-American (but actually British-born) entertainer Bob Hope was nearly killed when a car bomb exploded outside a Saigon hotel minutes before he arrived for the first of what would prove to be nine annual morale-boosting visits to the area. 'Holy shit!' the president exclaimed when watching coverage of the event that evening on the bank of three televisions – one tuned to each major network – in the Oval Office.

Early in the new year, Johnson's patience finally snapped with his 'panty-waisted' allies in Saigon, who now seemed to him to change their government on a near-weekly basis. From then onward, American planes began to systematically bomb North Vietnam. It wasn't necessary to do so every day; once or twice a week would be 'enough to keep morale up in Saigon', Johnson informed a meeting of his national-security staff. He added: 'We face a choice of going forward or running. We have chosen the first alternative. All of us agree on this, but there remains some difference in the government [and] the country as to how fast we should proceed.' This proved to be a significant understatement; America's collective agony in South East Asia had now officially begun.

About the one thing almost all Americans seem able to agree on today is that Washington doesn't work and their political system is broken. The seeds of this consensus had already been sown by late 1964. Johnson had decisively won the presidential race after he and his supporters had convincingly portrayed their Republican challenger as a dangerous fanatic and mortal enemy of the republic, almost a proto-Donald Trump figure. But the truth is that the country as a whole was hopelessly divided, not just by the escalating situation in Vietnam but by the first observable signs of identity politics, the primitive sense of an us-versus-them mindset largely determined by an individual's skin colour and the assumption – the throughline of all American politics today – that the only legitimate evidence of a non-racist society is equal outcomes for all, and that if necessary the state will step in to bring them about.

On 3 December 1964, police arrested some 800 students at the University of California in Berkeley following protests – riots, in some accounts – perhaps ambitiously demanding 'immediate civil rights and equality for all peoples of the world'. The trigger for the disturbances was the confrontation between university security staff and 24-year-old Jack Weinberg, a graduate student credited with the phrase 'Never trust anyone over 30', who had climbed onto the roof of a car in order to inform a large crowd about the pervasive racism on their campus. With the benefit of hindsight, the mass round-ups that followed were perhaps counterproductive. Normal business at Berkeley was effectively suspended for the rest of the year. When the US vice president-elect Hubert Humphrey came to visit the area, apparently in a bid to defuse tensions, he was met by demonstrators carrying signs asking, 'Lee Harvey Oswald, where are you now?' and using 'rustic language' to characterise Senator Humphrey and his family.

The tone of rhetoric was clearly souring in America as a whole. J. Edgar Hoover's FBI was now busy compiling thousands of dossiers on groups such as the Congress of Racial Equality (CORE) and Free Speech Movement (FSM), and other such 'radical-subversive cells that might jeopardize the normal democratic process of the country, [if] not imperil the life of the President and Vice President of the United States'. The FBI later reported that credible threats against the nation's two senior elected officials had risen from an average of six a day in December 1963 to 'upwards of 200' just a year later. This was serious, but the bureau remained confident that while 'CORE and FSM [may] use the race issue ... to divide the country ... we can match any challenge, though they may not think so.' The historian Robert Dallek adds: 'A result of the organized opposition was that Johnson became a prisoner in the White House, largely losing his freedom to travel in the country. It added to the distance between himself and the public, exacerbating tensions and increasing the "credibility gap".

Later in December, Hoover himself met the new Nobel laureate Martin Luther King at FBI headquarters in Washington in order to resolve 'any point [of] doubt or confusion that may have arisen between these two patriotic Americans' in the nuanced words of the press release. As understatements go, this was akin to remarking that Great Britain had had a trivial misunderstanding with Germany in the years 1914–18. King had previously said that the FBI had done a 'piss-poor job' of investigating civil rights abuses in the South, and Hoover in turn had called King 'the most notorious liar in America'. Perhaps the Washington talks spurred the veteran government man into action, because just two days later his agents picked up a group of twenty-one members of a rural Mississippi chapter of the Ku Klux Klan, including the local sheriff, whom they accused of having murdered three CORE activists earlier in the summer. Most of the charges were subsequently dismissed by a Mississippi judge who himself had Klan affiliations. The Justice Department eventually reinstated the indictments, and in 1970 seven men were tried and sentenced to terms of between three and nine years in federal prison.

On 7 December 1964, the US Supreme Court, 'prodding tradition as warily as a lion-tamer', in one account, narrowly voted to strike down a Florida law that prohibited a black man from living with a white woman. Some years earlier, a mixed-race Miami couple named Dewie McLaughlin and Connie Hoffman had each been sentenced to thirty days in jail for cohabitation, and their appeal had percolated up the judicial system until reaching the upper chamber in Washington. Other courts would soon come to interpret Johnson's Civil Rights Act in such a way as to make lawful discrimination in favour of what were termed 'protected minorities'. In time, an enormous race-quota compliance apparatus grew up, employing tens of thousands of people devoted to the ideal of what became known as affirmative action, the belief that it's permissible to extend preferential treatment to certain groups to atone for past injustice. All this began in 1964. The Supreme Court spoke again on 14 December of that year, when it ruled in Katzenbach v. McClung that Congress had acted within its power under the constitution in forbidding discrimination in restaurants, not so much on the grounds of equal rights, but because any such exclusion was to 'place an undue burden on interstate commerce ... Negroes typically spend less time eating at racially segregated restaurants, and thus segregation [there] imposes an artificial restriction on the flow of merchandise by discouraging negroes from making purchases.' Even in the uniquely charged world of America's race relations, it still ultimately came down to a question of the consumer dollar.

Just a few days later, the iconic actor John Wayne called a press conference at his home in Encino, California. The 57-year-old star of films like *Stagecoach* and *The Alamo* had nothing to say about civil rights per se (he did later), but instead shared the news that he had recently been treated for lung cancer, 'which I've now licked ... I know the big guy upstairs will pull the plug when he wants to, but I don't want to end my life being sick.'

Wayne further revealed that by going public in this way he'd gone against the advice of his family and long-time manager, who were concerned that any admission of serious illness could 'kill my image' at the box office. 'It's time for a new approach to these things,' he added. In the times ahead, dozens of lesser celebrities would follow this lead by sharing their various health struggles, or by writing newspaper articles recounting their painful but triumphant search for sobriety. One can surely applaud both Wayne himself and his fighting spirit – he lived for another fifteen years – even if his Christmas press conference marks the starting point of our own obsessive sharing of our daily ups and downs on Facebook, Instagram and other social media sites. Like the formalised race relations apparatus, this notion that others might be as intrigued by our mental or physical welfare as we are ourselves also has its roots in the events of 1964. John Wayne, on one level the personification of American frontier self-reliance, remains the unlikely harbinger of a particular kind of emotional incontinence.

★★★

While the West's sole superpower was busy redefining its idea of a model society, the Soviet Union also allowed itself a few modest reforms that year. Largely unnoticed at the time, a small article published on 25 December (a normal business day in the USSR) in the state-controlled newspaper *Izvestia* announced that the government would introduce a 'profit-based capitalist economic system in selected peoples' collectives in the Ukraine', effective from 1 January 1965.

According to the report, Leonid Brezhnev and his colleagues were not so much concerned with the nuances of free-market economics as they were anxious to produce practical results. By all conventional measurements, the USSR had fallen even further behind the industrial performance of its primary ideological rival during 1964. National price increases of as much as 35 per cent for meat and poultry products imposed overnight in the final days of the Khrushchev regime had led to an unprecedented wave of labour strikes around Moscow, Kiev and Leningrad. Some forty-seven years after the Bolshevik revolution, it had become painfully clear to Lenin's heirs in the Kremlin that there needed to be 'incentives' for increased manufacturing productivity that benefited those actually performing the work. Following the Ukraine experiment, Brezhnev announced a new scheme by which the profits of many concerns would go to a series of regional funds, which would be distributed according to strictly enforced central guidelines to individual farm or factory labourers. These same individuals could also be economically punished for falling below their planned quotas. A total of forty-three regional businesses shifted to the new model in the winter of 1964–65, and another 780 – representing about a third of total national economic output – followed within a year. It was the first tentative sign of the unravelling of the once rigidly enforced 1917 Soviet industrial blueprint.

The initiative could probably have taken place only under the Politburo led by Brezhnev and his reform-minded premier Alexei Kosygin, as opposed to that of their predecessor in office who towards the end had sometimes seemed not so much apathetic as cognitively impaired in his duties. Dropping in on the Moscow party boss Nikolai Yegorychev one Sunday afternoon in September 1964, Khrushchev had suddenly demanded to know what toilet seats in the city's new apartment blocks were being made of. 'Wood,' Yegorychev informed his head of state. 'Wood!' Khrushchev shouted:

I knew it. You're all wasters! You've got to use plastic. I was just in Poland. I lived in a villa. When you sit on a seat like the one there, it doesn't feel cold. So you take a trip there, check it out, and do the same thing with our crappers.

With that, the supreme leader of the USSR turned around and strode back to his waiting car. 'Those were the last instructions we ever received from Khrushchev about how to do things in Moscow,' Yegorychev reflected.

In the midst of this, Che Guevara, the 36-year-old czar of the Cuban economy, addressed the full majesty of the United Nations general assembly in New York, where he took the opportunity to predict a 'fast approaching hour of truth for Yankee monopoly capitalism', when the labour masses who 'turn the wheel of history' would 'awaken from the long, brutalising sleep to which they have been subjected.' In a notable show of magnanimity on his hosts' part, the man who had helped erect the first Cuban concentration camps for opponents of the regime, who referred to African Americans as 'magnificent beasts who have maintained their racial purity thanks to a lack of affinity with bathing', and dismissed some 80 million Mexican citizens as a 'band of illiterate savages', was rewarded by prolonged applause at the UN and the adulation of a segment of American liberal opinion. Jane Fonda once remarked that her biggest regret in life was not her decision to return from retirement to star in 2005's alleged comedy *Monster-in-Law*, but rather her failure to 'fuck Che Guevara'. The Church of England later went one further by publishing posters and leaflets bearing the face of Jesus Christ in the style of the iconic Guevara photograph, long hair flowing from under his trademark beret, apparently geared toward attracting 'young people' to attend worship services. Even Lyndon Johnson, not one of life's natural firebrands, thought the Cuban rebel a 'fine figure of a patriotic young man'.

Apparently not everyone shared in the Guevara cult, however, because during his UN address a heavy-duty anti-tank rocket was fired across the East River in an apparent assassination attempt. Three anti-Castro Cuban dissidents were later arrested for the attack, telling the police that they had bought their Second World War-era bazooka at a local military surplus store for $35. In the event, the shell missed its target by about 200 yards to land on the west bank of the river, sending up a spectacular plume of water and rattling the windows of the General Assembly. The New York supreme court later dismissed the indictments against the defendants, remarking that they had merely expressed a 'legitimate concern for their island, rather [than] attempt to cause mass casualties', and set them free. Three years later, Che Guevara was summarily executed by Bolivian army troops while on a mission to instil revolutionary fervour in their country, and remains widely revered as a martyr to idealism today.

It seems fairly clear that certain figures in public life become dangerously self-impressed from an early age. In time, even exposure to the outside world fails to adjust the flattering image of the distorting carnival mirror. It's not a phenomenon restricted to the United States, although it may be most pronounced there: the modern politician, wholly self-focused, who panders to the tastes of a class of society whom he or she privately despises.

In the case of Lyndon Johnson, who came up the hard way on a Texas farm with neither electricity nor indoor plumbing, the great motivating factor seems to have been not so much overweening pride as it was the nagging sense that he was adrift in a hostile world. Few occupants of the Oval Office are ever wholly free of some level of paranoia, but by late 1964 it had come to determine US national policy to an unusual degree. The president's principal speechwriter Dick Goodwin would remember his chief's reaction to the early opposition of the *New York Times* and others to his Vietnam policy: 'Don't they know I'm the only president they've got and a war is on?', before characterising his critics as 'sonsofbitches', 'shits', and close to being 'traitors'. In time, Goodwin grew increasingly alarmed about the gulf between the rational, self-confident commander-in-chief the world saw and the embittered loner he knew in private. 'I'm not going to have anything more to do with the panty-waists [liberals],' Johnson told Goodwin. 'They won't have anything to do with me. They all just follow the communist line – liberals, intellectuals, commies ... I can't trust anybody anymore.'

Bill Moyers was so concerned about the president's darkening state of mind that he phoned a colleague at close to midnight one evening to say 'he was extremely worried, that as he listened to Johnson he felt weird, almost as if he wasn't really talking to a human being at all'. Speaking to Goodwin about the dry arcana of the US social security budget, the president once suddenly broke off to remark, 'You know, Dick, the communists are taking over this country.' He interrupted another session of his domestic affairs staff to announce that 'the commies already control the three TV networks and the forty main news outlets in America'. Bill Moyers would later speculate that Johnson's cast of mind came down to 'the realisation, about which he was clearer than anyone else, that Vietnam was a road from which there was no turning back'. The president's mental state amounted to a 'pronounced, prolonged depression', Moyers would add. 'He would just go within himself, just disappear – morose, self-pitying, angry. He was a tormented man.'

Johnson was not the only one to succumb to a paranoid management style. One sure sign of this approach to governance lies in its concern with 'factuality', a piling up of random details that allows the injustice collector to always see themselves as the wronged party. Harold Wilson seems to have reached this point by around Christmas 1964, just ten weeks into his first term, by which time he was already convinced he was the target of a vast British establishment conspiracy to remove him from office. In time, his paranoia grew so acute that he became convinced that his enemies were following him even when he and his family went on their biennial holidays to the Scilly Isles, not generally known for their air of racy intrigue. When Wilson got back to Downing Street he promptly had his minister of defence, Denis Healey, make enquiries about whether there had been any 'unusual activity' by Soviet vessels in the vicinity of the Scillies while his family had been in residence, or if any 'foreign spy ships disguise[d] as trawlers' had perhaps been sent to keep watch. Was there even something a bit sinister about the profusion of seagulls seen circling above the Wilsons' modest three-bedroom bungalow in St Mary's, the PM wondered, perhaps in the way of miniature cameras or directional radio microphones fitted in the birds' wings?

All of this might seem to suggest that Wilson was cracking under the strain, although it's possible he was right to be concerned, if not about the Russians then some of his enemies closer to home. Prompted by CIA fears that the new Labour premier was actually a Soviet mole – put in place after KGB spooks had poisoned Hugh Gaitskell, the previous party leader – we know now that MI5 was burgling the homes of the PM's aides, bugging their phones, and spreading anti-Wilson gossip in the media. Of course, by definition most career politicians are abnormal. Both Wilson and Johnson were obviously highly motivated, fiercely intelligent men who were prepared to work gruelling hours at the expense of anything resembling a conventional home life to fulfil the duties for which destiny appeared to have chosen them. Each man would seem to have been an example of the high-functioning sociopath who displays a variety of paranoid or antisocial traits but otherwise remains perfectly competent, knows what he or she is doing and can be held responsible for their actions. The condition wasn't restricted to the Free World. In Moscow, Leonid Brezhnev was the latest in a long line of Soviet rulers for whom chronic suspicion, hypersensitivity and megalomania were the rule, and extended outbreaks of self-composure the exception. Even at this early stage of their terms in office, all three individuals were subject to a systematised and unshakeable delusional system, while retaining their ability to operate in the day-to-day world. Taken as a whole, it may be that some of the great geopolitical issues of the uniquely turbulent period of the mid 1960s were in the hands of a small number of psychologically flawed individuals who could, and did, play the cornered animal with the same degree of conviction as they showed in all the other political arts.

DEVIL'S DISCIPLES

Christmas sometimes seems to be the season for dark deeds in our public entertainment, a time when books and films often spill more blood than eggnog. There's a long tradition to this, stretching at least as far back as the 'sensation' novels of the mid-nineteenth century, with their characteristic gaslit atmosphere and sense of the macabre. At the end of 1964, however, Britain experienced a pair of real-life crimes, each in its way so depraved that no writer of fiction would have dared strain credulity by inventing the at once mundane and horrific events, taking place over a short period of time in separate parts of the country, that retain their power to both fascinate and shock us today.

The first incident came late on a snowy Christmas eve, in London's Regent's Park Road, when a young Fleet Street reporter named Michael 'Joe' Munnelly went to intervene in a drunken street brawl he'd seen from the window of his flat. Several youths had been evicted from a party at a nearby house and were not pleased at the outcome. One of these individuals threw some milk bottles at the front door of the property they had just vacated, and another one attacked an elderly man who came out onto the street to remonstrate, knifing him in the groin. At that point, Munnelly, his brother Jim and a friend named Don Smith had had a go, and with their arrival on the scene the original troublemakers had quickly started their waiting van and attempted to leave the area. Smith gave chase on foot, banging on the driver's-side door and demanding it stop. A moment later, the van did stop. Three or four youths promptly jumped out and began punching and kicking their pursuer into submission. It was a horrific assault. Staggering to his feet, screaming, running back and forth between his attackers like a trapped animal, Smith tried to fend them off with a poker he had seized on his way out of the flat. Struck from behind, he fell again to the street, bleeding and barely conscious.

Seeing this, Joe Munnelly ran to his friend's aid, and in the ensuing brawl received a fatal stab wound to the stomach, falling to the ground as the snow settled around his lifeless body and his assailants again climbed in their van and fled. Their victim was just 23 years old at the time of his death, and his killing would go on to trigger one of those cyclical national debates about the influence of televised violence, and more particularly if the country's youth might now be in the grip of a mass juvenile delinquency of the sort recently depicted in Anthony Burgess's novel *A Clockwork Orange*, the city streets apparently terrorised by feral gangs of young men in thrall to a routine of rape, theft and ultraviolence. An 18-year-old school leaver named Frederick Bishop was later found guilty of Munnelly's murder and sentenced to life imprisonment: either the forgettable villain in what could have been no more than the sort of routine punch-up of the type popularised by the seaside Mods and Rockers, or symptomatic of a baffling new youth culture in the United Kingdom that had the simple pleasures of *Top of the Pops* and *Ready Steady Go!* at one end, and the tragedy of the slain Joe Munnelly at the other.

Just two days later, a crime took place that would not only go on to fuel the controversy about the possible effect of moral permissiveness on the most impressionable members of society, but which was in itself barbaric even by the most ghoulish standards of Victorian gothic horror fiction. Hardened northern police officers blanched at the result.

Early on the morning of 25 December, a pretty 10-year-old girl with blue eyes and curly dark hair excitedly opened the gifts, including a doll and a miniature sewing machine, awaiting her under the small tree in her family's council flat at Charnley Walk, in Ancoats, central Manchester. The girl's name was Lesley Anne Downey, a bright, personable child who lived in the flat with her 34-year-old mother Ann, who was then four months pregnant, separated, and worked as a waitress, and her three brothers aged 12, 8 and 4. It was a normal enough Christmas Day of the sort being celebrated by tens of thousands of other local children, with snow carpeting the nearby streets, a high tea of fried sausage and cabbage with mince pies to follow, and then two hours sitting in paper hats in front of *Robinson Crusoe* on the black-and-white television set later that night.

Shortly after lunch the next day, Lesley Anne, wearing a red and green tartan skirt, pink sweater and short blue overcoat, walked across to the nearby Christmas fairground with sixpence in her pocket and her mother's instructions to be back again by the time it grew dark at five o'clock. Her older brother Terry was meant to accompany her, but had come down overnight with a cold, so she went instead with her 8-year-old friend Linda and Linda's young brother and sister. In time the other three children returned alone, after Lesley Anne had told them she wanted to have one more go walking among the brightly lit dodgems and candy-floss stalls to the penny-rolling track, where she apparently hoped to win a toy for her ailing big brother. According to later testimony, it was at this point, just as evening was falling, that a well-dressed young couple approached the child, deliberately dropping some shopping they were carrying, to ask her if she could help them retrieve the packages and load them into their nearby car. Again, it perhaps says something about the instinctive deference or credulity of the young of that era that she willingly agreed to do so. The couple were of course Ian Brady and Myra Hindley, and after bundling their victim into the back of the car they drove her the 10 miles back to their lair on Wardle Brook Avenue in suburban Hattersley. There can be few thoughts more disturbing than that of imagining the little girl's dawning fear as she came to realise what might be happening to her as she was taken away in the dark.

It's surely not necessary to linger over the terrible details of Lesley Anne Downey's ordeal that cold Boxing Day evening, except to say that they touched the depths of human abomination. But for the presence of certain modern-day technology, the scene could have been one of medieval barbarity. To add to the sheer sadism of the crime, the child's abductors saw fit to make a tape recording of her agony as she lay, bound and partly gagged on a bed, wearing nothing but her shoes and socks, one of Hindley's scarves wound tightly around her neck, pleading vainly for her life. It is a moot point whether both the child's torturers were present throughout. Hindley would later insist that she had left Lesley Anne alone in the room with Brady, who had proceeded to rape and strangle the child. Portions of the tape recording later harrowingly played in court would seem to refute this: at one point, a woman could be heard saying, 'Hush, hush, shut up or I will forget myself and hit you one', while, to a macabre backdrop of Christmas music playing on the gramophone, a small voice whimpers: 'I want to see my mummy ... Honest to God, I will swear on the Bible. I have got to go, because I am going out with my mum. Please, please help me, will you?'

When Ann Downey called the police at 10.30 that night, they told her that her daughter was probably still out larking around somewhere in the snow, but that if necessary they would start looking for her around the fairground area and nearby canal bank if she was still missing in the morning. Ten months later, the authorities found Lesley Anne's badly decomposed body buried in a shallow grave in the peat on Saddleworth Moor, on the opposite side of a small road to the remains of 12-year-old John Kilbride.

On the evening of 6 October 1965, Hindley drove Brady to Manchester's central rail station, where he accosted a 17-year-old apprentice engineer named Edward Evans, whom he found standing idly by a milk vending machine on the platform. Deploying his crude but serviceable gift for psychology, the murderer of Lesley Anne Downey swiftly suggested to his new acquaintance that they might assault and rob a 'businessman' somewhere in the darkened nearby streets and split the proceeds. After considering the proposal, Evans agreed to go outside with Brady and meet his 'sister' – Hindley – who was sitting at the wheel of the couple's latest car wearing a tight leopard-print dress, her bouffant hair carefully styled for the occasion. An air of sexual promise was apparently enough to persuade the young man to accompany the couple back to Wardle Brook Avenue prior to the commission of their crime. The three of them sat down to share a bottle of wine in the front room, and, following that, perhaps in keeping with her habit of absenting herself from the scene of the frenzy, Hindley decided to walk around the corner for a chat with her sister Maureen and Maureen's mentally slow but not wholly amoral husband David Smith.

In time, Hindley went on to ask her brother-in-law to walk her home again, and then suggested he wait outside on the street for a moment until he saw the lights of the house flick on and off three times, which would be the signal for him to enter. Evidently nothing about this arrangement struck Smith as particularly unusual or noteworthy, although a self-evidently hideous sight awaited him once inside.

'I stood there a minute or two,' Smith later told the police:

And then suddenly I heard a hell of a scream ... It sounded like a woman, really high-pitched. Then the screams carried on, one after another, really loud. Then I heard Myra shout, 'Dave, help him', very loud. When I ran in I just stood inside the living room and I saw a young lad. He was lying with his head and shoulders on the couch and his legs were on the floor. He was facing upwards, and Ian was standing over him, facing him, with his legs on either side of the young lad's legs. The lad was still screaming ... Brady had a hatchet in his hand ... He was holding it above his head and he hit the lad on the left side of his head with it. I heard the crack. It was a terrible sound.

After a total of fourteen such blows, Brady then wrapped a length of cord around the mortally wounded man's neck and pulled it tight, hissing 'You dirty bastard' as he did so. After that there was only a sort of gurgling sound – 'like when you brush your teeth and spit out the water' in Smith's words, as Edward Evans expired. Smith and Hindley then helped Brady wrap the body in a sheet and carry it upstairs to the spare bedroom, after which the three of them sat back down on the bloodstained couch and had a cup of tea. None of them immediately knew how to get Evans's corpse out of the house without drawing attention to themselves, so after a while Smith suggested that he return early the next morning with a pram. Instead, he went home and tearfully told his wife what had just happened before calling the police from a phone box across the road, holding a screwdriver in his hand as he did so in case Brady saw him.

Brady and Hindley were arrested, and, in May 1966, convicted. As the death penalty for murder had been abolished while they were on remand, each was given a life sentence. Brady was officially classified as a psychopath in 1985, a diagnosis many non-professionals might well have reached before that date. He died while in custody at a high-security prison hospital in 2017, at the age of 79; Hindley predeceased him by fifteen years. The whole ghastly saga again reignited the seemingly endless controversy about the link between 'permissiveness', or at least the availability of graphic pornography, and extreme antisocial behaviour, although perhaps in this case it was enough to say that when a materially and emotionally stunted childhood gives way to a half-baked adolescent grasp of nihilistic literature, and factors such as uncomplicated sex and cheap wine are added to the mix, normal standards of self-restraint can be relaxed to the point where tragic results follow. Some psychologists refer to this as a process of 'neutralisation', by which a manipulative personality like Brady rationalises his behaviour to make it seem morally acceptable. But that may just be hindsight. Most contemporary observers thought that Brady and Hindley were simply freaks of nature, whose twisted appetites had been formed long before any books or alcohol or other external stimuli had influenced them. 'Evil bastards' was the consensus.

★★★

The author Mario Vargas Llosa labelled our modern Western life the 'civilisation of the spectacle', describing the once inflexible guardians of public order abandoning their time-honoured duties to develop their own social media platforms or vainly lecture us on the looming apocalypse of climate change. Clearly, Britain had not quite reached this stage in its national fabric in 1964. But perhaps some of the ingredients, the seemingly permanent state of interlocking existential crises and the distractions of perpetual rainbow theatre, were already in place. For one thing, the nation was effectively bankrupt. No amount of tinkering by Harold Wilson or George Brown and their new Forward Plan unveiled that winter – 'We must pay our way in the world and produce more wealth inside this country,' ran the document's stark opening line – could disguise the fact that the United Kingdom was some £800 million in arrears in its trade account, while even then some of the nation's political masters appeared to be no more than marginally better-dressed social workers, rejecting thought in favour of wistful egalitarian dreaming. Of course, not everyone succumbed overnight to a headlong rush to self-aggrandisement and ineffectuality. Millions of ordinary Britons continued to cling to increasingly unfashionable virtues such as modesty, selfless dedication to a cause and service to others, took the phrase 'Mustn't grumble' as their motto, and watched with a mixture of horror and amusement as the country shifted gears from a secure and self-confident, if excessively uptight, society into one which had 'lost an empire and not yet found a role', to quote the American statesman Dean Acheson. Britain was still a world player in 1964 if measured by its nuclear capability, and more tangibly by its accomplishments in science, sport and the arts, as opposed to the dry terms of its GDP or currency exchange rates. Acheson himself visited London later in 1964 and wrote of his impression of 'some obscure sense of loss' about a country he saw as suspended between the two extremes of its post-war consensus and the perhaps spurious sense of modernism that rules today. Surveying the nation as a whole, the American was reminded of a magnificent medieval cathedral whose roof had fallen in, but whose current management drew one's attention to the notice board outside 'displaying the state of the great fundraising drive to implement exciting redevelopment plans for the future'.

In the meantime, the Beatles continued their irreverently radiant progress into the realm of permanent regard with their latest single 'I Feel Fine', a worldwide smash for several weeks over the winter of 1964–65, accompanied by an enjoyably cut-price promotional video in which George Harrison sang into a gym's punch-ball while Ringo pretended to energetically pedal an exercise bike. As we've seen, Donald Campbell, having promised to break both land- and water-speed records in the same year, managed to do so when steering his boat *Bluebird K7* across a lake in Western Australia on the final day of 1964. He would die just two years later when seeking to break his own record at Coniston Water, the setting for Arthur Ransome's once ubiquitous novel *Swallows and Amazons*, still then mandatory reading for many British children and their parents. In a sign of the evolving culture, the mystery writer Ruth Rendell published *From Doon With Death* in 1964, marking the first appearance of the celebrated Inspector Wexford. The book's shocking-seeming twist of a fatal lesbian obsession gave notice that the acceptable idea of popular middlebrow literature might be under review. At around the same time, Joseph Losey's *King and Country* became the rare war film with no battlefield scenes, but which instead explored some of the graded snobberies of the nation's class system, and, perhaps more daringly, the mental health issues of men in uniform.

The Rolling Stones were back on the road that winter, and to pass the time in between shows the group's bass player Bill Wyman bought himself one of the new Polaroid cameras and, in a not unrelated development, had the band's road manager Tom Keylock deliver groupies to his hotel room in shifts – although the word 'groupie' didn't exist yet, so Bill resourcefully gave his activities a series of innocuous-sounding code names, casually enquiring of Keylock, for example,

'Did you arrange my laundry yet, Tom?' While Wyman did most of the randy shagging, the Stones's creative unit was about to knock out a song called '(I Can't Get No) Satisfaction', which the arts critic on the *New York Times* went on to extol as a 'quasi-Marxist attack on Western consumerism' and which Mick Jagger and Keith Richards themselves used to go out and acquire a large English country house and a chauffeured Bentley S3 Continental saloon, respectively. It wasn't all suddenly pneumatic guitar and snarled lyrics, however, because 20 million viewers still tuned in each week to watch Val Doonican, a vocal star with more traditional values, already in a rocking chair in his mid 30s, crooning away about Paddy McGinty's goat. He was unapologetically and gloriously square.

That same winter, Stanley Matthews was still turning out on the wing for second division Stoke City at the age of 49, for what was then the eye-watering wage of £50 a week. On New Year's Eve, he became the first ever footballer to be knighted while an active player, which was either a welcome sign of social progress or the first step down the road to a degraded national honours system increasingly prone to reward the cloaca-tongued celebrity chef or overexposed supermodel whose chief creativity would seem to lie in their personal tax avoidance schemes. Harold Wilson later wrote in a foreword to Matthews's autobiography: 'He was a symbol of English sportsmanship in the days when that was a quality acknowledged worldwide.'

When Wilson and his Cabinet colleagues met again after the Christmas holidays in 1964, their first orders of business were the funding crisis in the Post Office, the issue of council care for children, the array of 'trade disputes that [appear] imminent' among a 'troubled' industrial landscape as a whole, and the government's plan to 'restore much-needed confidence in the nation's economic soundness', even if this involved 'difficult' spending decisions at home and an 'urgent brake' on aid overseas. The overall state of the nation's finances was 'precarious', Wilson later admitted, but there remained much to celebrate in Britain's ability to change and yet remain true to its values – 'our ability to make light of adversity, our eternal inventiveness, our acceptance of fundamental progress without mayhem'. These were the 'abiding points of distinction', he added; and such was national life in 1964.

SOURCES AND CHAPTER NOTES

This brief section shows at least the formal interviews, published works, and/or primary archive material used in the preparation of the book. As well as those listed, I also spoke to a number of people who prefer not to be named. Where sources asked for anonymity, usually citing a healthy respect for the UK's libel laws, every effort was made to get them to go on the record. Where this wasn't possible, I've used terms such as 'a friend' or 'a colleague' as appropriate, and once or twice resorted to the use of an alias. (The reader should be assured that every fact stated in the book has nonetheless been sourced, and for obvious reasons corroborated, to the very fullest extent possible before publication.) No acknowledgement thus appears of the help, encouragement and kindness I received from a number of quarters, some of them, as they say, household names.

INTRODUCTION

I'm grateful for the help of the UK National Archives, and more particularly their collection of Cabinet Papers dealing with everything from international relations in war and peace to successive ministers' pay awards to themselves, which proved a sustaining source for the book. The specific quote by Harold Wilson remarking that television was 'open to abuse by any charlatan ...' appears in Tony Judt, *Postwar: A History of Europe Since 1945* (New York: Penguin Group, 2005), p.346. The brief excerpts from the likes of the UK *Daily Express* and *Daily Telegraph* can be found by subscribing to the British Newspaper Archive, essentially the successor (and now fee-requiring) organisation to the much-missed British Library Newspaper repository in Colindale, north London. Mary Quant's remark about contemporary women dressed in 'a bouillabaisse of clothes and accessories ...' appears in Miriam Akhtar and Steve Humphries, *The Fifties and Sixties: A Lifestyle Revolution* (London: Macmillan, 2002), pp.39–40. The reaction of the new Labour chancellor of the exchequer on discovering the true state of the nation's finances appears in James Callaghan, *Time and Chance* (London: Collins, 1987), p.162. The evocative words of the government health campaign of 1963–64 can be found in the article 'Smoking and the New Health Education in the Britain of the 1950s–1970s', published in the *American Journal of Public Health*, June 2005. The peerless Dominic Sandbrook's quote beginning 'Avocados, aubergines and courgettes …' appears in his book *White Heat*, as cited in the bibliography, p.196; and the Marriage Guidance Council's 1964 advice to young women is quoted in Cate Haste, *Rules of Desire* (London: Chatto & Windus, 1992), pp.144–145.

I. WINTER

I should particularly thank the late Ted Dexter, as well as Tony Gill, Arthur Gregory, the late Johnny Johnson, the late Alan Kennington, the late Victor Lownes, James Morton, Bill Payne, Cecilia Page, Roman Polanski, Don Short and the late Tom Wolfe, in addition to the trustees and staff of the John F. Kennedy Presidential Library and Museum, Boston, Massachusetts, for their input. Without them there would have been a very different Chapter 1, or no chapter at all.

The quote beginning 'We all went to bed with Victor …', attributed to an anonymous young employee of the Playboy Club, appears in the profile of Victor Lownes published in *Casino Life* magazine of 23 January 2017. A compelling account of the critical misunderstanding between Randolph Churchill and *Private Eye* appeared in *The Spectator* of 22 March 1963. President Johnson's unanswerable remark beginning, 'Well, what is the difference?' appears in the US State Department's *Foreign Relations of the United States: Diplomatic Papers* (1964) (Washington DC: US Government Printing Office, undated), p.546. Johnson's remark beginning, 'There's one of three things we can do [about Vietnam] …' can be found in the document classified as 'Telephone Tape, February 3 1964' in the LBJ Presidential Library and Museum, Austin, Texas. Tom Wolfe's recollection of the '4,000 screaming youths' running past him in the New York airport terminal building – heralding the arrival in America of the Beatles – was included in Wolfe's letter to me of 7 January 2011.

The account of the activities of Mods and Rockers in the otherwise benign streets of Margate appeared on the BBC News website under the headline 'Margate Capitalises on 1964 Riots' on 1 October 2011. The reference to the early activities of Radio Caroline and others appears in the government paper 'Report on a Survey Conducted on the Radio Audience for Pirate Stations' held by the UK National Archives, ref. UKNL/HO 255/1001. The quote beginning 'Princess Margaret and [Lord Snowdon] broke new ground socially …' appears in *The Guardian*'s obituary of Princess Margaret, 10 February 2002; the line similarly describing Snowdon as 'part of the royal family, and yet not royal …' is from *The Guardian*'s obituary of Snowdon, published on 13 January 2017. The quote beginning 'Almost overnight lensmen became invested with glamour and prestige …' appears in Jonathan Aitken, *The Young Meteors* (New York: Atheneum, 1967), pp.36–37.

Juliet Nicolson's account of having her bottom pinched by the 75-year-old John Profumo appears in her wonderful book *Frostquake*, as cited in the bibliography, p.283; while the closely following quote about the greater, set-piece Profumo scandal remarking 'Authority, however disinterested ...' appears in Richard Davenport-Hines, *An English Affair: Sex, Class and Power in the Age of Profumo* (London: HarperCollins, 2013), p.345. For an account of the deathless Argyll scandal, the reader might consider the article entitled 'The Scarlet Duchess of Argyll' published in *The Independent* on Sunday of 17 February 2013. President Kennedy's private remarks on the nuclear test-ban talks held in Moscow in the summer of 1963 appear in the folder 'JFK Cable to Harold Macmillan, July 23 1963' found in the 'UK: General' file of the John F. Kennedy Presidential Library and Museum. Macmillan's own quote confiding that he had had 'a bad time, and I can't understand what they' – the Queen and Queen Mother – 'are saying' appears in the *Harold Macmillan Diaries*, Vol. 11 (London, Pan Macmillan, 2012), entry for 12 October 1963. The remark of the UK foreign secretary noting 'All ministers should refrain from commenting on McLeod's article ...' appears in the minutes of the UK Cabinet meeting of 17 January 1964 held in the UK National Archives, ref. CAB 195/23/33. The transcript of Edward Heath's remarks on the legislation introduced to parliament as the Retail Prices Act appears in *Hansard*, Vol. 691, recording the Commons sitting of 10 March 1964. For the UK consumer price index of that same period, see the tables included in the Macrotrends.net website under the title 'UK Inflation Rates 1960–2022'. The 'cut-price cancer' line appears on the front cover of *Private Eye* No. 55, dated 24 January 1964. Richard Burton's appreciation of Elizabeth Taylor's 'round belly' and other assets appears in Sam Kashner and Nancy Schoenberger, *Furious Love* (New York: HarperCollins, 2010). For a – surely definitive – account of the early days of the London Playboy Club, see the article headlined 'Playboy in London' by Bill Prince, *GQ* magazine of 1 June 2011. Cecil Beaton's remarks about the Fanny Hill proceedings and other matters are found in *Beaton in the Sixties: More Unexpurgated Diaries*, introduced by Hugo Vickers (London: Phoenix, 2003), p.7. The sporting reference beginning 'No one who attended matches in those days ...' appears in Tony Judt, *Postwar*, as cited, p.782.

II. SPRING

I was once lucky enough to lurk on the outer fringes of what could be called the Rolling Stones set, and I'm grateful to Patricia 'P.P.' Arnold, the late Hal Ashby, Bob Beckwith, the late Hal Blaine, Stanley Booth, Bebe Buell, Allan Clarke, Lol Creme, Janice Crotch, Sam Cutler, Micky Dolenz, the late Adam Faith, Chris Farlowe Jeff Griffin, Bob Harris, Peter Holland, the late Joe and Eva Jagger, Tommy James, the late Tom Keylock, Nick Lowe, Dave Mason, May Pang, Wayne Perkins, the late Harold Pinter, David Scutts, Chris Spedding, the late Mary Wilson and Tony Yeo, among others, who put their recollections of that group and the era at my disposal. I'm grateful, too, for the help of the late Tony Benn, Rob Boddie and Sussex C.C.C., John Bond, the late Terence Conran, Tony Gill, John Knowles, Bobby Simpson, Peter Wilson and Alan Yentob. I visited Milton Keynes.

For an account of Tony Benn and the maiden flight of the Concorde, see Benn in *The Independent* of 17 October 2003, as well as his earlier remarks to the author; the various challenges of the UK housebuilding supply can be found in the paper 'Ministry of Housing and Local Government, South-East Study, 1964' in the UK National Archives. The remark beginning 'The goal was simply to clear urban slums ...' is from Tony Judt, *Postwar*, as previously cited, p.387. For at least some of the background detail on Terence Conran found in this chapter, see Mark Rozzo's article 'Conran Country' in *Vanity Fair* of May 2019. The late – and I might add great – Jim Laker's remark beginning, 'Just why the selectors wanted Ted Dexter sent out ...' appears in Laker's book *Over to Me* (London: Muller, 1960), p.51; Dexter's own somehow characteristic line stating 'I was fascinated by an adorable Danish girl ...' is from his early memoir *Ted Dexter Declares* (London: Stanley Paul, 1966), p.35.

Ken Russell's observation, 'A script by a couple of West End revue writers ...' is from that director's memoir *The Lion Roars* (London: Faber, 1994), pp.71–72. Arthur C. Clarke's impression that 'Stanley [Kubrick] was in some danger of believing in flying saucers ...' appears in John Baxter, *Stanley Kubrick: A Biography* (New York: Carroll & Graf, 1997), pp.205–206. I had the pleasure to interview Harold Pinter in November 1999, when he spoke about *Tea Party* and other matters. The registrar at the London School of Economics kindly put some of the details of their graduation dates and ceremonies at my disposal. The intense debate about the UK's apple and pear quotas can be found in the minutes of the Cabinet meeting of 4 June 1964, held in the UK National Archives, ref. CAB 195/24/10. For Lyndon Johnson's ambition to 'outdo Kennedy' and create a program 'different in tone, fighting and aggressive', see Public Papers of the President, Vol. 1, 1963–64 held at the LBJ Presidential Museum and Library. The same source describes the meeting between Richard Goodwin and Eric Goldman that, at least in part, led to the concept of Johnson's 'Great Society' initiative. For Johnson's speech concluding 'For a century, we have laboured to settle and to subdue a continent. For half a century we have called upon unbounded invention and untiring industry ...' see Robert Dallek, *Flawed Giant: Lyndon Johnson and His Times*, as cited in the bibliography, p.82. Bill Moyers's own memory of Johnson remarking 'The commies think with Kennedy dead ...' appeared in *Newsweek* magazine of 10 February 1975.

Johnson's subsequent National Security Order No. 308, effectively kick-starting the American intervention in Vietnam, can be found in the US National Security Files held in the Gelman Library, George Washington University, Washington DC, document NASM 308, dated 22 June 1964. Saul Bellow's remarks beginning 'The lives of southern Negroes are not protected by law ...' are quoted in Zachary Leader, *The Life of Saul Bellow, Love and Strife 1965–2005* (New York: Knopf, 2018), p.30. Leonid Brezhnev's protestation of eternal love for Nikita Khrushchev, an effusion followed by Khrushchev's abrupt removal from power six months later, is found in William Taubman, *Khrushchev: The Man and His Era* (New York: Norton, 2003), p.615. Khrushchev's own earlier remark insisting to Western diplomats, 'We will bury you' was quoted in *The Times* of 19 November 1956, though not curiously enough in any of the contemporary Soviet media. For an account of Khrushchev and the chickens, see the article 'An Early Lesson in Capitalism' of 17 October 2008 on the online page The Poultry Site.

There are many published accounts detailing the horrors of the Moors Murders, and I've drawn here on Robert Wilson's book *Devil's Disciples*, as cited, among others.

III. SUMMER

I'm especially grateful to the late Tony Judt, who spoke to me about some of his impressions of Western Europe in 1964 in the course of a correspondence not long before his untimely death in 2010. I was also at one time lucky enough to interview Selwyn Lloyd, who held the posts of chancellor and foreign secretary among numerous other offices of state, and on a different but hardly less consequential note both Mal Evans and Tom Keylock, as well qualified as anyone for the role of the Fifth Beatle and Sixth Rolling Stone respectively. Bobby Simpson and Ted Dexter among others gave me their impressions of the 1964 England–Australia Test series, as did Paul Heppe of pre-enlightenment central Wolverhampton, where as a child I too sometimes liked to loiter on a Saturday afternoon. A number of those I interviewed at the time of writing two slim books on the John F. Kennedy administration again kindly put their recollections of the era at my disposal, and I'm grateful both to them and to the Kennedy and Lyndon Johnson presidential libraries, as previously cited. My late uncles Bob and Jack Prins hosted me as a young English schoolchild when visiting the Oz of colour television and backyard swimming pools that seemed to characterise the USA of 1964, an experience I'm unlikely soon to forget. At that age the mind perhaps turns more naturally to the question of cheeseburgers and cartoons than to the affairs of state then leading the US into its decade-long national nightmare in South East Asia, but I hope the reader won't find the former unduly emphasised over the latter in the text. I should again particularly acknowledge the UK National Archives, the British Newspaper Archive and the University of Cambridge Library, where I spent significantly longer researching this book than I did in three years as a Cambridge undergraduate.

Tony Judt's remarks beginning 'British Leyland's car plants [then] counted 246 different unions ...' are from his book *Postwar*, as cited, p.358. Ray Gunter's statement to parliament on the number of days historically lost to industrial disputes was quoted in *Hansard* of 1 February 1966. Similarly, *Hansard* of 28 July 1964 has the text of Alec Douglas-Home's tribute to the retiring Winston Churchill. For Evelyn Waugh's comment to Ann Fleming beginning 'For the past fortnight my drive has been worn into pot-holes ...' see *The Letters of Evelyn Waugh*, edited by Mark Amory (London: Weidenfeld & Nicolson, 1980), 27 January 1965. The UK Cabinet memo of 20 February 1964 beginning 'It is not clear whether Cairncross could, in fact, be returned ...' is in the Cabinet Papers of the UK National Archives, ref. CAB 301-270. The FBI's characterisation of the young Rolling Stones as 'liberals [who] have announced their intention to financially support Dr. Martin Luther King', a commitment that seems to have subsequently slipped the band members' minds, was found in a '1964: Subversives' file obtained under a Freedom of Information Act request. I once had the pleasure of interviewing Mick Jagger's parents, Joe and Eva, then living in retirement in Kent.

James Callaghan's remarks in parliament beginning 'The government has now increased the price of energy ...' are quoted in *Hansard* of 20 July 1964. The figures about the relative health or ill health found in different regions of the UK were published in *The Guardian* of 9 October 2006. Jack Nicklaus spoke to me of his impression of Tony Lema and others while on a mutual visit to the newly opened St Mellion Estate golf course in Cornwall in April 1986. Paul Heppe, as cited, similarly put his memories of visiting the Black Country in 1964 at my disposal. President Johnson's necessarily private remarks about wanting to teach 'these nigras that don't know anything how to work for themselves ...' are quoted in Robert Dallek's *Flawed Giant*, as cited, pp.119–120. The line beginning 'The president couldn't lose, in other words: if the bill failed to pass ...' is from the same book, p.115.

The remarks of the captain of the USS *Maddox*, unusually potent under the circumstances, beginning 'Review of action makes many reported contacts and torpedoes appear doubtful ...' are included in *Foreign Relations of the United States 1964, Vol V* (Washington, DC: US Department of State, Office of the Historian, 1965), pp.607–609. For Robert McNamara's policy on answering unwanted questions, see *Fog of War: Eleven Lessons from the Life of Robert S. McNamara* (Sony Pictures, 2003). President Johnson's remark insisting 'Now I'll tell you what I want ....' appears in William C. Gibbons, *US Government and the Vietnam War* (Princeton, New Jersey: Princeton University Press, 1995), pp.288–289. Johnson's remark to McNamara beginning 'I consider it a matter of the highest importance ...' is similarly in *Foreign Relations of the United States*, as cited, Document 440. The UK Cabinet's note including the line 'The Americans need our support for their policies in South-East Asia ...' is found in the Foreign Office paper 'An Anglo-American Balance Sheet', presented to Cabinet on 2 September 1964, UK National Archives, ref. CAB 129/118/64. I interviewed Keith Richards, briefly but memorably, on 12 February 1977.

For the UK's reported crime figures of 1964, see the Home Office paper 'A Summary of Recorded Crime Data for England and Wales 1898–2022', via the Home Office website at www.gov.uk. While the figures as a whole don't make for happy reading, it's at least salutary to note that the incidence of such late Victorian or Edwardian offences as 'Householder permitting defilement of girls' or 'Larceny of horses and cattle' are no longer quite such a prominent part of daily life as was once the case. Again, for the peculiar horrors of the Moors Murders, see Robert Wilson's *Devil's Disciples*, as cited, pp.33–35, among numerous other sources.

Cecil Beaton's line noting 'A pre-nuptial gaiety in cold dark King's Cross station ...' is from *Beaton in the Sixties: More Unexpurgated Diaries*, as previously cited, pp.8–9. Beaton's subsequent line remarking, 'For myself I am grateful ...' is from the same source, pp.168–169. For the account of long-term sufferers of prescription drugs see the story 'Agony of the Very Unlikely Addicts' published in *Mail Online* on 23 March 2010. The description of the principal architects behind the launch of *The Sun* on 15 September 1964 is from Christopher Booker, *The Neophiliacs*, as cited in the bibliography, p.247. For an account of the contentious Smethwick parliamentary election of 1964 see the story headlined 'Britain's Most Racist Election 50 Years On' in *The Guardian* of 15 October 2014. The description of Cathy McGowan wearing the 'latest trendy shifts and mini-dresses' is in Dominic

Sandbrook, *White Heat*, as cited, p.101. For an account of the iconic 'Daisy ad' of the 1964 US presidential election, see Edwin Diamond and Stephen Bates, *The Spot: The Rise of Political Advertising on Television* (Cambridge, Massachusetts: MIT Press, 1984), p.127. President Johnson's remark noting 'Reporters are just puppets ...' is quoted in Doris Kearns, *Lyndon Johnson and the American Dream* (New York: Signet, 1976), pp.246–247. Nikita Khrushchev's 'It always sounded good in public speeches to say ...' is from that individual's *Khrushchev Remembers* (Boston: Little, Brown, 1974), p.47. Khrushchev's apparent willingness to visit West Germany, forestalled by events, was reported in the *Chicago Tribune* of 4 September 1964.

For an account of Harold Wilson's preferred image at the time of the UK's general election of October 1964, see Anthony Howard and Richard West, *The Making of a Prime Minister* (London: Jonathan Cape, 1965); Richard Crossman kindly gave me his views on the effects of the Gallup Poll findings on his Labour Cabinet colleagues when as a young but reasonably eager school magazine editor I had the good luck to interview him in July 1973.

IV. AUTUMN

I should again thank Kate Armstrong, the Collections of the Chicago Public Library, Tony Gill, Tommy James, Edith Keep, the executive committee of the LBJ Presidential Library and Museum, Alexei Leonov, the late Selwyn Lloyd, Diana Pryce and the late Tom Wolfe, all of whom provided interviews or other direct input to this chapter, as well as both the collections of the Rare Books Room of the British Library and the Margaret Herrick Library in Los Angeles. Every effort has been made to comply with the copyright provisions involved. For all the challenges of successfully mining the material, the FBI Freedom of Information Division holds important files on the political, commercial and criminal backdrop to the United States of 1964, as do the archives of the US State Department and Treasury Department. I'm grateful for the help of all these individuals and groups.

The line comparing the attempts of Alec Douglas-Home to speak at the riotous political rally in Birmingham to that of 'a single flute in a Wagner storm scene ...' appears in Anthony Howard and Richard West's *The Making of a Prime Minister*, as cited, p.195; Rab Butler's comment of that same week noting 'We're running neck and neck ...' was quoted in the column by George Gale in the *Daily Express* of 9 October 1964; Ted Dexter's admission that 'At that time I knew more about Italian politics than English ...' is from *Ted Dexter Declares*, as cited, p.113.

Nikita Khrushchev's quote beginning 'I am old and tired ...' appears in Sergei Khrushchev, *Khrushchev on Khrushchev* (Boston: Little, Brown, 1990), pp.150–152; Leonid Brezhnev's portrayal of the Berlin Wall as a 'public humiliation' was made to the cosmonaut Alexei Leonov in November 1964, and later made available to the author; the inimitable enquiry by the Chinese diplomat as to why exactly so many Communists around the world had for so long considered 'some sort of shit' – as he characterised Josef Stalin – to be their leader appears in Vladislav Zubok's article in the *Cold War International Press Bulletin*, issue 10 (1988), p.158. The

US Defence Department brief of 24 November 1964 beginning 'The Soviet lack [of cooperation] has delayed ...' can be found in the paper 'An Assessment of the CHICOM Ability to Produce and Deliver Nuclear Weapons' in the LBJ Library, file no. E.O. 13526/ ISCAP 2007-014. Brezhnev's remark noting 'This individual [Mao] may be a communist ...' was provided direct to Alexei Leonov.

Enoch Powell's constituency address about the need to 'introduce control over the number of immigrants ...' is quoted in Simon Heffer, *Like the Roman: The Life of Enoch Powell* (London: Weidenfeld & Nicolson, 1998), p.360. The letter of David Ormsby-Gore noting 'almost anything could have tipped the electoral scale ...' is quoted in John W. Young, 'International Factors of the 1964 Election', published in *Contemporary British History 21* (2007), pp.361–362; Harold Wilson's remarks to Cabinet ruing that 'De Gaulle had indicated that negotiations for our membership of the EEC might be prolonged ...' appear in the Cabinet minutes of the UK National Archives, ref. CAB 128/42/41. The details of the Queen's reception of the newly elected Wilson at Buckingham Palace are quoted in Ben Pimlott, *The Queen: A Biography* (London: HarperCollins, 1996) p.342.

The lines by the late Tom Wolfe, who kindly also responded to my enquiries on the subject, beginning 'The girls have Their Experience ...' first appeared in Wolfe's 'The Girl of the Year' included in his book *The Kandy-Kolored Tangerine-Flake Streamline Baby* (New York: Farrar, Straus & Giroux, 1965). The acceptance speech by Martin Luther King Jr at the Nobel ceremony of 11 December 1964 can be read on the website www.nobelprize.org, among other sources. President Johnson's remarks on the 1964 election campaign trail noting 'I am going to repeat here ...' are quoted in Robert Dallek, *Flawed Giant*, as cited, p.183; Johnson's more guarded remark noting, 'Jack Kennedy tried to get Castro, but Castro got him first' appears in Dallek, p.53; the quote by Bill Moyers recalling 'there were times when [Johnson] didn't want to step off the campaign plane ...' also appears in Dallek, p.53.

The UK Cabinet minutes of 12 November 1964 are held by the UK National Archives, ref. CAB 128/39/8. The late and much missed Tom Keylock generously put his memories of Allen Klein, among other subjects, at my disposal. Etta James's remarks about the state of Sam Cooke's body as seen at his funeral appear in Etta James, *Rage to Survive* (New York: Da Capo, 2003), p.151. The ambitious plans announced by Douglas Houghton in the British Cabinet meeting of 15 December 1964 are found in the UK National Archives, ref. CAB 128/39/15. Tom Fraser's remarks in the House of Commons noting that Dr Beeching would be 'returning to his former role ...' were reported in Hansard of 23 December 1964.

The unusually consequential remarks by President Johnson about whether or not to send 'American boys 9 or 10,000 miles away from home ...' are found in the Personal Papers of the President 1963–64, Vol. II, pp.1126–1127, at the LBJ Presidential Library and Museum. Johnson's complaint beginning 'They don't want to help the poor and the negroes ...' is quoted in Doris Kearns, *Lyndon Johnson and the American Dream*, as previously cited, pp.251–252. Johnson's remark indicating it would be sufficient to bomb North Vietnam only once or twice a week 'to keep morale up in Saigon' is quoted in William C. Gibbons, *The US Government and Vietnam*, as previously cited, p.65. The line beginning 'A result of the organised opposition was that Johnson became a prisoner ...'

appears in Dallek, *Flawed Giant*, p.452. Nikita Khrushchev's interest in the composition of Moscow apartment-block lavatories appears in Egorychev, Beseda S. Egorychevym N.G., interview by Nikolai Barsukov, pp.299–300.

President Johnson's complaint, 'Don't they know I'm the only president they've got and a war is on?' appears in Eric F. Goldman, *The Tragedy of Lyndon Johnson* (New York: Knopf, 1969), pp.418–420. Johnson's remark indicating 'the commies already control the three major networks ...' appears in Richard Goodwin, *Remembering America* (New York: Open Road Media, 2014), pp.397–402. It's a necessarily repulsive task, but further details of the Moors Murders can be found in Jean Ritchie, *Myra Hindley: Inside the Mind of a Murderess* (Sydney: Angus & Robertson, 1988), in particular the account of the death of Edward Evans that appears on p.78 of that book.

For details of the new Labour government's response to the UK's perennial balance of payments crisis, see the paper entitled 'The National Plan for Economic Development' in the UK National Archives, ref. PREM 13/274.

SELECT BIBLIOGRAPHY

Alex, Peter, *Who's Who in Pop Radio* (London: New English Library, 1966)

Banting, Keith, *Poverty, Politics and Policy: Britain in the 1960s* (London: Macmillan, 1979)

Beaton, Cecil, *The Unexpurgated Beaton* (London: Weidenfeld & Nicolson, 2002)

Bogdanor, Vernon, and Skidelsky, Robert, eds, *The Age of Affluence* (London: Macmillan, 1970)

Bohlen, Charles E., *Witness to History: 1929–1969* (New York: Norton, 1973)

Booker, Christopher, *The Neophiliacs* (London: Pimlico, 1992)

Brown, Callum, *The Death of Christian Britain* (Abingdon, Oxon: Routledge, 2001)

Butler, David, and King, Anthony, *The British General Election of 1964* (London: Macmillan, 1965)

Butler, R.A., *The Art of the Possible* (London: Hamilton, 1971)

Cannandine, David, *Class in Britain* (New Haven: Yale University Press, 1998)

Cherry, Gordon E., *Town Planning in Britain Since 1900* (Oxford: Blackwell, 1996)

Crosland, Anthony, *The Future of Socialism* (London: Jonathan Cape, 1956)

Dallek, Robert, *Flawed Giant: Lyndon Johnson and His Times* (New York: Oxford University Press, 1998)

Davenport-Hines, Richard, *An English Affair* (London: HarperPress, 2013)

Ferris, Paul, *Sex and the British: A Twentieth-Century History* (London: Michael Joseph, 1993)

Foot, Paul, *The Politics of Harold Wilson* (London: Penguin, 1968)

Gaddis, John Lewis, *The Cold War* (New York: Penguin, 2005)

Gilbert, Martin, *'Never Despair': Winston S. Churchill, 1945–65* (London: Heineman, 1988)

Gillett, Charlie, *The Sound of the City* (London: Sphere, 1971)

Green, Jonathan, *All Dressed Up* (London: Jonathan Cape, 1998)

Hitchcock, William I., *The Struggle for Europe: The Turbulent History of a Divided Continent 1945–2002* (New York: Doubleday, 2002)

Karnow, Stanley, *Vietnam: A History* (New York: Viking, 1983)

Lycett, Andrew, *Ian Fleming* (London: Weidenfeld & Nicolson, 1995)

Matusow, Allen J., *The Unraveling of America: A History of Liberalism in the 1960s* (New York: Harper, 1984)

Nicolson, Juliet, *Frostquake* (London: Chatto & Windus, 2021)

Oldham, Andrew Loog, *Stoned* (London: Secker & Warburg, 2000)

Sakharov, Andrei, *Memoirs* (New York: Knopf, 1990)

Sandbrook, Dominic, *White Heat* (London: Little, Brown, 2006)

Shellard, Dominic, *British Theatre Since the War* (New Haven: Yale University Press, 1999)

Taubman, William, *Khrushchev: The Man and His Era* (New York: Norton, 2003)

Wilson, Bryan R., *Religion in a Secular Society* (Londonw: Watts, 1966)

Wilson, Robert, *Devil's Disciples* (London: Express Newspapers, 1986)

Zhai, Qiang, *China and the Vietnam Wars, 1950–1975* (Chapel Hill: University of North Carolina Press, 2000)

INDEX

British Railways 21–2, 252
Brockway, Fenner 231
Brook Advisory Centres 98
Brooke, Henry 123
Brown, George **146**, 210, 221, 224,
    234–5, 247–8
Bruce, Lenny 131–2, **152**
Bueno, Maria 104
Bundy, McGeorge 35–6
Burge, Peter 174
Burton, Richard 78–9, **147**
Butler, Rab 73–4, 191, 215, 217
Byrne, Johnny 104

Café Au Go Go, New York 131–2
Caine, Michael 24, **151**
Cairncross, John 164–6
Callaghan, James 23, 170–1, 215–16, 224
Campbell, Donald 111–12, **150,** 268
Campbell, Ian, Duke of Argyll 64
Cancer, lung 172
Caras, Roger 83
Carnaby Street 21
Caroline, Radio 52–5, **143**
Cars, price of 20
Carter-Ruck, Peter 31–2
Castle, Barbara 224
Channel Tunnel 36
Chatto, Lady Sarah 57
Chesser, Eustace 26
Christmas 248–9, 251
Churchill, Randolph 30–2
Churchill, Winston **153,** 162–4
Civil rights (US) 178–9, 255–6; *see also*
    Racial discrimination
Clark, Jim 104–5
Clark, Roger 230
Clarke, Allan 120
Clay, Cassius (aka Muhammad Ali) 86,
    148
Cleopatra (film) 79, 82
Clothing, price of 20
Common Market, European *see*
    European Community
Compton Group (film company) 250
Computers 99–100
Concorde aircraft 89–90
Congo, Democratic Republic of 238–9
Congress of Racial Equality (CORE) 255–6
Connery, Sean **154**
Conran, Terence 26, 95–7, **149**
Conservative party 73–7
Constantine, Learie 131
Contraceptive pill 96

Cook, Peter 117, **152**
Cooke, Sam **158,** 240–4
Cornell, George 177
Coups 239, 253
Coward, Noël 57–8, 85
Crewe, Quentin 58
Cricket 84–5, 101–2, 105–10, 173–4, 185
Crime statistics 188–9
Crosland, Anthony 234
Crossman, Richard 209, 211
Crossroads (ITV) 237
Cubi-Klub, Rochdale 44
Cudlipp, Hugh 197
Cup Final, FA football 103–4
Cyril Lord carpet company 19

Dahl, Roald 72
Daily Express newspaper 19
Daily Herald newspaper 19
Daily Sketch newspaper 34–5, 67, 249
Daily Telegraph newspaper 19
'Daisy' TV commercial (US) 205
Daltrey, Roger 84
Dardi, Harbhajan 199–200
Davenport-Hines, Richard 63
Davies, Mr Justice Edmund 69
Davis, Fred 110
Davis, L. D. 'Bubba' 131
De Gaulle, General 161, 223, 237–8
De Wet, Quartus 132–3
Dee, Simon 54
Defence of the Realm Act, 1914 99
Design Museum, London 97
Dexter, Ted 85, 105–8, **150,** 173–4, 215–16
Diet 24–5
Dilhorne, Viscount (Reginald
    Manningham-Buller) 161–2
Disputes, industrial 160–1
Divorce laws 65–6
Doonican, Val 269
Douglas-Home, Robin 59–60
Douglas-Home, Sir Alec 17, 74–6, 112,
    123–4, 135, **145,** 190–2, 213–15
Downey, Lesley Anne 263–5
Dr Strangelove (film) 82–3
Drones over China, American 238
Dullea, Keir 115
Dunbar, John 167
Dunn, Miss Olivia 44
Duvalier, François 'Papa Doc' 239
Dylan, Bob 203

Easton, Eric 120
Eastwood, Clint **156,** 201–2